HENRY BRADSHAW SOCIETY

ﬀounded in the ﬄear of ﬀur ﬂord 1890
for the editing of ﬃare ﬂiturgical ﬄerts

Volume CXXIV

ISSUED TO MEMBERS FOR THE YEAR 2015
AND
PUBLISHED FOR THE SOCIETY
BY
THE BOYDELL PRESS

THE MARTYROLOGY OF THE
REGENSBURG *SCHOTTENKLOSTER*

Edited by
Pádraig Ó Riain

LONDON
2019

First published for the Henry Bradshaw Society 2019
by The Boydell Press
an imprint of Boydell & Brewer Ltd
PO Box 9, Woodbridge, Suffolk IP12 3DF, UK
and of Boydell & Brewer Inc,
668 Mt. Hope Avenue, Rochester, NY 14620-2731, USA
website: www.boydellandbrewer.com

ISBN 978-1-90749-736-0

ISSN 0144-0241

A CIP catalogue record for this book is available
from the British Library

The publisher has no responsibility for the continued existence or accuracy of
URLs for external or third-party internet websites referred to in this book, and
does not guarantee that any content on such websites is, or will remain, accurate
or appropriate

This publication is printed on acid-free paper

Printed and bound in Great Britain by
TJ International Ltd, Padstow, Cornwall

MIX
Paper from
responsible sources
FSC   FSC® C013056
www.fsc.org

CONTENTS

For Alexandra

PUBLICATION SECRETARY'S PREFACE

It is a well-recognised feature of expatriate communities that their members, while enthusiastically open to integration with their new setting, are at the same time inclined not only to bring with them the more dearly-held features of their native culture but also to preserve those features, sometimes with greater care than the compatriots they have left behind. So it is that when a group of Irish monks came to Regensburg from Ulster in the later eleventh century, and established a community there, they brought with them the cults of the saints of Ireland whom they venerated. They would thus have set considerable store by any written record of those saints' feast-days, such as that enshrined in a martyrology, a type of document for which the Irish church had an especial fondness, as many past volumes produced for the Henry Bradshaw Society attest. The earliest Irish martyrology was compiled in prose and verse at Tallaght, near Dublin, around the year 830; the verse version, the 'Martyrology of Óengus', was edited for the Society by Whitley Stokes (volume XXIX) and the edition of the prose by Richard Best and Hugh Lawlor appeared as volume LXVIII in 1931. Hitherto, evidence for the circulation of the Tallaght martyrology before the mid twelfth century, the date of the earliest surviving copy of the prose version, has been in short supply. That gap in our knowledge has now been filled to a considerable degree by the painstaking efforts of Professor Pádraig Ó Riain, the world's authority on Latin hagiography and saints' cults in Ireland, not to mention on the Irish tradition of martyrologies. His edition of the martyrology of the Regensburg *Schottenkloster* (Irish monastery), offered in the present volume on the basis of a seventeenth-century manuscript which is still at Regensburg, provides crucial evidence that a copy of the metrical version of the martyrology from Tallaght had reached southern Germany by at least the eleventh century when it was used by the Irish monks at Regensburg. The *Schottenkloster* martyrology contains very many entries relating to Ireland and shows a striking correspondence with feasts commemorated in the Martyrology of Óengus, even to the extent of misreading some Irish forms used in its verse so as to create a couple of non-existent saints whose names consist only of honorific titles. A thorough scrutiny of other local German martyrologies, from Tegernsee and Reichenau, shows that they too drew upon the Tallaght material for entries on Irish saints. A further important point can be drawn out from the Regensburg martyrology as it is preserved, namely that the Scottish Benedictines who succeeded the Irish inhabitants at the *Schottenkloster* in the sixteenth century, in conservatively transmitting references to Irish saints into their seventeenth-century version of the martyrology, saw themselves as embodying cultural and liturgical continuity with their predecessors, or wished to represent themselves as doing so. The edition of the martyrology is fully annotated with cross-reference to other martyrologies, thus making it an invaluable addition to the array of scholarly tools Professor Ó Riain has provided for students of the Irish church, and it is with considerable gratitude to him and great pleasure that the Publications Committee issues this volume to members of the Henry Bradshaw Society for the year 2015. The Society is grateful for generous financial support towards the cost of producing this volume provided by the Publications Committee of the National University of Ireland.

Rosalind Love
on behalf of the Publications Committee
23 July 2019

PREFACE AND ACKNOWLEDGMENTS

The importance of the text edited here is threefold. Firstly, its entries on Irish saints prove that a copy of the early ninth-century martyrology of Óengus of Tallaght had reached Regensburg in Bavaria by the late eleventh century, at the latest. Secondly, comparison of its entries on Irish saints with similar entries added to several Bavarian martyrologies reveals that a Latin adaptation of Óengus's text was circulating for more than a century in the region about Regensburg. Thirdly, the close agreement between its entries on Irish saints and those of Óengus's martyrology supports the view that the Scottish Benedictines, who were given control of the Regensburg *Schottenkloster* (Irish monastery) in the early sixteenth century, were concerned with presenting themselves as heirs to the Irish monks who had preceded them.

Although begun in the early 2000s, the preparation of this edition has taken many years to complete, mainly due to other commitments. In the course of my work on the text, I have incurred many debts, both in Regensburg and elsewhere. In Regensburg, my study of the manuscript was facilitated by the following members of staff of the library, past and present: Dr Marina Bernasconi-Reusser, who allowed me to view a copy of her catalogue of the manuscript, Dr Raymond Dittrich, who, among other acts of kindness, provided me with a digitized copy of the manuscript, and Monsignor Paul Mai, former director of the library, who gave me permission to work on the manuscript. I am also very grateful to Dr Rachel Butter of the University of Glasgow for the digitized copy she provided of Hermann Greven's manuscript copy of his edition of Usuard's martyrology, now Darmstadt Universitäts- und Landesbibliothek MS 1021, 173–208. Sincere thanks are also owed to Dr Rosalind Love, Council Member and Publications Secretary of the Henry Bradshaw Society, for her advice and assistance in seeing this volume through the press. Last, but not least, I wish to thank both my wife Dagmar, who first drew my attention to the Regensburg martyrology, and my son Diarmuid, both of whom have an intimate knowledge of the history of the German and Austrian *Schottenklöster*.

EDITORIAL APPROACH

The present edition is mainly concerned with the manuscript's martyrological entries, with necrological and diary notices relegated to an appendix. Although drawing mainly on Molanus's *auctarium* of MU for its entries on non-Irish saints, cross-references in the notes to the text are to Jacques Dubois's edition of MU, which can be easily consulted.The few abbreviations that occur in the manuscript, for example *S.* for *sancti*, are expanded and the ending *-ij* is read throughout as *-ii*. When dealing with the Irish names of his *vorlage*, the seventeenth-century scribe had particular difficulty with some vowel or consonant clusters, such as *ae/ai* in *Baethin/Baithin* and *rr* in *Bairrinn*, which become *Battin-/Bartinn-*. All such scribal misreadings are noted and, where appropriate, corrected in line with readings in the Martyrology of Óengus (MO), which, together with the corresponding forms in the Tegernsee (T) and Hermann the Lame martyrologies (CSOW), are appended throughout. Punctuation and use of capital letters are editorial and, as already noted, bold is used here within entries to represent the scribe's red lettering. Notes are usually added to entries that are not in MU, and where *auctaria* other than Molanus record feasts of Irish saints, these too are noted. This applies especially to the Cologne *auctaria*, Grevenus and Lübeck/Cologne, mostly as in Sollerius's edition but, in the case of Grevenus, corrections have been made to the spelling in accord with the compiler's manuscript, now Darmstadt Universitäts- und Landesbibliothek MS 1021, 173–208.[1]

---

[1]   J. B. Sollerius/Du Sollier edited Usuard's text, together with additions from the various *auctaria* in *AASS* Iunii VI and VII. Among the *auctaria* were that published in 1490 in Lübeck and Cologne and that prepared by the Carthusian Hermann Greven, whose edition, printed in Cologne in 1515 and 1521, was closely studied by Baudouin de Gaiffier in *Analecta Bollandiana* 54 (1936), 316–58. Rachel Butter very kindly provided me with a digitized version of Greven's manuscript.

The indexes are designed to be as complete as possible but reference to the subject as *confessor*, which is normal in cases where martyrdom did not occur, is usually omitted.

ABBREVIATIONS

AASS	*Acta Sanctorum quotquot toto orbe coluntur*, ed. J. Bolland et al. (Antwerp and Brussels, 1643–)
ab.	*abbas*
anch.	*anchorita*/anchorite
App.	Appendix.
Apr.	*Aprilis*/April
archidiac.	*archidiaconus*
archiep.	*archiepiscopus*
Aug.	*Augustus/August*
b.	barony
BiblSS	*Bibliotheca Sanctorum*, 12 vols (Rome, 1962–9).
Bruxellensis	*Auctarium* of MU, ed. Sollerius, *Martyrologium Usuardi Monachi*
C	Version of the Martyrology of Hermann the Lame (Munich, Bayerische Staatsbibliothek Clm 5256)
Co./co.	county
conf.	confessor
Dec.	December
diac.	*diaconus*
DIS	Ó Riain (P.), *A Dictionary of Irish Saints*
disc.	*discipulus*
E	Martyrology of St Emmeram, Regensburg (Augsburg, University Library I, 2 fo. 8; ed. Freise, Geuenich and Wollasch, *Das Martyrolog-Nekrolog*)
E.	East
ed./eds	edited
edn	edition
EF	Eichstätt fragment of Regensburg martyrology (The fragment is now Dublin, TCD 11463; ed. Hochholzer, 'Ein Martyrologfragment')
ep.	*episcopus*

EncASE	*The Blackwell Encyclopaedia of Anglo-Saxon England*, ed. M. Lapidge, J. Blair, S. Keynes and D. Scragg (Oxford, 1999)
f. (ff.)	folio (folios)
Feb.	*Februarius*/February
Florarium	*Auctarium* of MU, ed. Sollerius, *Martyrologium Usuardi Monachi*
Florus	Martyrology of Florus, ed. Dubois and Renaud, *Martyrologes*
FSHIM	Ó Riain (P.), *Feastdays of the Saints*
Grevenus	*Auctarium* of MU, ed. Sollerius, *Martyrologium Usuardi Monachi*
HDGP	Ó Riain, Ó Murchadha and Murray, eds, *Historical Dictionary of Gaelic Placenames*
Ian.	*Ianuarius*
Iun.	*Iunius*
Iul.	*Iulius*
Jan.	January
LegSS	*Legends of Scottish Saints*, ed. Macquarrie
Lübeck/ Cologne	*Auctarium* of MU, ed. Sollerius, *Martyrologium Usuardi Monachi*
Mar.	*Martius*/March
m.	mille/milia
m./mm.	*martyr/martyres*
MA	Martyrology of Ado, ed. Dubois and Renaud, *Martyrologes*
Mai.	*Maius*
MenScot	Menologium Scotorum, in Forbes, *Kalendars*, 173–230
MG	Martyrology of Gorman, Brussels, Bibliothèque royale 5100–5104, ff. 124–97; ed. Stokes
MH	*Martyrologium Hieronymianum*, ed. De Rossi and Duchesne/Delehaye and Quentin
MO	Martyrology of Óengus, ed. Stokes
Molanus	*Auctarium* of MU, ed. Sollerius, *Martyrologium Usuardi Monachi*
mon.	*monachus*
MR	*Martyrologium Romanum*, ed. Delehaye et al.
MReg	Martyrology of the *Schottenkloster*
MS	manuscript

MT	Martyrology of Tallaght (Dublin, TCD MS 1339, ff. 355–65 and Brussels, Bibliothèque royale 5100–5104, ff. 209–224; ed. Best and Lawlor)
MU	Martyrology of Usuard, ed. Dubois
N.	North
Nov.	November
Oct.	October
O	Version of the Martyrology of Hermann the Lame (Munich, Bayerische Staatsbibliothek Clm 1071)
p.	page/parish
P	Martyrology of Prüll (Munich, Bayerisches Hauptstaatsarchiv Kl. Lit. Weltenburg 8; ed. Freise, Geuenich and Wollasch, Das Martyrolog-Nekrolog)
pr.	*presbyter*
Pulsanensis	*Auctarium* of MU, ed. Sollerius, *Martyrologium Usuardi Monachi*
r.	river
repr.	reprinted
rev.	revised
S	Version of the Martyrology of Hermann the Lame (Linz, Oberösterreichische Landesbibliothek 332)
S.	South
Sep.	September
St	*sanctus*/saint
TCD	Trinity College, Dublin
tl.	townland
T	Martyrology of Tegernsee (Augsburg, University Library I, 2 quarto 20)
v./vv.	*virgo/virgines*
W	Version of the Martyrology of Hermann the Lame (Munich, Bayerische Staatsbibliothek Clm 22058)
W.	West

INTRODUCTION

The first known group of Irish monks in Regensburg, Muireadhach mac Robhartaigh (alias Marianus Scotus) and his companions, had arrived from their native Ulster by the 1070s.[1] Allegedly on a pilgrimage to Rome, the monks were persuaded to remain on as scribes in the employ of the royal convents of Obermünster and Niedermünster, before being put in charge of a small church named Weih Sankt Peter. This building soon proved inadequate to the needs of a growing number of recruits from Ireland, and a new monastery had been constructed in proximity to the west gate of the city by the late eleventh or early twelfth century; 1112 is the date of the charter granted by Henry V to the monastery.[2] Following the Benedictine rule and dedicated to St James and St Gertrude, this monastery became known as the *Schottenkloster* (Irish monastery) and over the following decades a number of dependencies were founded; Würzburg (St James; c. 1138), Nuremberg (St Giles; c. 1140), Constance (St James; c. 1142), Erfurt (St James; c. 1150), Vienna (St Mary; c. 1155), Eichstätt (Holy Cross; c. 1155), Memmingen (St Nicholas; c. 1167/1180) and Kelheim (St

---

[1]   What follows here in the Introduction is a much modified form of Chapter 10 of my *Feastdays of the Saints*. The definitive work on the *Schottenklöster* is Flachenecker, *Schottenklöster*. For an up-to-date discussion of the history and architecture of the *Schottenklöster*, see Ó Riain (D.), 'The Early History and Architecture of the Irish Benedictine Monasteries in Medieval Germany', and idem, 'The *Schottenklöster* and the Legacy of the Irish *sancti peregrini*'. For references to manuscripts and previous work in the field, see Ó Riain-Raedel, 'Irish Benedictine Monasteries on the Continent'; eadem, 'Cashel and Germany'.

[2]   Flachenecker, *Schottenklöster*, 83–95; Weber, *Iren auf dem Kontinent*, 443–53; Ó Riain (D.), 'The Early History and Architecture', 40–2.

John the Evangelist; c. 1232).[3] Recruits, mainly from Munster, were provided by one or more religious houses, most notably by St Mary's in Rosscarbery, Co. Cork.[4]

From the beginning, the Irish abbots of these mainly southern German foundations worked tirelessly towards integration into their new environment, in the process achieving the protection of kings, emperors and popes, as well as attaining the support of local bishops, aristocracy and citizens. In line with well-established practice in neighbouring German houses, they also insisted on obtaining written confirmation of their privileges, and used the recognized scribal skills of their communities to good effect in creating a library of standard literary and liturgical works. About the middle of the twelfth century a necrology of the *Schottenkloster* began to be kept, containing some 1,000 names of benefactors, lay and clerical, Irish and German, as well as monks of the entire congregation and of other associated monasteries.[5] Contact with the homeland continued at all times. A number of fund-raising trips were made by Regensburg abbots to Munster, and important Irish events were duly noted in *Schottenkloster* annals, a set of which was kept at St Mary's in Vienna.[6]

Once in place, the network of Benedictine *Schottenklöster* provided an ideal vehicle for the propagation of cults of Irish saints. Also, the fact that from the early twelfth century onwards the monks were mostly recruited in the southern province of Munster meant that the Irish saints of greatest interest to the *Schottenkloster* communities tended to be of southern background.[7] Among the Lives of Irish saints copied, and arguably compiled, in Regensburg was that of St Flannán of Killaloe in Co. Clare, which is datable to shortly after 1163 by reference to an event witnessed 'recently' at Lismore in Co. Waterford by Gregory,

---

3   Flachenecker, *Schottenklöster*, 153–236; Ó Riain-Raedel, 'Das Nekrolog', 14–17; Ó Riain (D.), 'The Early History and Architecture'.
4   Ó Riain (D.), 'New Light on the History of St Mary's Priory'; Flachenecker, 'Benedictine Monks from Rosscarbery'.
5   Ó Riain-Raedel, 'Das Nekrolog', 7–119.
6   Ó Riain-Raedel, 'Twelfth- and Thirteenth-Century Irish Annals', 27–36.
7   Ó Riain-Raedel, 'Das Nekrolog', 19; eadem, 'Aspects of the Promotion', 225.

abbot of St James.[8] Among other southern Lives in the *Schottenkloster* collection were those of Íde of Killeedy in Co. Limerick and of Seanán of Scattery Island and Mochuille of Tulla, both in Co. Clare, thus underlining a particular concern with churches on either side of the Shannon estuary during the second half of the twelfth century.

The mid to late twelfth century coincided both with the abbacy of Gregorius (c. 1156–1185), who may have begun his ecclesiastical career at the Augustinian priory of Clare Abbey, near Ennis in Co. Clare, and with the priorship of Magister Marianus (c. 1160–1180), the likely author of the Lives of Flannán and Mochuille, who also composed a Life of his namesake, the founder of the *Schottenkloster* congregation.[9] Almost all of these texts are extant in copies of a collection containing over five hundred Lives, and traditionally known as the *Magnum Legendarium Austriacum*, which was begun, probably at Admont in Styria, during the second half of the twelfth century.[10] Among other texts produced by the Regensburg *Schottenkloster* in the course of the twelfth century were *Visio Tnugdali* and *Vita Albarti*.[11] A century later a foundation-chronicle, entitled *Libellus de fundacione ecclesie Consecrati Petri*, which traces the history of the *Schottenklöster*, was also written in Regensburg.[12] It is against this background of continuing devotion to their native saints, exemplified by the above-mentioned Lives, together with a fragmentary calendar and a recently discovered litany, now in the Boole Library at University College Cork, that the martyrology edited here for the first time from a revised and updated seventeenth-century copy was compiled at some point in the late eleventh or early twelfth century.[13]

---

8 Ó Riain-Raedel, 'Cashel and Germany', 211; Weber, *Iren auf dem Kontinent*, 589–90.
9 The Life has most recently been edited in Weber, *Iren auf dem Kontinent.*
10 Ó Riain (D.), 'The *Magnum Legendarium Austriacum*'.
11 Picard and de Pontfarcy, *Vision of Tnugdal*; Pfeil, *Die 'Vision des Tnugdalus'*; Ó Riain-Raedel, 'Das Nekrolog'; Hennig, 'St. Albert of Cashel'; Weber, *Iren auf dem Kontinent*, 732–4; Ó Riain, *Beatha Ailbhe*, 38–9.
12 Breatnach, *Die Regensburger Schottenlegende.*
13 UCC, Boole Library MS 331; see now Ó Riain-Raedel and Ó Riain, 'Irish Saints in a Regensburg Litany'. The calendar is now Regensburg, Bischöfliche Zentralbibliothek MS 8; see Dold, 'Wessobrunner Kalendarblätter'.

Following the transfer of control of the Regensburg *Schottenkloster* from Irish to Scottish Benedictines in the early sixteenth century, some of the manuscripts previously written and kept in the monastery were dispersed. Some liturgical manuscripts continued in use under the new ecclesiastical regime, however, subject to rewriting. One example is the above-mentioned necrology of the *Schottenklöster*, which is preserved in the Vatican Library in two late copies, the earlier of which was written at Würzburg in 1617.[14] This text commemorated not only deceased Irish members of the *Schottenklöster* but also Scottish monks, and examination of the names has shown that the necrology, while begun in the twelfth century, was added to until after 1600.[15] The names of the day in the necrology would have been remembered at an assembly of the monks in the chapter house of the monastery, which explains why texts of this kind are often preserved in *libri capituli*, 'chapter books'. In these, the necrology would normally have been accompanied by a calendar of the feasts most highly regarded by the community, together with a copy of a martyrology containing mainly feasts of the universal church, and a copy of the rule of the order to which the community belonged, all of which would have required and received daily reference. While the main necrology of the *Schottenklöster* is now preserved independently, the seventeenth-century martyrology of the Regensburg *Schottenkloster* edited here is accompanied by excerpts from the rule of St Benedict and some necrological notices.[16]

THE MANUSCRIPT

Manuscript 40 of the Bischöfliche Zentralbibliothek in Regensburg, a *Liber officii capituli* used for reading in the local *Schottenkloster* at prime, contains martyrological entries for each day of the year from 20 January until 19 December together with extracts from the rule of St Benedict, likewise for each day, up to folio 171 of 178, where the extracts begin to be taken from the pseudo-Bernard text *Documenta*

---

[14] Ó Riain-Raedel, 'Das Nekrolog'.

[15] Ibid., 52–6.

[16] During visits to Regensburg in February 2004, July 2015 and October 2018, I transcribed and checked the readings of the text with the kind permission of Monsignor Paul Mai and Dr Raymond Dittrich. Unfortunately, the lists from 20 December to 19 January are lacking.

pie seu religiose vivendi.[17] The entries for the remaining days of the year are now lacking due to the loss of several leaves at the beginning and end of the manuscript. Scattered throughout the text of the martyrology are entries relating mainly to deceased members of various monastic communities, comprising Rottenburg (presumably the place so named on the river Laaber); St Emmeram, close by the *Schottenkloster* in Regensburg; the *Schottenkloster* in Erfurt and the abbeys of Oberaltaich and Niederaltaich in the diocese of Regensburg, which account for most of the entries.[18] In addition, some benefactors of the monastery are named, and there are references to duties performed by the community for other local communities, such as Sarching, Obermünster and Niedermünster. Red lettering is used throughout for the Roman notation of the martyrology, whereas dominical letters (A–G), which are in brown ink, appear to have been added later. Red lettering is also used to indicate feasts important to the community, many of which relate to Ireland. Shown in the edition by the use of bold lettering, the use of red lettering is less frequent towards the end of the text.

There are 178 folios in all, foliated on the recto pages, and, due to the loss of folios at the beginning and end, the martyrology, rule and pseudo-Bernard texts are now incomplete. The same hand is visible throughout, with some variation in style, sometimes hasty, more often careful and orderly, but a few necrological entries may have been added by a different hand. Frequent confusion in the spelling of Irish names indicates a lack of familiarity on the part of the seventeenth-century scribe with many of the names contained in his exemplar.[19] Preserved on the spine of the manuscript is a piece of vellum bearing the incomplete inscription *Martirologium et ... pia hoc monasterio an.* 1651, and this date is supported by the Regensburg watermark, which is similar to other seventeenth-century local styles.

---

[17] A catalogue of the manuscripts by Dr Marina Bernasconi Reusser, who kindly made available her description of MS 40, is as yet unpublished. Cf. Ó Riain-Raedel, 'Das Nekrolog', 43. For the extracts from the rule of St Benedict and the pseudo-Bernard text, see Appendix 3 below. Cf. *S. Bernardus*, PL 184, 1173–4.

[18] Most of those named in these entries have proved untraceable, but a full list is given below in Appendix 1.

[19] For example: *l* is often confused with *c*; 7 February (*comani* for *lomani*), 18 April (*Casreani* for *Lasreani*).

SOURCES OF NON-IRISH ENTRIES

The basic text of the non-Irish entries in MReg is that of the Martyrology of Usuard (MU), albeit in a much abbreviated form. The extent of the abbreviation may be illustrated by reference to the entries for 18 December:

> *Apud Macedoniam, ciuitate Philippis sanctorum martyrum Rufi et Sozimi.*
> *In Africa, passio sancti Moysetis martyris.*
> *Turonis, sancti Gatiani episcopi et confessoris.*

The second entry only corresponds exactly to that of MU, which devotes five and three (printed) lines respectively to the first and third entries. Although clearly based on MU, therefore, the entries in MReg are reduced to the minimum necessary for some understanding of the historical background of the saints commemorated. The version of MU lying at the base of the martyrology was the *auctarium* of Usuard's martyrology prepared by Jan Vermeulen (Molanus) and published first in 1567 and again in 1573 and 1583.[20] Numerous entries agree with Molanus in having the same wording and equally numerous entries are otherwise found either only in Molanus or in very few *auctaria*, but including Molanus.[21] By way of contrast, only three passages in entries absent from Molanus but present in other *auctaria* are included for the months of January and February.[22] A few saints were added on the basis of their connections with churches in southern Germany or with Irish-connected abbeys of the Benedictine order. These include Gunthildis of Suffersheim (28 September) and Gallus, founder of the monastery of St Gall (23 October). Some Irish saints commemorated by Molanus in the first edition only of his martyrology, for example Celsus and Malchus (6, 10 April), were also omitted from MReg, whereas other entries confined to the first edition, for example Felix (23 March), are included. On the other hand, several entries are otherwise found only in the later editions of Molanus, for example, Macarius (10 April) and Basilius (12 April).

---

[20] Grosjean, 'Sur les éditions'.
[21] E.g. for the month of February: 2.4, 3.2, 6.2, 7.4, 15.1, 18.2, 21.2, 23.2, 25.4, 26.3, 27.3. Also, spellings characteristic of Molanus are often shared by MReg, e.g. *Maimbodi* (Jan. 23.4), *Ephesi* (Jan. 24.1), *Bassiani* (Dec. 9.2).
[22] E.g. January 23.1, 30.2 and February 25.1.

In view of the fact that the 1584 edition of the *Martyrologium Romanum* had been sanctioned by Pope Gregory XIII for use in the whole Church, one might well ask why Molanus's version was chosen as a source of the non-Irish entries. Possibly the redactor was concerned with giving his work a semblance of antiquity in line with the entries on Irish saints in his text, which were drawn almost exclusively from the martyrology previously used by the Irish monks of the *Schottenkloster*. The Scottish redactor responsible for MReg may well have wished to create the impression that he and his fellow monks were in direct line of descent from the earlier occupants of the monastery. On the other hand, when compared with the much earlier Eichstätt fragment (EF), which may be taken to represent the martyrology used in the Regensburg *Schottenkloster* until it was replaced by MReg, with retention only of the entries on Irish saints, there is a marked difference in the sources used for non-Irish saints.[23] As is shown here by the entries for 15 and 16 April, which are respectively based on the Martyrology of Ado and the Martyrology of Jerome, EF drew its non-Irish entries variously from historical and Hieronymian sources.[24]

> 15 April: *In ciuitate Cordula natale Olimpiadis, et Maximi nobilium. Qui iubente Decio fustibus cesi et inde plumbatis ad ultimum capita eorum securibus tunsa sunt donec spiritum emitterent.*
> 16 April: *In Achaia natale sanctorum Petri diaconi et Hermogenis ministri Petri.*

The first entry is an abbreviated version of the Martyrology of Ado (MA), whereas the second brings together saints commemorated in

---

[23] For the full text of the Eichstätt fragment, see Hochholzer, 'Ein Martyrologfragment', 48–52. The single-leafed fragment was discovered some years ago in the local antiquarian bookshop of Armin Jedlitschka, and is now Dublin, TCD, MS 11463. It has full entries for the period from 15 to 24 April together with the end and beginning respectively of the entries for 14 and 25 April. On six days (14, 15, 17, 19, 21, 23 April), the same hand that wrote the main text added entries relating to Irish saints, and on one day (18 April) an entry has been added on the dedication of the church of Weih Sankt Peter in Regensburg which corresponds closely to the entry on that day in MReg.

[24] The distribution is as follows: MA: 14, 15, 18 (part), 20 (part), 21–23, 24 (part), 25. MH: 16, 17, 18 (part), 19, 20 (part). As a rule, the entries from MH are taken back from the following day in the source. Abbreviations are expanded silently in the examples cited here.

the Hieronymian martyrology on 16 and 17 April. Also to be noted is the fact that the readings from MA in EF are close to those in the martyrology of the Regensburg church of St Emmeram, which was compiled in 1036.[25] This, together with the prominence given in both texts to the feasts of Adalbert and George on 23 April, would suggest that both martyrologists were using the same, or a very similar version of MA. On the other hand, the lack of agreement between the two texts in their selection of saints from the Hieronymian martyrology shows that EF was not drawing directly on the St Emmeram text.

SOURCES OF IRISH ENTRIES

The provenance of the text of MReg from among the community of Irish monks in Regensburg is clearly indicated by several references to anniversaries of such events as the dedication of an 'altar of Irish saints' (30 January), presumably in the church of 'St Peter outside the Walls' (Weih Sankt Peter), and the dedication of the church itself on 18 April; as already stated, this was the first foundation in Regensburg to be occupied by Irish monks.[26] Likewise indicative of Irish influence is the inclusion of an otherwise unknown feast of the translation of the remains of Flannán of Killaloe, as well as some red-letter feasts of Erhard, patron of Regensburg, who was thought to be Irish, and the uncommonly recorded octave of the feast of St Gall.[27] Moreover, on almost every day of the year feasts of Irish saints were added to the text, as was also the case, albeit to a lesser extent, in two other martyrologies produced in the late twelfth century in southern Ger-

---

[25] Freise, Geuenich and Wollasch, *Das Martyrolog-Nekrolog.*

[26] Ó Riain (D.), 'The *Schottenklöster* and the Legacy of the Irish *sancti peregrini*', 159n.

[27] The texts of these entries are as follows: 30 January (*dedicatio altaris sanctorum Hyberniorum*); 18 April (*Ratisbonae, dedicatio ecclesiae sancti Petri extra muros*); 26 August (*In Hybernia, translatio sancti Flannani episcopi et confessoris*); 8 October (*Eodem die, translatio sancti Erhardi episcopi et confessoris*); 15 October (*Et octaua translationis sancti Erhardi*); 23 October (*Eodem die, translatio sancti Galli confessoris*). The words '*sancti Erhardi*' are in red letters in MReg, and the Erhard entry is also in the Lübeck/Cologne version of MU (*AASS*, Iunii VII, 587), which has the same wording. For this saint's Irish associations, see Breatnach, *Libellus*, 207–8; Flachenecker, *Schottenklöster*, 63–9; Weber, *Iren auf dem Kontinent*, 732–3.

man monasteries, namely the Bavarian recension of the martyrology of Hermann the Lame (*Contractus*) of Reichenau, who died in 1054, and the Tegernsee Martyrology.[28]

The Bavarian recension of Hermann the Lame's martyrology is preserved in four manuscripts (CSOW), all of which share a common exemplar, distinguished from Hermann's archetype by the presence of some four hundred entries added after 1144 and reflective of a wide geographical spread, covering Germany, Italy, Prussia, Poland, Bohemia, Hungary, France, Denmark, Norway, England and Ireland.[29] John McCulloh has described the attention paid by the Bavarian redactor of the text to English and Irish saints as particularly noteworthy, with no fewer than twenty-seven entries relating to native Irish saints.

The Tegernsee martyrology, here distinguished as T, was kept in one of the most important Benedictine monasteries of Bavaria. Within a few years of its foundation, about 765, Tegernsee had received from Rome the relics of St Quirinus, and the various feasts of this saint are duly given prominence in its martyrology, where the patron's name is written in capitals on no fewer than four occasions (24 and 25 March, 16 June, 20 October).[30] Two textual characteristics of T led McCulloh to conclude that the martyrology was not written in Tegernsee itself.

---

[28] Hermann the Lame's still unpublished martyrology is based on the earlier martyrologies of Notker (†912), Ado (†875) and Hrabanus Maurus (†856), with some additions of names of saints who died after Notker. Attention has been drawn previously to the additions in the Bavarian recension of Hermann's text by various scholars, including John McCulloh, Dagmar Ó Riain-Raedel and Elmar Hochholzer, and I have also discussed them in my *Feast-days of the Saints*, 228–44.

[29] McCulloh, 'Herman the Lame's Martyrology', 351–3.The four manuscripts are as follows: (1) Munich, Bayerische Staatsbibliothek Clm 5256, from the monastery of Chiemsee (C); (2) Linz, Oberösterreichische Landesbibliothek cod. 332 (olim 258), from the monastery of Suben am Inn (S); (3) Munich, Bayerische Staatsbibliothek Clm 1071, from the monastery of Oberaltaich (O); and (4) Munich, Bayerische Staatsbibliothek Clm 22058, from the monastery of Wessobrunn (W). The *terminus post quem* of the text is based on the inclusion of the feast of William of Norwich, who died in 1144 (McCulloh, 'Jewish Ritual Murder'). I owe all the citations from these manuscripts to the kindness of John McCulloh, who forwarded a copy of his edition in preparation.

[30] This is now Augsburg, University Library MS I, 2, quarto.

One of these characteristics is its very close textual relationship to the martyrologies of St Emmeram (E) and Prüll (P), which points to a Regensburg provenance.[31] The other is the fact that the vast majority of the additions to the text, which are written in a hand close to – indeed in many instances indistinguishable from – that of the original scribe, consist of names of Irish saints. Taken together, these characteristics suggest that the martyrology was written at the Irish Benedictine monastery of St James in Regensburg, and this conclusion is supported by the spelling of the added Irish names, which is generally correct. Such was the reputation of the *Schottenkloster* scriptorium for the quality of its scribal work that, as Helmut Flachenecker has pointed out, it seems to have become a matter of course for other monasteries in the city and surrounding region to commission work from it.[32] The political importance of Regensburg within the wider region had led to its becoming the seat of many monastic *Stadthöfe* or 'town-houses', one of which, the *Tegernseehof*, founded in 1002, may have played a role in commissioning a new martyrology from the *Schottenkloster*.[33] Alternatively, the monastery of St Emmeram, whose necrology has several entries relating to the *Schottenkloster* and even more commemorating deceased members of the Tegernsee community, could have acted as an intermediary.[34]

The two Regensburg martyrologies, E and P, which served as the main source of T, are essentially abbreviated versions of the Martyrology of Ado (MA), with some additions from MH together with some recently deceased saints.[35] The Tegernsee martyrology (T) is even more drastically abbreviated, with little left of its source beyond bare names, together with occasional initial letters, such as *e.* for *episcopus* and *a.* for *abbas/apostolus*. However, by comparison with E and P, T sought out names far more widely, once more in full versions of MA and MU, in one or more of the several full and abbreviated versions of

---

31 Freise, Geuenich and Wollasch, *Das Martyrolog-Nekrolog*.
32 Flachenecker, 'Monastischer Austausch', 107.
33 Morsbach, *Ratisbona Sacra*, 93–5.
34 The necrologies of Tegernsee and St Emmeram have numerous entries representative of one another but, whereas that of St Emmeram has some entries relating to the *Schottenkloster*, that of Tegernsee has none (Baumann, *Necrologium*).
35 Freise, Geuenich and Wollasch, *Das Martyrolog-Nekrolog*, 12.

the Hieronymian martyrology, and in many other, as yet unidentified, sources. The result was a martyrology containing some six thousand names, mostly bare, spread over the 365 days of the year. Included in this number are some 125 additions of mainly Irish saints.[36] McCulloh has argued that T was compiled sometime during the last quarter of the twelfth century.[37]

As already stated, the additional Irish feasts in T are in regular agreement with those in CSOW. Similarly, the Irish additions in both T and CSOW regularly agree with the more numerous names in MReg. In the following collation of the feasts of Irish saints common to MReg and either CSOW or T for the month of March, I have placed alongside them the corresponding entries in the Martyrology of Óengus (MO), a copy of which, with its names rendered in Latin, is the source from which the Irish entries were drawn.[38] The entry on Patrick, which MReg took from an *auctarium* of MU, is omitted here. Also, where appropriate, the MO reading is accompanied within brackets by a form taken from the list of variant readings provided by Whitley Stokes, the editor of MO.[39] All additions of Irish names in CSOW and T are again noted below in the full edition of MReg.

March

5. *In Hybernia, sanctorum Karthagii et Kiarani* MReg / *Kyarani, Karthagi* T / *Carthach ... Ciarán* MO.
8. *In Hybernia, sancti Senani episcopi et confessoris. Ibidem, sanctorum episcoporum et confessorum Beoani et Mochonni* [MS *Machoaeni*] MReg / *In Hibernia* [*autem* W], *sancti Senani episcopi et confessoris*? CSOW / *Senani confessoris*? T / *Senan ... Conandil (Conna) ... Beó-áed* MO.[40]

---

[36] In addition to the transcript of the text kindly provided by John McCulloh, I have also used a photocopy.
[37] In a lecture delivered in St Patrick's College, Maynooth in July 1989, McCulloh dated it to after 1170, on the basis that it contained the feast of Thomas Becket.
[38] For a full collation, see Ó Riain, *Feastdays of the Saints*, 233–43.
[39] Stokes, ed., *Martyrology of Óengus*, provides a very full list of variant readings.
[40] *Conna* (for *Conandil*) is in the notes to MO.

11

16. *In Hybernia, sanctorum confessorum Abbani et Finnani* MReg / *Finani, Patricii* T / *Abbán ... Fínán* MO.

19. *In Hybernia, sancti Lachteani abbatis et confessoris* MReg / *Lactani* T / *MoLachtóc (Lachténe)* MO.[41]

21. *In Hybernia, sancti Ennae* [MS *Cunae*] *abbatis* MReg / *Enneni* T / *Éndae* MO.

22. *In Hybernia, sancti Falbi abbatis et confessoris* MReg / *Albani* T / *Failbe* MO.[42]

24. *In Hybernia, sanctae Scirae uirginis. Item, sanctorum Camini, Mochtani, et Domangarti abbatum et confessorum* MReg / *Camini, Moctani* T / *Scíre ... Mochtae (... Domangart)* MO.[43]

26. *In Hybernia, sancti Synchilli abbatis. Item, sancti Mochelloki confessoris* MReg / *Sinchellini* T / *mo Chellóc ... Shinchill* MO.

30. *In Hybernia, sanctorum abbatum et confessorum Mochua, Colmani, et Tolani* [MS *Totani*] MReg / *Mochuani, Colmani, Tolani* T / *mo Chuae ... Colmán ... Tolai* MO.[44]

CONCLUSIONS

Comparison of the list of Irish feasts in MReg, which are spread over 177 days of the year, with the corresponding entries of the Martyrology of Óengus (MO) reveals a remarkable level of conformity. The extent of the agreement is shown by the fact that forty-three of the fifty entries relating to Ireland for the period 20 January to 31 March correspond to entries on Irish saints in MO.[45] Moreover, of the remaining seven feasts in MReg, two – at 27 January (*Maeda*) and 18 March (*Mochtanus*) – commemorate ghost saints whose names derive from misunderstood words in the corresponding quatrains of MO, respectively *moéda*, 'my Lord', and *mochtae*,

---

[41] The name *Lachténe* is in the notes to MO.

[42] '*Albani*' (for *Abbani*, i.e., *Abán*?) of T may refer to the octave of the feast on 16 March.

[43] The name *Caimín* occurs in the notes of the following day in MO.

[44] MReg's '*Colmani*' is corrected in the manuscript from '*Colamani*'.

[45] Exceptions are the entries in MO for 28 February (*Siollán*) and 11 March (*Libhréan, Seanán, Custaintín*).

'glorified'.[46] The other five were taken either from Dempster's *Menologium Scotorum* (*MenScot*), presumably by the Scottish scribe of the manuscript, or from MU, which contains a number of entries relating to Ireland.[47] Also, wherever MO is without a commemoration of an Irish saint during this period, this is almost invariably also the case in MReg.[48] On this evidence, there can be no doubt but that the bulk of the Irish feasts recorded in MReg, CSOW and T were taken from a copy of MO brought from Ireland and kept in all likelihood by the community of Irish monks in Regensburg, where the names of those commemorated in the text were given Latin forms.

When is this copy of MO likely to have reached Regensburg? A *terminus post quem* is provided by the date of the first known presence of a group of Irish monks in Regensburg, which is usually placed in the period extending, roughly, from 1050 to 1070.[49] Similarly, a *terminus ante quem* of the mid twelfth century is provided by the use made of MO in the compilation of the Irish additions to Hermann the Lame's martyrology. A much closer dating in the mid to late eleventh century has recently been suggested by Elmar Hochholzer on the palaeographical evidence of the manuscript fragment containing EF, which Hartmut Hoffmann has dated to the third quarter of the eleventh century, at the very latest. Premised on the basis that the scribe's hand shows no insular features, this dating gives no consideration to the fact that all Irish names in EF are spelt correctly, despite the presence in them of minims and other features likely to have confused a continental scribe.[50] This would suggest that the scribe must indeed have been Irish, in which case he could well have learned to write in non-insular

---

[46] The latter term proved to be a stumbling block for the martyrologist, who used it to create yet another ghost saint at 12 August (*Mochteus*). Similarly, at 2 January, the ghost saint *Muchullinus* in T was created from a placename (*Disert Meic Ciluirn / Cuilinn*) mentioned in a note to MO.

[47] Thomas Dempster, *Menologium Scotorum* [or *Scoticum*] (1622), in Forbes, ed., *Kalendars*, 173–230 (*MenScot*). The three entries from *MenScot* are at 29 and 30 January (*Wallach, Glass*) and 16 February (*Fionán*).

[48] E.g. January: 23–26; February: 3, 5, 12, 14–16, 20, 22–23, 25–26; March: 4, 6–7, 9–10, 12, 14, 20, 25, 27–28, 31.

[49] Individual Irish ecclesiastics may have arrived earlier. For the most recent discussion of this question, see Hochholzer, 'Ein Martyrologfragment', 35–48.

[50] Ibid., 33–5, 46.

style from eleventh-century manuscripts, thus allowing for the possibility that he himself was at work at a somewhat later date. Much the same 'backwardness' was later to be a feature of the Irish Gothic hand which tended to lag a generation or more behind its English model and counterpart.[51]

Whichever dating is accepted, there is little option but to conclude that a copy of MO was brought to Regensburg by an early group of *Schottenmönche*. Interestingly, internal evidence in MReg and T shows that the Regensburg copy of MO had already been subjected to some annotation, mainly, it would seem, in the form of alternative versions of names. Among the examples of names in MReg that occur in glosses on MO and not in the main text are *Féchine* for *Moecu* (20 January); *Ternochus* for *Haue ind écis* (8 February); *Mochonna* for *Conandil* (8 March); and *Lacteanus* for *Molachtóc* (19 March). There is also some evidence to suggest that the version of MO that was taken to Germany was in a line of transmission which appears to have originated in Armagh.[52] Possibly, therefore, a copy of the version of MO kept in Armagh had already been procured during the period when northern monks, led by Marianus, formed the first group of Irish ecclesiastics to arrive in Regensburg.

One would expect the author of the 'Bavarian' recension of Hermann the Lame's martyrology (CSOW) to have used the same source as MReg and T. There is usually little to distinguish its entries from those of MReg, when both are present on the same day. Moreover, the fact that CSOW has *Merobus* instead of *Berchanus* (MReg) at 4 December, describing him erroneously as Irish, may well be due to the fact that both names occur in MO on that day.[53] John McCulloh has made a strong case for regarding the Bavarian text as the work of either Paul of Bernried or of his close associate, Gebhard, who founded the canonry of Sankt-Mang in Regensburg.[54] Either Paul or Gebhard, both of whom were dead by 1156, must have made their selection of over twenty-five Irish feasts, therefore, from a list provided directly or indirectly by the community of the Regensburg *Schottenkloster*.

[51] Ó Riain, '*Codex Salmanticensis*', 96–7.
[52] Ó Riain, *Feastdays of the Saints*, 173–203.
[53] The editors of MH describe the name, which is also written *Metropus*, as *nudum nomen* (*AASS*, Nov. II / 2, 634).
[54] McCulloh, 'Jewish Ritual Murder', 724–8.

Finally, the six entries on Irish saints in EF are in such close agreement with MReg that, had the full earlier manuscript survived, the agreement would doubtless have been maintained throughout, thus underlining the likelihood that the full martyrology lying behind EF was the source of the entries on Irish saints in MReg.[55] Also, the use made of MO in Regensburg represents one of the few surviving traces of evidence for the circulation of the text in the period between its composition in about 830 and its reception of an extensive preface and commentary in the late twelfth century.[56]

---

[55] The only major difference is the omission in MReg of the reference in EF at 17 April to Donnán's martyrdom having taken place, not on Eigg, as is usually said, but on '*insula alasina*', which appears to refer to Ailsa Craig in the Firth of Clyde. On the other hand, the misspelling at 17 April in MReg of *Lasreani* as *Casreani* may have been caused by the form in EF of the initial *L* (with rounding of the ascender and elongation of the top bar), which arguably may have seemed like a *C* to the eye of the Scottish scribe of MReg, unfamiliar as he was with Irish names.

[56] See Ó Riain, *Feastdays of the Saints*, 197.

MARTYROLOGY OF THE REGENSBURG
SCHOTTENKLOSTER

[1–19 January are missing from the manuscript, but see Appendix 2]

[20 January] Decimo Tertio Calendas Februarii 1. Die 20 F

1. **Romae**, natalis beati Fabiani papae et martyris.
2. Eodem die, apud Catacumbas, passio sancti Sebastiani martyris.
3. Lugduno Galliae, sancti Clementis praesbiteri.
4. In Hybernia, sanctorum Fecheni abbatis, Oeni et Molacki confessorum.

4   *Fechini, Molacini* (*in marg.*) T (19 January), *mo Laca, mo-Ecu ... Óenu* MO.

1, 2. MU 1, 2. MReg's *apud Catacumbas* agrees with Molanus.
3. This feast, otherwise extant in some *auctaria* of MU, including the similarly worded Molanus, is already present in MH.
4. While the main text of MO uses the hypocoristic form *Moecu* for Féichín, who was patron of Fore in Co. Westmeath, the radical form was added as a gloss. Aona was abbot of Clonmacnoise in Co. Offaly, whereas Molaga was patron of Aghacross, near Mitchelstown in Co. Cork, and of a number of other churches in the same area.

Sources: **1, 2**. Dubois, *Martyrologe*, 164; *AASS*, Iun. VI, 46. **3**. *AASS*, Iun. VI, 48; Overgaauw, *Martyrologes*, 584; *BiblSS*, iv, 28. **4**. Stokes, *Martyrology*, 37; Best and Lawlor, *Martyrology*, 10; Ó Riain, *Corpus*, §217; *DIS*, 77, 309–11, 480–2.

17

[21 January] G Duodecimo Calendas Februarii 1. Die 21

1. **Romae**, passio sanctae Agnetis, uirginis et martyris.
2. Eodem die, sancti Publii episcopi et martyris.
3. **In Hybernia**, sanctae Fanchae uirginis.
4. In **Scotia**, sancti Vimini episcopi et confessoris.

3 *Fanche* T, *Fuinche* MO.

1, 2. MU 2, 1.
3. Fuinche was patron of the unidentified church of Cluain Caoi, which lay among the Eoghanacht of Cashel, probably in Co. Tipperary.
4. *MenScot* (*In Scotia, Vvimini episcopi*) seems to be the source of this entry. The saint is 'Wynnin/Winning' of Kilwinning, in Ayrshire, whose feast fell on this day. Winnin(g) is taken to represent the same cult as Irish Finnian, alias Fionnbharr of Movilla in Co. Down, but the latter does not have a day in January.

Sources: **1, 2**. Dubois, *Martyrologe*, 165. **3**. Stokes, *Martyrology*, 37; Best and Lawlor, *Martyrology*, 10. **4**. Forbes, *Kalendars*, 190 (XXI), 463–6; Watson, *Celtic Placenames*, 165, 187; *DIS*, 321–4; *LegSS*, 42–5, 422–3.

[22 January] Undecimo Calendas Februarii 1. Die 22 A

1. **Apud** ciuitatem Valentiam, natalis sancti Vincentii leuitae et martyris.
2. **Romae**, ad aquas Saluias, sancti Anastasii monachi et martyris.
3. **In Scotia**, sancti Columbani et sanctarum filiarum Comgalli.

2 *Salinas* MS.
3 *Comgalli* (with a dot over the *m*) MS; *Colmani* T; *Estecht ingen Comgaill, Colmán maccu Béognai*, 'The deaths of the daughters of Comhghall, Colmán of Maca Beoghna', MO.

1, 2. MU 2, 3.
3. Colmán, patron of the Offaly church of Lynally, belonged to a branch of the Ulaidh of N.E. Ulster, as did the three daughters of Comhghall, named Bogha, Laisre and Colum, of whom little else is known.

Sources: **1, 2**. Dubois, *Martyrologe*, 166. **3**. Stokes, *Martyrology*, 37; Best and Lawlor, *Martyrology*, 11; Ó Riain, *Corpus*, §§ 151, 311; *DIS*, 203–5.

[23 January] B Decimo Calendas Februarii 1. Die 23 Januarii

1. **Romae**, natalis sanctae Emerentianae uirginis et martyris, quae erat collactanea sanctae Agnetis.
2. **Philippis**, beati Parmenae, qui fuit unus de septem diaconibus.
3. Apud **Alexandriam**, natale sancti Joannis patriarchae.
4. In **Burgundia**, sancti Maimbodi martyris.

4 *Maibodi* MS.

1, 2. MU 2, 1. The description of Emerentiana as a *collactanea* of Agnes, which is absent from MU, is already in MA, whose wording is followed by MReg.
3. The relics of John of Alexandria were translated to Pressburg (Bratislava) in Slovakia on 23 January 1632, which may explain the inclusion of the feast here. The wording corresponds closely to that of Molanus.
4. The Life of this saint, who was patron of a church near Besançon in Burgundy, describes him as having been born in Ireland. The wording of the entry, and the spelling of the saint's name, correspond closely to Molanus, which is the only other *auctarium* to notice the feast.

Sources: **1, 2**. Dubois, *Martyrologe*, 167; *AASS*, Iun. VI, 54. **3**. *AASS*, Iun. VI, 55; *BiblSS*, vi, 750–56, at 754. **4**. *AASS*, Iun. VI, 55; *BiblSS*, viii, 561–2.

[24 January] Nono Calendas Februarii 1. Die 24 C

1. **Natalis** sancti Timothei, discipuli sancti Pauli. Hic, ab eodem apostolo, episcopus ordinatus Ephesi, post multos pro Christo agones, martyrio coronatus est.
2. **Aruernis**, sancti Artemii episcopi et confessoris.

1. MU 1 (22 January). The wording (*sancti* for *beati*) and spelling (*Ephesi* for *Epheso*) are those of Molanus. Like MReg, Molanus also displaces this feast by two days.

2. Alone of the *auctaria* of MU, Molanus, which has the same wording, also notices the feast of Artemius, bishop of Clermont.

Sources: **1**. Dubois, *Martyrologe*, 165; *AASS*, Iun. VI, 51. **2**. *AASS*, Iun. VI, 57; *BiblSS*, ii, 488.

[25 January] D Octauo Calendas Februarii 1. Die 25

1. **Conuersio** sancti Pauli.
2. Eodem die, sancti Ananiae, qui eundem apostolum baptizauit.
3. Ciuitate **Aruernis**, sancti Praeiecti episcopi et confessoris.

1, 2, 3. MU 1, 2, 3.

Sources: **1–3**. Dubois, *Martyrologe*, 168.

[26 January] Septimo Calendas Februarii 1. Die 26 E

1. **Apud Smyrnam**, natalis sancti Policarpi episcopi, discipuli sancti Joannis apostoli.
2. **Treuiris**, sancti Mari episcopi et confessoris.

1. MU 1.
2. Marus, bishop of Trier, is commemorated in several *auctaria*, including Molanus.

Sources: **1**. Dubois, *Martyrologe*, 168. **2**. *AASS*, Iun. VI, 57; *BiblSS*, viii, 1192.

[27 January] F Sexto Calendas Februarii 1. Die 27

1. **Natalis** beati Joannis Chrisostomi, episcopi Constantinopolitani.
2. In **Bethlem Judae**, dormitio sanctae Paulae.
3. **Romae**, sancti Uitaliani papae, qui cantum Romanum composuit et dulcisono organo concordauit.
4. In **Hybernia, sanctae Maidae virginis**.

[4] The *i* of *Maidae* was rewritten in black ink. *Carais moéda*, 'My Lord loved', MO.

1, 2. MU 1, 3.
3. This entry is in some *auctaria* of MU, including Molanus, which has much the same wording.
4. Despite MReg's red lettering, there is no such saint; the second word of the first line of the quatrain in MO (*moéda* < *mo fhiadha*, 'my Lord') was mistakenly taken to be the name of a saint.

Sources: **1, 2**. Dubois, *Martyrologe*, 169. **3**. *AASS*, Iun. VI, 64–5; Overgaauw, *Martyrologes*, 593. **4**. Stokes, *Martyrology*, 38.

[28 January] Quinto Calendas Februarii 1. Die 28 G

1. **Romae**, natalis sanctae Agnetis secundo.
2. **Alexandriae**, beati Cyrilli episcopi, qui catholicae fidei praeclarissimus extitit propugnator.
3. In **Hybernia**, sancti **Acobrani** abbatis et confessoris.

[3] *Scobrani*? MS; *La hAccobrán*, 'With Acobhrán', MO.

1, 2. MU 1, 3. Unusually for MReg, both entries represent the full text of MU.
3. Acobhrán was patron of a church named Kilrush (*Ceall Rois*), now either Kilrush in the Clare barony of Moyarta, or Kilrush in the Kildare barony of Offaly West.

Sources: **1, 2**. Dubois, *Martyrologe*, 170. **3**. Stokes, *Martyrology*, 38; Best and Lawlor, *Martyrology*, 13; Stokes, *Martyrology of Gorman*, 24; *DIS*, 53.

[29 January] A Quarto Calendas Februarii 1. Die 29

1. **Treuiris**, depositio beati Ualerii episcopi, discipuli sancti Petri apostoli.
2. In **Britannia**, sancti Gildae abbatis et confessoris.
3. In Hy**bernia**, sancti Maknolocki episcopi et confessoris.

1. MU 2.

2. This entry, in much the same wording, is also in Molanus.

3. *MenScot* (*Makvvoloci episcopi et confessoris*) appears to be the source of this entry. Volocus (Makwoloch), later Wallach, gave name to the parish of St Walach in Aberdeenshire. Watson suggested a derivation from the 'rather rare' Irish name Uallach, but a possible Pictish origin has also been proposed. An office Life of the saint has been preserved in the Breviary of Aberdeen.

Sources: **1**. Dubois, *Martyrologe*, 170. **2**. *AASS*, Iun. VI, 69. **3**. Forbes, *Kalendars*, 191 (XXIX), 459–61; Watson, *Celtic Placenames*, 336; *LegSS*, 44–7, 421.

[30 January] Tertio Calendas Februarii 1. Die 30 B

1. **Apud Antiochiam**, passio beati Hyppoliti martyris.

2. **Hierosolimis**, sancti Mathiae episcopi, qui octauus post sanctum Jacobum rexit ecclesiam.

3. Eodem die, in **Hybernia**, sancti Maglastiani episcopi.

4. Ibidem, sancti Aenani abbatis.

5. Die 30, dedicatio altaris sanctorum Hyberniorum.

⁴   *Enán Roiss*, 'Éanán of Ros', MO.

1, 2. MU 1, 2. The reference to Mathias being eighth after James, although absent from MU, is otherwise also found in some *auctaria*, but not in Molanus.

3. *MenScot* (*in Kyntyre, Maglastiani episcopi*) is again the probable source here. The saint is associated with Kinglassie (from *Cill Glaise*, 'church of the brook') in Fife, near which is a well called St Glass's. As Watson points out, the saint may have taken his name from the stream.

4. Éanán was patron of Rosminogue in the Wexford barony of Gorey.

5. This altar stood probably in Weih Sankt Peter in Regensburg. The feast is nowhere else recorded.

Sources: **1, 2**. Dubois, *Martyrologe*, 171; *AASS*, Iun. VI, 71–2; Overgaauw, *Matryrologes*, 597. **3**. Forbes, *Kalendars*, 191 (XXX), 356–7; Watson, *Celtic Placenames*, 320. **4**. Stokes, *Martyrology*, 39; Best and

Lawlor, *Martyrology*, 13; *DIS*, 452. **5**. Ó Riain (D.), 'The *Schotten-klöster* and the Legacy of the Irish *sancti peregrini*', 159n.

[31 January] C Pridie Calendas Februarii 1. Die 31

1. **Natalis sancti** Julii confessoris.
2. Eodem die, translatio sancti Marci euangelistae ab Alexandria Aegipti ad Venetias.
3. In **Hybernia**, sancti Maedochii episcopi.
4. Item, beati Melanphni Scoti abbatis et confessoris.

3, 4 *Madochii?* MS. *Medoci* T; *Aed ... Ferna, Mael-anfaid*, 'Aodh of Ferns, Maol Anfaidh.', MO.

1, 2. The Molanus version of MU also has these two entries in much the same wording. Overgaauw describes Julius as a German addition, to be distinguished from the Milan saint of the name who is also commemorated on this day.
3, 4. Maodhóg, alias Aodh, is patron of the Wexford diocesan see of Ferns, whereas Maol Anfaidh was attached to Dairinis, now Molana Abbey on the river Blackwater, near Youghal in Co. Cork. Maodhóg's feast is also in two Cologne *auctaria* of MU (Lübeck/Cologne and Grevenus), which read: *Edani episcopi et confessoris*.

Sources: **1, 2**. *AASS*, Iun. VI, 74; Overgaauw, *Matryrologes*, 601; *BiblSS*, vi, 1237–8. **3**. Stokes, *Martyrology*, 39; Best and Lawlor, *Martyrology*, 13; *AASS*, Iun. VI, 74; *DIS*, 432–6.

[1 February] Calendis Februarii 1. Die 1 Februarii D

1. **Natalis** beati Ignatii episcopi et martyris, qui, tertius post Petrum apostolum, Antiochenam rexit ecclesiam.
2. In **Scotia**, sanctae **B**rigidae uirginis, cuius uita miraculis claruit.

1, 2. MU 1, 5. The wording of both entries is exactly the same as that of MU. Brighid, Ireland's second 'national' saint after Patrick, had already been introduced to the universal martyrological tradition in the early eighth century in Willibrord's calendar and in the Echternach

copy of the Hieronymian martyrology, as also in Bede's martyrology (c. 730).
Sources: **1**, **2**. Dubois, *Martyrologe*, 172–3; *AASS*, Nov. II/2, 71–2; Wilson, *Calendar*, 4; *DIS*, 123–5.

[2 February] E Quarto Nonas Februarii 1. Die 2

1. **Purificatio beatae Mariae** Uirginis.
2. Apud **Cesaream**, beati Cornelii centurionis, quem beatus Petrus baptizauit.
3. In **Hybernia**, sanctae Finnichae uirginis.
4. **Cantuariae** in **Anglia**, natalis sancti Laurentii episcopi et confessoris.

3 *la Finnig nDuirn*, 'with Finneach of Dorn', MO.

1, **2**. MU 1, 2. Most *auctaria* of MU agree with the wording here.
3. Finneach of Dorn, who appears also to have been known as Sineach, gave name to the church of Killinny (from *Ceall Fhinnche*, 'church of Finneach'), in the Kilkenny barony of Kells.
4. Of the *auctaria* of MU, only Molanus and Grevenus otherwise commemorate Laurence of Canterbury, albeit in different words.

Sources: **1**, **2**. Dubois, *Martyrologe*, 173; *AASS*, Iun. VI, 79; Overgaauw, *Matryrologes*, 604. **3**. Stokes, *Martyrology*, 58; Best and Lawlor, *Martyrology*, 14; *HDGP*, iii, 172; *DIS*, 564. **4**. *EncASE*, 279; Farmer, *Dictionary*, 238–9.

[3 February] Tertio Nonas Februarii 1. Die 3 F

1. **Apud Sebasten**, passio sancti Blasii episcopi et martyris.
2. **Viennae**, sancti Euentii gloriosi episcopi.
3. In **Africa**, natalis beati Celerini diaconi.

3 *et diaconi* MS.

1. Following Ado, Usuard placed Blasius's feast on 15 February, but it is on the present day in most liturgical calendars and *auctaria* of MU, including Molanus.

2. This entry, drawn from MA, is in most *auctaria*, including Molanus, which has much the same wording as here.
3. MU 1.

Sources: **1**. Dubois, *Martyrologe*, 180; *AASS*, Iun. VI, 80–2; Overgaauw, *Matryrologes*, 606–7. **2**. Dubois and Renaud, *Martyrologes*, 79; *AASS*, Iun. VI, 80–2; Overgaauw, *Matryrologes*, 607. **3**. Dubois, *Martyrologe*, 174.

[4 February] G Pridie Nonas Februarii 1. Die 4

1. In ciuitate **Aegypti**, passio beati Phileae episcopi.
2. **Romae**, sanctorum martyrum Aquilini, Magni et Donati.
3. **In Hybernia**, sancti Cuanni abbatis et confessoris.

3   *Cúannae* MO.

1, 2. MU 1, 2, with characteristic omission in MReg of the precise locations of the martyrdoms (*Thmuis, Forum Simpronii*).
3. Cuanna (†701) was attached to the church of Lismore, in the Waterford barony of Coshmore and Coshbride.

Sources: **1, 2**. Dubois, *Martyrologe*, 174. **3**. Stokes, *Martyrology*, 58; Best and Lawlor, *Martyrology*, 14; *DIS*, 53.

[5 February] Nonis Februarii 1. Die 5 A

1. Apud Ciciliam, ciuitate Catanensium, natalis sanctae Agathae, uirginis et martyris.
2. Viennae, beati Auiti episcopi et confessoris.

1, 2. MU 1, 2.

Sources: **1**. Dubois, *Martyrologe*, 175; *AASS*, Iun. VI, 84–6.

[6 February] B Octauo Idus Februarii 1. Die 6

1. Apud Cesaream Cappadociae, natalis sanctae Dorotheae virginis et martyris.
2. **Romae**, uia Appia, passio sanctae Sotheris uirginis.

3. **In Hybernia**, sancti Melini episcopi et confessoris.

3 *epscop Mel*, 'bishop Mel', MO.

1. MU 1.
2. Although absent from MU, this feast is present in a number of *auctaria*, including Molanus which agrees closely with MReg's wording.
3. Mel was patron of the Longford church and diocesan see of Ardagh.

Sources: **1**. Dubois, *Martyrologe*, 175. **2**. *AASS*, Iun. VI, 87–8. **3**. Stokes, *Martyrology*, 59; Best and Lawlor, *Martyrology*, 15; *DIS*, 450–1.

[7 February] Septimo Idus Februarii 1. Die 7 C

1. In **Britanniis**, ciuitate Augusta, natalis beati Auguli episcopi et martyris.
2. **In Hybernia**, sancti Mellani abbatis.
3. Ibidem, sanctorum Lomani et Ronani episcoporum et confessorum.
4. In **Anglia**, sancti Odonis episcopi et confessoris.

2 *Mellán Inse ... maccu Cuinn*, 'Meallán of Inchiquin', MO. **3**. *Comani* MS; *Lommán ... Locha Uair*, 'Lomán of Lough Owel', MO.

1. MU 1.
2. Meallán was connected with Inchiquin, an island on Lough Corrib (GY).
3. Lomán's church was on Lough Owel in Co. Westmeath, where Portloman (earlier Teach Lomáin, 'Lomán's house/church') bears his name. As to Rónán, no saint of that name figures in the Irish record on this day. However, a Rónán of Lismore was commemorated on 9 February. Furthermore, *MenScot* commemorates *Ronnani episcopi, qui in Levinia excessit* on this day, and he may be the same as the eponym of Kilmaronock near Dumbarton. His name, but no legend, is preserved in the Breviary of Aberdeen.
4. Of the *auctaria* of MU, only Grevenus (Feb. 7.4) and Molanus, both of which have the same wording as MReg, refer here to Odo. The saint intended is presumably Odo (Oda) of Canterbury, whose feast otherwise fell on 2 June.

Sources: **1**. Dubois, *Martyrologe*, 176. **2**. Stokes, *Martyrology*, 59; Best and Lawlor, *Martyrology*, 15; *DIS*, 451–2. **3**. Stokes, *Martyrology*, 59; Best and Lawlor, *Martyrology*, 15; Forbes, *Kalendars*, 191 (VII); Watson, *Celtic Placenames*, 309; *LegSS*, 56, 410–11; *DIS*, 401– 2. **4**. *AASS*, Iun. VI, 89; *EncASE*, 339–40; Farmer, *Dictionary*, 296–7.

[8 February] D Sixto Idus Februarii 1. Die 8

1. Apud **Armeniam minorem**, natalis sanctorum Dionisii, Emiliani et Sebastiani.
2. Ciuitate **Corduba**, Salomonis martyris.
3. In **Hybernia**, sancti Ternochi confessoris.
4. Item Fiachrai abbatis.

3 *Ternochi* T; *Haue ... ind ecis*, 'descendant of the sage', MO. **4**. *Fiachraij* (with line through *j*) MS; *Fiachrae ... abb Irarda*, 'Fiachra abbot of Ullard', MO.

1, 2. MU 1, 3, with the omission here in 2, as in Molanus, of the name of the province (*Lusitania*).
3. Little is known of Téarnóg, other than his description in MT as an anchorite. The form of the name in MReg is also in a note in MO.
4. Fiachra's church, Ullard (Irish Iorard) in the Carlow barony of St Mullin's Lower, was sometimes confused with Clonard (Irish Cluain Ioraird) in the Meath barony of Moyfenrath.

Sources: **1, 2**. Dubois, *Martyrologe*, 176–7. **3**. Stokes, *Martyrology*, 59; Best and Lawlor, *Martyrology*, 15. **4**. Stokes, *Martyrology*, 59; Best and Lawlor, *Martyrology*, 15; *DIS*, 316.

[9 February] Quinto Idus Februarii Die 9 E

1. Apud **Alexandriam**, passio sanctae Apolloniae virginis, cui persecutores primum dentes excusserunt, deinde, cum nolebat cum eis impia uerba proferre, repente se de manibus eorum liberauit et in ignem prosiliuit.
2. In **Hybernia**, Mochuaroch abbatis.
3. Item Cairech Dergan uirginis.

4. In Hoyo, sancti Mangoldi ducis et martyris, regis Gugonis Anglorum filii.

² *Mochnaroch* MS; *Mo Chúaróc* MO. 3. *Cairec Dernae* MS; *Cáirech Dergan* MO.

1. MU 1. Much more is retained here of Usuard's entry on Apollonia, patron of toothache, than is usual in this highly abridged text.
2. This saint, styled *Cuaranus sapiens* by MT, was patron of a number of churches, mainly in Munster.
3. Caoireach Deargáin was patron of Cloonburren in the Galway barony of Moycarn.
4. Alone of the *auctaria* of MU, Molanus likewise contains this entry, with *Maingoldi* and *Hugonis* for the variant readings here. The saint may be the same as the Blessed *Magilmumensis, qui Doctor Scotorum audit*, whom *MenScot* places *in Anglia* on this day.

Sources: **1.** Dubois, *Martyrologe*, 177. **2.** Stokes, *Martyrology*, 59; Best and Lawlor, *Martyrology*, 15. **3.** Stokes, *Martyrology*, 59; Best and Lawlor, *Martyrology*, 15; Stokes, *Martyrology of Gorman*, 32; *DIS*, 150–1. **4.** *AASS*, Iun. VI, 93; Forbes, *Kalendars*, 192 (IX).

[10 February] F Quarto Idus Februarii [10]

1. Apud **Cassinum**, **sanctae Scholasticae** uirginis, sororis sancti Benedicti abbatis.
2. Romae, uia Lauicana, decem militum.
3. **In Hybernia**, sancti Cronani abbatis et confessoris.

³ *Cronán ... Glasse Máre*, 'Crónán of Clashmore', MO.

1, 2. MU 4, 3, with the omission here of *castrum* before *Cassinum*.
3. Crónán son of Meallán, patron of Clashmore in the Waterford barony of Decies within Drum, is said to have been a disciple of Mochuda of Lismore. Grevenus's *In Hibernia, Trouani* [recte *Cronani*?] *episcopi et confessoris* on the previous day may refer to Crónán.

Sources: **1, 2.** Dubois, *Martyrologe*, 178. **3.** Stokes, *Martyrology*, 59; Best and Lawlor, *Martyrology*, 16; *AASS*, Iun. VI, 95; *DIS*, 233.

[11 February] Tertio Idus Februarii Die 11 G

1. Apud Lugdunum, natalis sancti Desiderii episcopi et confessoris.
2. **In Hybernia**, sancti Etcheni episcopi.
3. Et sancti Mogobochi abbatis et confessoris.

2 *Eicheni* MS; *Etchini* T; *epscop Etchen*, 'bishop Éidchéan', MO. **3.**
Mogopnat MO.

1. MU 1.
2. Éidchéan, patron of Clonfad in the Westmeath barony of Farbill,
was also one of the Irish saints commemorated in Grevenus's version
of MU, which reads: *In Hibernia, Eciani episcopi et confessoris.*
3. By choosing to commemorate Moghobóg, who is first of the list in
MT for this day, MReg failed to follow MO, whose saint of the day,
Gobnaid, was patron of the Cork church of Ballyvourney. Moghobóg
was identical with Gobán of Killamery in the Kilkenny barony of
Kells, whose usual feast fell on 6 December.

Sources: **1.** Dubois, *Martyrologe*, 178. **2.** Stokes, *Martyrology*, 60;
Best and Lawlor, *Martyrology*, 16; Stokes, *Martyrology of Gorman*,
34; *AASS*, Iun. VI, 97; *DIS*, 288–9. **3.** Stokes, *Martyrology*, 60; Best
and Lawlor, *Martyrology*, 16; *DIS*, 367–8.

[12 February] A Pridie Idus Februarii Die 12

1. In Hispaniis, natalis sanctae Eulaliae uirginis.
2. In Affrica, sanctorum martyrum Saturnini presbiteri, Datiui et sociorum.
3. Item, passio sancti Damiani militis.

1, 2. MU 1, 2.
3. Many *auctaria*, including Molanus, which, apart from placing the
saint in Africa, has the same wording as MReg, include here the feast
of Damianus, of whom little else is known.

Sources: **1, 2.** Dubois, *Martyrologe*, 179. **3.** *AASS*, Iun. VI, 99; *BiblSS*,
iv, 444.

[13 February] Idibus Februarii Die 13 B

1. Apud Antiochiam, natalis sancti Agabi prophetae.
2. **Romae**, sancti Gregorii papae secundi.
3. **In Britannia, sanctae** Ermenildae uirginis.
4. **In Hybernia, sancti** Modomnochi abbatis et confessoris.

4   *mo Domnóc* MO.

1. MU 1, with *Apud Antiochiam* placed first by MReg, as in the Molanus version of MU.
2. The feast of Gregory II (†731), who supported the missionary work of Boniface in northern Europe, figures in a number of *auctaria*, including Molanus.
3. Some *auctaria*, including Molanus, commemorate Ermengild/Ermenilda, queen of Mercia and abbess of Ely, on this day. Although described as a virgin, she reputedly had issue, a daughter named Werburga, who succeeded her at Ely.
4. Modhomhnóg was patron of Tibberaghny in the Kilkenny barony of Iverk. He is said to have brought bees to Ireland.

Sources: **1**. Dubois, *Martyrologe*, 179. **2**. *AASS*, Iun. VI, 100; Kelly, *Dictionary*, 86–7. **3**. *AASS*, Iun. VI, 100; Overgaauw, *Martyrologes*, 623; Farmer, *Dictionary*, 135. **4**. Stokes, *Martyrology*, 60; Best and Lawlor, *Martyrology*, 16; *DIS*, 477–8.

[14 February] C Decimo Sexto Calendas Martii Die 14

1. **Romae, natalis** beati Ualentini presbiteri, qui, post multa tormenta, sub Claudio Caesare decollatus est.
2. Apud Alexandriam, sanctorum martyrum Bassi et Antonii, qui in mare mersi sunt.

Heading   *sexto* corrected from *quinto* MS. **2**. *mari* MS.

1, 2. MU 1, 4, with some variant readings here, including the placing of *sub Claudio Caesare* before *decollatus est* in 1 and the omission in 2 of the third martyr (Protolicus).

Sources: **1, 2**. Dubois, *Martyrologe*, 180.

[15 February] Decimo Quinto Calendas Martii Die 15 D

1. Ciuitate **Brixia**, sanctorum martyrum Faustini et Jouitae uirginis.
2. **Romae**, sancti Cratonis martyris.
3. **Antiochiae**, Joseph diaconi.

1 *martyrum* for *uirginis* MS.

1. MU 3, with *Brixia* here for *Brixa*, as in Molanus, which also places the entry first.
2. MU 2.
3. Of the *auctaria* consulted by Sollerius, Bruxellensis and Molanus likewise commemorate Joseph on this day. The entry is already in MH.

Sources: **1, 2.** Dubois, *Martyrologe*, 180. **3.** *AASS*, Iun. VI, 104; Overgaauw, *Martyrologes*, 626; *AASS*, Nov. II/2, 97.

[16 February] E Decimo Quarto Calendas Martii Die 16

1. Natalis beati Onesimi, de quo sanctus Paulus scribit Philemoni.
2. Apud **Aegyptum**, sancti Juliani martyris, cum aliis numero quinque millibus.
3. **In Scotia**, sancti Finnani episcopi.

1, 2. MU 1, 3.
3. *MenScot* (*In Anglia, Finnani episcopi et gentis illius apostoli*) is probably the source of the present entry. Intended is Fíonán, successor of Aidan at Lindisfarne, whose feast normally falls on the following day. His Legend is preserved in the Breviary of Aberdeen.

Sources: **1, 2.** Dubois, *Martyrologe*, 181–2. **3.** Forbes, *Kalendars*, 192 (XVI); Farmer, *Dictionary*, 150; Ó Riain, *Anglo-Saxon Ireland*, 9; *LegSS*, 56–8, 363.

[17 February] Decimo Tertio Calendas Martii Die 17 F

1. **In Scotia**, sancti Fintani praesbiteri et confessoris, magnae uirtutis uiri.

2. Claromonte, sancti Lupini confessoris.
3. In **Hybernia**, sancti Cormaki confessoris.

1 *Fintani abbatis* T. **3**. *féil Chormaicc*, 'Cormac's feast', MO.

1. MU 3. Fiontan, patron of Clonenagh in the Laois barony of Mary-borough West, was one of a small number of Irish saints introduced by Usuard to the continental martyrological tradition. The wording is the same as that of MU. Grevenus has a notice which reads: *In Scotia, Fintani presbyteri et confessoris*.
2. Lupianus, whom Gregory of Tours noticed in *De gloria confessorum*, may have been the saint venerated at Clermont-Ferrand on this day. He is commemorated in some *auctaria*, including Molanus which uses the same words.
3. Cormac, who is elsewhere described as a bishop, was attached to the church of Trim in the Meath barony of Moyfenrath Lower.

Sources: **1**. Dubois, *Martyrologe*, 182; *DIS*, 339–41. **2**. *AASS*, Iun. VI, 109; *BiblSS*, viii, 378. **3**. Stokes, *Martyrology*, 61; Best and Lawlor, *Martyrology*, 17; *DIS*, 227.

[18 February] G Duodecimo Calendas Martii Die 18

1. Hierosolimis, beati Symeonis episcopi et martyris.
2. In Affrica, sanctorum Lucii, Syluani et Maximi.
3. In **Hybernia**, sancti Columbani abbatis.
4. Et sanctae Moliuae uirginis.

3, 4 *Colmán, mo Liba* MO.

1. MU 1, with precedence given here to the location of the bishop's see.
2. Alone of the *auctaria* of MU, Molanus likewise reads *Lucii* for the more usual *Rutuli*.
3. This Colmán, whose office Life is preserved in the Breviary of Aberdeen, was attached to Moray and Tarbat in Ross-shire. Grevenus (*Culani episcopi et confessoris, Berethei*) notes the feasts of Cúlán of Coolaun and Bearach of Kilbarry on this day.

4. Molioba, alias Libhear, was attached to various churches in East Ulster, including Annahilt in the Down barony of Lower Iveagh. Despite MReg, whose compiler may have been confused by the ending of the saint's name in *-a*, Molioba was a male.

Sources: **1**. Dubois, *Martyrologe*, 183. **2**. *AASS*, Iun. VI, 111; Overgaauw, *Martyrologes*, 629. **3**. Stokes, *Martyrology*, 61; Best and Lawlor, *Martyrology*, 17; Forbes, *Kalendars*, 128; Watson, *Celtic Placenames*, 278–9; *LegSS*, 58–61, 336; *AASS*, Iun. VI, 111; *DIS*, 94–6, 197–8, 246. **4**. Stokes, *Martyrology*, 61; Best and Lawlor, *Martyrology*, 17; Ó Riain, *Corpus*, §722.102; *DIS*, 396–7.

[19 February] Undecimo Calendas Martii Die 19 A

1. **Romae**, natalis sancti Gabini et martyris.
2. In Affrica, sanctorum Publii, Juliani et Marcelli.
3. **In Hybernia**, sancti Baitheni abbatis et confessoris.

3 *Battheni* MS; *Bartheni* T; *Baethíne ... macc ... Cuanach*, 'Baoithín son of Cuana', MO.

1. MU 1, with the omission here of Usuard's description of the saint as *presbyter*.
2. MU 2. The addition here of *et Marcelli* is at one with several versions of MU, including Molanus.
3. This saint was patron of Taghboyne, which took its name from him, in the Westmeath barony of Rathconrath.

Sources: **1**. Dubois, *Martyrologe*, 184. **2**. *AASS*, Iun. VI, 112; Overgaauw, *Martyrologes*, 630. **3**. Stokes, *Martyrology*, 61; Best and Lawlor, *Martyrology*, 18; Stokes, *Martyrology of Gorman*, 38; *DIS*, 89–90.

[20 February] B Decimo Calendas Martii Die 20

1. Apud Tyrum, quae est urbs maxima Phoenicis, beatorum martyrum, qui, iubente Diocletiano, multis tormentorum suppliciis occisi sunt.
2. In Cypro insula, sanctorum Pothamii et Nemesii.

1. MU 1. Despite its normally abbreviated character, MReg added here from MA *quae est urbs maxima Phoenicis*, which is not in Molanus.

2. MU 2.

Sources: **1, 2**. Dubois, *Martyrologe*, 184; Dubois and Renaud, *Martyrologes*, 90.

[21 February] Nono Cale[nd]as Martii Die 21 C

1. Nono calendas Martii, apud Siciliam, sanctorum martyrum septuaginta nouem.
2. Mediolani, festum sancti Ambrosii, pro uictoria, ipso inuocato, adepta.
3. **In Hybernia, sancti Fintani abbatis**.

3   *Togairm Fintain choraig*, 'The calling of Fiontan Corach', MO.

1. MU 1. The reference to the ninth calend is not in MU, but is, of course, the heading of the list for this day.
2. Alone of the *auctaria* of MU, Molanus also records this feast, in the same words, but adds the name of the place of victory, *ad Parabiagum*, and the date 1338.
3. The epithet *corach* is commonly attached to this saint's name; Fiontan was remembered in the Laois church of Clonenagh and, as such, may have been identical with its like-named patron, whose feast fell four days earlier.

Sources: **1**. Dubois, *Martyrologe*, 184. **2**. *AASS*, Iun. VI, 116. **3**. Stokes, *Martyrology*, 61; Best and Lawlor, *Martyrology*, 18; *DIS*, 340.

[22 February] D Octauo Calendas Martii Die 22

1. Apud **Antiochiam**, cathedra sancti Petri.
2. **Alexandriae**, sancti Abilii episcopi.
3. Viennae, sancti Pascasii.

1, 2. MU 1, 4.
3. Most *auctaria*, including Molanus, follow MA's listing of Paschasius on this day.
Sources: **1**. Dubois, *Martyrologe*, 184. **2**. *AASS*, Iun. VI, 116; Overgaauw, *Martyrologes*, 623; Dubois and Renaud, *Martyrologes*, 91–2.

[23 February] Septimo Calendas Martii Die 23 E

1. Vigilia beati Mathiae apostoli.
2. In **Anglia**, sanctae Milburgis uirginis, filiae regis Merciorum.
1. Several *auctaria*, including Molanus which, like MReg, uses *beati* to describe Matthew, have this feast.
2. Of the *auctaria* of MU, only Grevenus and Molanus agree with MReg in describing Mildburg as a daughter of the king of Mercia.

Sources: **1**. *AASS*, Iun. VI, 120; Overgaauw, *Martyrologes*, 634. **2**. *AASS*, Iun. VI, 120; *EncASE*, 313; Farmer, *Dictionary*, 279.

[24 February] F Sixto Calendas Martii Die 24

1. Natalis beati Mathiae apostoli, qui post Ascensionem Domini ab apostolis sorte electus est.
2. Item, inuentio capitis Praecursoris Domini.
3. **In Hybernia**, sancti Cumini abbatis et confessoris.

3   *abb Híae ... Cummine find*, 'Abbot of Í (Iona), fair Cuimín', MO.

1, 2. MU 1, 2.
3. Cuimín Fionn (fair) held the abbacy of Iona between 657 and 669.

Sources: **1, 2**. Dubois, *Martyrologe*, 186. **3**. Stokes, *Martyrology*, 62; Best and Lawlor, *Martyrology*, 19; *DIS*, 245–6.

[25 February] Quinto Calendas Martii Die 25 G

1. Natalis sanctae Walpurgae uirginis.
2. Item, sanctae Aldetrudis uirginis.
3. In Sicilia, sancti Gerlandi ex Burgundia, episcopi Agrigentini, tempore Rogerii comitis.

1. The feast of Walburga, sister of Winnebald and abbess of Heidenheim, is listed on this day in several versions of MU, but not in Molanus, which notes the feast at 1 May and again at 4 August.
2. Aldetrudis, supposedly the daughter of Vincentius Madelgarius, was abbess of Maubeuge. The entry in Molanus, which otherwise

agrees with the wording here, goes on to describe her as *filiae sanctae Waldetrudis*.

3. Gerlandus, bishop of Agrigento in Sicily, a native of Besançon, died on 25 February 1100. The final translation of his relics occured in 1630. Molanus has the same wording as here.

Sources: **1**, *AASS*, Iun.VI, 124; Overgaauw, *Martyrologes*, 636; *EncASE*, 464; Farmer, *Dictionary*, 395. **2**. *AASS*, Iun. VI, 124; *BiblSS*, i, 750–1. **3**. *AASS*, Iun. VI, 124; *BiblSS*, vi, 224–5.

[26 February] A Quarto Calendas Martii Die 26

1. Apud Alexandriam, sancti Alexandri episcopi.
2. Item, Fortunati, Faelicis, cum aliis viginti septem.
3. Eodem die, sancti patris Porphyrii, archiepiscopi Gazae.

1. MU 2.
2. This feast, which was borrowed from MH, is found in several *auctaria* of MU, including Molanus.
3. MR was the first western martyrology to commemorate Porphyrius, bishop of Gaza, but the feast is also in Molanus, whence its inclusion here.

Sources: **1**. Dubois, *Martyrologe*, 187. **2**. *AASS*, Iun. VI, 126; Overgaauw, *Martyrologes*, 637. **3**. *AASS*, Dec., Propyleum, 77–8; *AASS*, Iun. VI, 126; *BiblSS*, x, 1039–43.

[27 February] Tertio Calendas Martii [Die] 27 B

1. Alexandriae, passio sancti Juliani martyris.
2. In **Hybernia**, sancti Comgani abbatis et confessoris.
3. Eodem die, in Nortmannia, beatae Honorinae uirginis et martyris.

² *Conigani* MS; *féil Chomgain*, 'feast of Comhghán', MO.

1. MU 1.
2. Comhghán was patron of Killeshin in the Laois barony of Slievemargy.

3. This is one of several entries relating to Normandy which MReg took from Molanus. Honorina, patron of a church in Conflans, was also a patron of mariners.

Sources: **1.** Dubois, *Martyrologe*, 187. **2.** Stokes, *Martyrology*, 63; Best and Lawlor, *Martyrology*, 19; *DIS*, 220–1. **3.** *AASS*, Iun. VI, 126; *BiblSS*, ix, 1211–12.

[28 February] C Pridie Calendas Martii Die 28

1. In territorio Lugdunensi, sancti Romani abbatis.
2. Papiae, translatio sancti Augustini episcopi et confessoris.

1. MU 1, with omission here of the precise location (*in locis Iurensibus*).
2. This entry on the translation of the relics of St Augustine is found in several *auctaria* of MU, including Molanus which has much the same wording.

Sources: **1.** Dubois, *Martyrologe*, 187. **2.** *AASS*, Iun. VI, 130; Overgaauw, *Martyrologes*, 639.

[1 March] Calendis Martii Die 1 D

1. Natalis sancti Donati martyris.
2. **In Britannia**, Dauid episcopi et confessoris.
3. **In Hybernia**, sancti Sennani episcopi, et sancti Moinenni abbatis et confessoris.

1   *Donat* MS. **3.** *Sennooni ... Maemnani* (with a third *m* expunged) MS; *Senán, Moinenn* MO.

1. MU 2.
2. The entry on David could have come from a number of possible sources, including MO whose commentary locates the saint in Britain. However, the feast is also in several *auctaria*, including Molanus which likewise places the saint *in Britannia*.
3. Seanán and Maoineann were thought to be bishops. The former saint, whose more usual feast fell a week later (see below at 8 March), was regarded as patron of the church and former diocese of Inis Cathaigh (Scattery Island in Co. Clare). Maoineann, who is usually described as

a psalmist and Briton, figures prominently in the first Life of Brendan of Clonfert, where he and a *puer* named Seanán are brought together. Grevenus reads: *In Scocia, Monani abbatis et confessoris* on this day and *In Hibernia, Tedgnae et Monendabis abbatum* on the following day. Despite Sollerius's caustic comment – *Hibernis ipsis ignotorum* – this may refer, however corruptly, to Seanán and Maoineann.

Sources: **1**. Dubois, *Martyrologe*, 188. **2**. *AASS*, Iun. VI, 132–3; Stokes, *Martyrology*, 86. **3**. Stokes, *Martyrology*, 80; Best and Lawlor, *Martyrology*, 20; Plummer, *Vitae*, i, 145; *AASS*, Iun. VI, 134; *DIS*, 436, 557–60.

[2 March] E Sexto Nonas Martii Die 2

1. **Romae**, uia Latina, sanctorum martyrum Jouini et Basilei.
2. In **Hybernia**, sancti Fergnani abbatis et confessoris.
3. Item, sancti Marnani archidiaconi.

² *Fregnani* MS; *féil ... Fergnai Íae*, 'feast of Feargna of Í (Iona)', MO.

1. MU 1, with untypical inclusion here of the precise location.
2. Feargna held the abbacy of Iona until his death in 623. Adhamhnán refers to him on several occasions under the guise of *Virgnous*. He is sometimes provided with the epithet *Briot*, 'Briton'.
3. *MenScot* lists here *Marnani*, describing him as *episcopi*. However, on the previous day we find *Minnani archidiaconi*, which may have caused the confusion. The Breviary of Aberdeen has Marnan's office Life at 1 March.

Sources: **1**. Dubois, *Martyrologe*, 188. **2**. Stokes, *Martyrology*, 80; Best and Lawlor, *Martyrology*, 20; Anderson and Anderson, *Adomnan's Life of Columba*, 129; *DIS*, 308. **3**. Forbes, *Kalendars*, 193 (I, II); *LegSS*, 64–5, 398; *AASS*, Iun. VI, 133; *DIS*, 453.

[3 March] Quinto Nonas Martii Die 3 F

1. Bambergae, sanctae Kunigundis uirginis.
2. **In Hybernia**, sanctorum Cele et Moacra abbatum et confessorum.
3. Item, sancti Ceddei episcopi.

1   *Kunegundis* MS. **2.** *Céle Críst ... mo Macru macc Senain*, 'Céile Críost ... Momhagra son of Seanán', MO.

1. This feast is in several *auctaria*, but only Molanus (*Babenbergae*, more correctly *Bambergae*) otherwise prefaces the entry with a reference to the place of burial. Kunigundis died in 1033 and is buried in Bamberg.

2. Some versions of MO render the second name *Moacru*, as in MReg. Moshagra was attached to Saggart in the Dublin barony of Newcastle. The later Irish martyrologies, beginning with MG, identify Céile Críost as the eponym of Ceall Chéile Chríost in Uí Dhúnchadha, now probably Kilteel in the Kildare barony of South Salt.

3. Chad's feast fell on the previous day, where it is noticed by most *auctaria* of MU, but *MenScot* refers to the transfer of the saint's relics on this day.

Sources: **1.** *AASS*, Iun. VI, 136; Overgaauw, *Martyrologes*, 643. **2.** Stokes, *Martyrology*, 80; Best and Lawlor, *Martyrology*, 20; Stokes, *Martyrology of Gorman*, 46; *DIS*, 165, 498–9; *HDGP*, iii, 141. **3.** *AASS*, Iun. VI, 133; Forbes, *Kalendars*, 193 (III).

[4 March] G Quarto Nonas Martii Dei 4

1. Romae, natalis beati Lucii papae et martyris.
2. **Nicomediae**, sancti Hadriani, cum aliis viginti tribus.

1. MU 1, with omission here of the precise location (*via Appia*).

2. This entry, which was borrowed from the second recension of MA, is in many *auctaria* of MU, including the similarly worded Molanus.

Sources: **1.** Dubois, *Martyrologe*, 188. **2.** *AASS*, Iun. VI, 137–8; Overgaauw, *Martyrologes*, 645; Dubois and Renaud, *Martyrologes*, 98.

[5 March] Tertio Nonas Martii Die 5 A

1. Apud Antiochiam, natalis beati Phocae martyris.
2. **In Hybernia**, sanctorum Karthagii et Kiarani.

2   *Karchagii* MS. *Kyarani, Karthagi* T; *Carthach ... Ciarán ... Saigre*, 'Carthach, Ciarán of Seirkieran', MO.

1. MU 1.

2. Both Ciarán and Carthach were attached to Seirkieran in the Offaly barony of Ballybrit and, according to Ciarán's Life, Carthach was his disciple. The shared *natalis* is not unusual in the Irish record. Brighid and her successor Darlughdhach were remembered on 1 February, as were Colum Cille and his successor Baoithín on 9 June. Grevenus reads: *In Hibernia, Kyriani episcopi et confessoris.*

Sources: **1**. Dubois, *Martyrologe*, 190. **2**. Stokes, *Martyrology*, 80; Best and Lawlor, *Martyrology*, 20; Plummer, *Vitae*, i, 227; Heist, *Vitae*, 351; *DIS*, 158–9, 172–3.

[6 March] B Pridie Nonas Martii Die 6

1. **Nicomediae**, natalis sanctorum Uictoris et Uictorini, qui, multis tormentis afflicti et in carcerem retrusi, ibidem cursum uitae impleuerunt.

1. MU 1, with a fuller than usual text here.

Sources: **1**. Dubois, *Martyrologe*, 190.

[7 March] Nonis Martii Die 7 C

1. In Terracina **Campaniae** ciuitate, monasterio Fossae Nouae, natalis sancti Thomae Aquinatis doctoris et confessoris.
2. Eodem die, natalis, apud **Cartaginem**, Perpetuae et Faelicitatis.

1 *Tarracina* MS.

1. Thomas Aquinas died in 1274 and was canonized in 1323. MReg follows very closely the text of Molanus.
2. MU 1. In MU, the saints are assigned to Mauretania [in Africa]. The reference to Carthage is otherwise also in the Martyrology of Bede.

Sources: **1**. *AASS*, Iun. VI, 142–3; Overgaauw, *Martyrologes*, 647–8.
2. Dubois, *Martyrologe*, 190; Quentin, *Martyrologes historiques*, 88.

[8 March] D Octauo Idus Martii Die 8

1. **In Anglia**, sancti Faelicis episcopi et confessoris, qui, de Burgundia veniens, nationi Anglorum orientalium Christum annunciauit.
2. **In Hybernia**, sancti Senani episcopi et confessoris.
3. Ibidem, sanctorum episcoporum et confessorum Beoani et Machonni.

[2] *In Hibernia, sancti Senani episcopi et confessoris* COW; *Senani ?confessoris?* T; *Senan Inse Cathaigh*, 'Seanán of Inis Chathaigh', MO. **3.** *Machoaeni* MS; *Conandil ... epscop Beoáed*, 'Conainnil ... bishop Beoaidh', MO.

1. This entry is in agreement with Molanus. Of Gaulish origin, Felix of Dunwich preached among the people of East Anglia, and gave his name to Felixstowe in Suffolk.
2. Seanán, who was already commemorated above at 1 March, was patron of Scattery Island in the Clare barony of Moyarta. Grevenus lists *Cenani* here with *C* in error for *S* (see also next entry).
3. The form *Conna* is used of Conainnil in notes to MO. The saint was attached to Assylin in the Roscommon barony of Boyle. Beoán, alias Beoaidh, was patron of Ardcarn, at one stage the seat of a diocese, in the same barony. The full entry in Grevenus for this day is: *In Hibernia, Cenani* [recte *Senani*], *Conalli* [recte *Conandli*], *Crouani* [recte *Cronani*], *episcoporum et confessorum*.

Sources: **1.** *AASS*, Iun. VI, 145; Farmer, *Dictionary*, 147. **2.** Stokes, *Martyrology*, 81; Best and Lawlor, *Martyrology*, 21; *DIS*, 557–60. **3.** Stokes, *Martyrology*, 81, 90; *DIS*, 103, 269–70.

[9 March] Septimo Idus Martii Die 9 E

1. Apud Sebasten Armeniae minoris, natalis sanctorum quadraginta martyrum, tempore Licini regis.
2. Apud Nissenam, depositio sancti Gregorii episcopi, fratris beati Basilii Caesariensis.

1. MU, following MA, displaced this entry to 11 March, but MReg again follows Molanus (and many other *auctaria*) in bringing it back to the earlier date of 9 March. Molanus also places it first, but reads *militum* for *martyrum*.

2. MU 1.

Sources: **1.** Dubois, *Martyrologe*, 192; *AASS*, Iun. VI, 145–6; Overgaauw, *Martyrologes*, 649. **2.** Dubois, *Martyrologe*, 191.

[10 March] F Sexto Idus Martii Die 10

1. In Perside, natalis sanctorum quadraginta duorum.
2. Parisiis, depositio sancti Droctouei abbatis.

1, 2. MU 2, 3.

Sources: **1.** Dubois, *Martyrologe*, 192.

[11 March] Quinto Idus Martii Die 11 G

1. In Carthagine, natalis sanctorum martyrum Heraclii, Sosimi, et aliorum uiginti.
2. Eodem die, sancti patris Sophronii patriarchae Hierosolimorum.

1. This feast, originally drawn from MH, is in most *auctaria*, including Molanus in much the same wording.
2. Alone of the *auctaria* of MU, Molanus also has the feast of this seventh-century patriarch of Jerusalem, with similar wording.

Sources: **1.** *AASS*, Iun. VI, 149–50; Overgaauw, *Martyrologes*, 650–1.
2. *AASS*, Iun. VI, 150; *BiblSS*, xi, 1283–5.

[12 March] A Quarto Idus Martii Die 12

1. **Romae**, beati pontificis Gregorii, doctoris et apostoli Anglorum.
2. Apud Nicomediam, passio sancti Petri martyris.
3. In Brittania minori, sancti Pauli Leonensis episcopi.

1, 2. MU 1, 2, with omission here, as in Molanus, of the second pontiff, i.e., *Innocentis*, in MU 1.
3. This entry, otherwise found in some *auctaria* only, is close to Molanus. The relics of Paul Aurelian were translated to the monastery of

Fleury-sur-Loire about the middle of the tenth century. Some were kept in Brittany, where the saint gave his name to Saint-Pol-de-Léon.

Sources: **1, 2**. Dubois, *Martyrologe*, 192–3. **3**. *AASS*, Iun. VI, 151–2; *BiblSS*, x, 296–9.

[13 March] Tertio Idus Martii Die 13 B

1. In Nicomedia, natalis sanctorum martyrum Macedonii presbiteri, Patriciae et Modestae.
2. In Hybernia, sanctorum Mochaemochi et Cuangusi abbatum et confessorum.

2   *mo Chóemóc ... Cuangus ... ó Liath mór*, 'Mochaomhóg ... Cuanghas of Leigh', MO.

1. MU 1.
2. Mochaomhóg was patron of Leigh (Liath Mór) in the Tipperary barony of Eliogarty. Cuanghas, likewise attached to Leigh, is otherwise little known. Grevenus reads on this day: *In Hibernia, Mothomogi confessoris*.

Sources: **1**. Dubois, *Martyrologe*, 193. **2**. Stokes, *Martyrology*, 82; Best and Lawlor, *Martyrology*, 23; *AASS*, Iun. VI, 153; *DIS*, 459–61.

[14 March] C Pridie Idus Martii Die 14

1. Romae, passio sanctorum martyrum quadraginta et septem, qui a beato Petro apostolo baptizati fuerunt, cum in custodio tenerentur.
2. Eodem die, beati Zachariae pontificis.

1. MU 1, with some slight adjustments here to the wording.
2. Several *auctaria*, including Molanus, have an entry here – as well as on the following day – on Pope Zacharias, who took a special interest in Boniface's mission in Germany.

Sources: **1**. Dubois, *Martyrologe*, 193. **2**. *AASS*, Iun. VI, 155–6; Overgauuw, *Martyrologes*, 655; Kelly, *Dictionary*, 89–90.

[15 March] Idibus Martii [Die] 15 D

1. In Caesarea Cappadociae, passio sancti Longini, qui latus Domini lancea perforauit.
2. In Hybernia, natalis septem filiorum Nesani.

1 *qui* corrected from *quia*. 2. *maicc Nessáin ónd inis*, 'sons of Neasán from the island', MO.

1. MU 1. In line with MO and some *auctaria*, Longinus is provided with a second feast at 24 October.
2. The sons of Neasán were patrons of the island named Inis Mac Neasáin, now Ireland's Eye, off Howth in Co. Dublin.

Sources: **1.** Dubois, *Martyrologe*, 194; *BiblSS*, viii, 89–95. **2.** Stokes, *Martyrology*, 82, 98; Best and Lawlor, *Martyrology*, 23; *DIS*, 265.

[16 March] E Decimo Septimo Kalendas Aprilis Die 16

1. **Romae**, natalis sancti Ciriaci.
2. **In Hybernia**, sanctorum confessorum Abbani et Finnani.

2 *Finani, Patricii* T; *Abbán ... Fínán ... lobur*, 'Abán ... Fíonán the leper', MO.

1. MU 2.
2. Abán was patron of Adamstown in the Wexford barony of Bantry, and the subject of a *vita* written in the early thirteenth century, whereas Fíonán Lobhar was attached to the church of Swords in Co. Dublin. This feast was also that of Fíonán of Kinnity in Co. Offaly, whose cult mostly flourished on the Iveragh peninsula in Co. Kerry. Grevenus commemorates both saints as follows: *In Scotia, ... Albani episcopi et confessoris ... In Hibernia, Finiani abbatis et confessoris.*

Sources: **1.** Dubois, *Martyrologe*, 194. **2.** Stokes, *Martyrology*, 82; Best and Lawlor, *Martyrology*, 24; Ó Riain, 'St Abbán'; *DIS*, 51–2, 330.

[17 March] Decimo Sexto Calendas Aprilis Die 17 F

1. **In Scotia**, natalis sancti Patricii episcopi et confessoris, qui, tempore Celestini papae ad predicandum missus in Hyberniam, Euangelium Christi praedicauit.

1 *in Hyberniam* (corrected from *Hibernia*) MS.

1. Already remembered by Bede, Patrick was one of the first Irish saints to be commemorated outside Ireland and, uniquely, to be given precedence in his list. The latter part of the text here, from *qui* on, varies considerably from that of MU, but resembles part of the more extensive entry in the Bruxellensis *auctarium* of MU. Despite its presence in MU and Molanus, MReg has no notice here of the feast of Gertrude, co-patron with James of the Regensburg *Schottenkloster*.

Sources: **1**. Dubois, *Martyrologe*, 195; Dubois and Renaud, *Martyrologes*, 50; *AASS*, Iun. VI, 160; *DIS*, 526–31.

[18 March] G Decimo Quinto Calendas Aprilis 18

1. Natalis beati Alexandri episcopi.
2. **In Britannia**, sancti Eduardi regis.
3. **In Hybernia**, sancti Mochtani confessoris.

3 *fiche miled mochtae*, 'twenty glorious soldiers', MO.

1. MU 1.
2. The entry on Edward the Martyr, who was murdered in 978, is also in several *auctaria*, including Molanus.
3. MReg, in common with some versions of MO, extrapolated this ghost saint from the final word of the quatrain in MO, the adjective *mochtae* meaning glorious.

Sources: **1**. Dubois, *Martyrologe*, 196. **2**. *AASS*, Iun. VI, 161–2; *EncASE*, 163. **3**. Stokes, *Martyrology*, 83.

[19 March] Decimo Quarto Calendas Aprilis 19 A

1. Natalis beati Joseph sponsi beatissimae **Virginis Mariae**.
2. Vezzelliaco monasterio, translatio sanctae Mariae Magdalenae.
3. In Hybernia, sancti Lachteani abbatis et confessoris.

² *Verselliaco* MS. **3.** *Lactani* T; *MoLachtóc* MO.

1. Joseph's cult was popular in Ireland at a very early stage, the feast being attested in both MT and MO. However, the wording here is that of Molanus.
2. Beginning in the eleventh century, the community at Vézelay laid claim to possession of the relics of Mary Magdalene. Most *auctaria* contain an entry on the translation, but only Molanus (*Vercelliaco monasterio*) has a formulation similar to *Vezzeliaco monasterio*.
3. Laichtín was founder-patron of Freshford in the Kilkenny barony of Crannagh. Two Cologne *auctaria*, Grevenus and Lübeck/Cologne, bear witness to the feast, with the former reading: *In Hibernia, sancti Lactini episcopi et confessoris*.

Sources: **1.** Stokes, *Martyrology*, 83; Best and Lawlor, *Martyrology*, 25; *AASS*, Iun. VI, 163; Grosjean, 'La prétendue', 357–62. **2.** *AASS*, Iun. VI, 163; Overgaauw, *Martyrologes*, 662. **3.** Stokes, *Martyrology*, 83; Best and Lawlor, *Martyrology*, 25; *AASS*, Iun. VI, 163; *DIS*, 387–8.

[20 March] B Decimo Tertio Calendas Aprilis Die 20

1. Apud **Britanniam**, depositio sancti Cuthberti, qui ex anachorita factus est episcopus Lindisfarnensis.
2. Eodem die, sancti Joachim, patris beatae **Mariae uirginis**.

1. MU 2, with slight adjustments here in the wording.
2. Molanus, which adds *confessoris* to Joachim, is one of very few *auctaria* of MU to have this entry.

Sources: **1.** Dubois, *Martyrologe*, 197. **2.** *AASS*, Iun. VI, 165.

[21 March] Duodecimo Calendas Aprilis Die 21 C

1. Apud castrum **Cassinum**, natalis **sancti Benedicti abbatis**, cuius uita in uirtutibus et miraculis gloriosa extitit.
2. **In Hybernia**, sancti Ennae abbatis.

2 *Cunae* (with confusion of *c* and *e*) MS; *Enneni* T; *Éndae* ... *Árne*, 'Éanna of Aran', MO.

1. MU 1, with slightly different wording in MReg.
2. Éanna was particularly associated with the island of Aran, off the Galway coast. Grevenus reads here: *In Hibernia, Endei abbatis*.

Sources: **1.** Dubois, *Martyrologe*, 198. **2.** Stokes, *Martyrology*, 83; Best and Lawlor, *Martyrology*, 25; *AASS*, Iun. VI, 167; *DIS*, 281–3.

[22 March] D Undecimo Calendas Aprilis Die 22

1. In Affrica, sancti Saturnini et aliorum nouem.
2. **In Hybernia**, sancti Falbi abbatis et confessoris.

2 *Failbe* ... *Íae*, 'Fáilbhe of Í (Iona)', MO.

1. Several *auctaria* of MU, including Molanus, have this entry, which was originally drawn from MH.
2. Fáilbhe, abbot of Iona, died in 679 and was succeeded by Adhamhnán. The Tegernsee (T) martyrology has an entry here on Albanus (for Abbanus?), which may refer to the octave of the feast of Abán (16 March above).

Sources: **1.** *AASS*, Iun. VI, 168; Overgaauw, *Martyrologes*, 665. **2.** Stokes, *Martyrology*, 83; Best and Lawlor, *Martyrology*, 26; *DIS*, 301.

[23 March] Decimo Calendas Aprilis Die 23 E

1. In Africa, natalis sancti Faelicis.
2. **In Hybernia**, sancti Momedochi confessoris et filiae Feradaigae uirginis.

2 *filiae eius* MS; *Ingen* ... *Feradaig* ... *moMaedóc mind nAlban*, 'Daughter of Fearadhach, Momhaodhóg, Alba's diadem', MO.

1. The first edition of Molanus, which adds *et aliorum viginti*, is among the few *auctaria* to have an entry here on Felix, who is taken to have been a companion of the more widely commemorated Fidelis. **2**. In line with MO, Momhaodhóg , patron of Fiddown in the Kilkenny barony of Iverk, is provided with two other feasts, at 18 May and 13 August. Despite MO on this day, the saint does not appear to have had a church in Scotland. Although recorded on this day in most Irish martyrologies, including MO, the daughter of Fearadhach is otherwise unknown.

Sources: **1**. *AASS*, Iun. VI, 169–70. **2**. Stokes, *Martyrology*, 83; Best and Lawlor, *Martyrology*, 26; *DIS*, 494–5.

[24 March] F Nono Calendas Aprilis Die 24

1. In Phrigia, sancti Agapiti.
2. In monasterio Vuasteno, sanctae Catharinae abbatissae, filiae beatae Brigittae.
3. **In Hybernia**, sanctae Scirae uirginis.
4. Item, sanctorum Camini, Mochtani et Domangarti abbatum et confessorum.

1   *Agapeti* MS. **2**. *Buasteno* MS. **3**. *Scíre* MO. **4**. *Camini, Moctani* T; *Mochtae* MO.

1. MU 4, with *Ph*– here as in Molanus.
2. Alone of the *auctaria* of MU, Molanus also commemorates Catherine on this day, in exactly the same words. Although never proclaimed a saint, Catherine of Sweden (†1381), daughter of Birgitta, and abbess of Vadstena, became the subject of a cult.
3. Scíre was patron of the church named Kilskeer (Ceall Scíre) in the Meath barony of Kells Upper.
4. Mochta, patron of Louth in the county, parish and barony of the same name, at one stage also a diocesan see, was the principal native saint commemorated on this day. However, reference is made to Domhanghart, who gave name to Slieve Donard (Sliabh Domhanghairt) in County Down, in notes to MO, as also, albeit in some manuscripts only, to Caimín, patron of Inishcaltra or Holy Island on

Lough Derg in the county of Galway. Grevenus's *Kanini confessoris* probably refers to Caimín.

Sources: **1**. Dubois, *Martyrologe*, 198. **2**. *AASS*, Iun. VI, 171; *BiblSS*, iii, 994–6. **3**. Stokes, *Martyrology*, 84; Best and Lawlor, *Martyrology*, 26. **4**. Stokes, *Martyrology*, 84, 100; Best and Lawlor, *Martyrology*, 26–7; *AASS*, Iun. VI, 171; Grosjean, *Notes* 5, 106–7; *DIS*, 465–7, 551.

[25 March] Octauo Calendas Aprilis Die 25 G

1. **Jesus Christus Dominus** noster passus est.
2. Apud Nazareth, ciuitatem Galileae, annunciatio beatae **Mariae** uirginis.
3. Eodem die, immolatio Isaac.
4. Et transitus filiorum Israel per Mare Rubrum.

4 *Israell* MS.

1. MO likewise commemorates this feast, with the words: *Crochad ocus chombert Issu Críst*, 'Crucifixion and conception of Jesus Christ', adding a note that reads: *Iesus ... pas[s]us est*. However, the wording here is exactly that of Molanus and Grevenus.
2. MU 1, with specification here of Mary the virgin, as against Usuard's *dominica*.
3. The immolation of Isaac is also in some *auctaria* of MU, including Molanus, which has the same words.
4. Like **3** above, this is also in some *auctaria*, including the similarly worded Molanus.

Sources: **1**. Stokes, *Martyrology*, 84; Best and Lawlor, *Martyrology*, 27; *AASS*, Iun. VI, 172; Overgaauw, *Martyrologes*, 668. **2**. Dubois, *Martyrologe*, 200. **3**. *AASS*, Iun. VI, 173–4. **4**. *AASS*, Iun. VI, 173–4; Overgaauw, *Martyrologes*, 668.

[26 March] A Septimo Calendas Aprilis Die 26

1. Romae, uia Lauicana, sancti Castuli martyris.
2. **In Hybernia**, sancti Synchilli abbatis.
3. Item, sancti Mochelloki confessoris.

² *Sinchellini* T; *in t-Shinchill ... Cille ... Achid*, 'Sincheall of Killeigh', MO.
³ *Il-Letha ... mo Chellóc*, 'In Leatha Mocheallóg', MO.

1. MU 2.
2. Sincheall was attached to the church of Killeigh in the Offaly barony of Geashill.
3. Mocheallóg gave name to the church of Kilmallock (Ceall Mocheallóg) in the Limerick barony of the same name. Grevenus (*In Hibernia, Mottelogi abbatis et confessoris*) also commemorates the saint, as does the other Cologne *auctarium*, Lübeck/Cologne.

Sources: **1.** Dubois, *Martyrologe*, 201. **2.** Stokes, *Martyrology*, 84; Best and Lawlor, *Martyrology*, 27; *DIS*, 562–3. **3.** Stokes, *Martyrology*, 84; Best and Lawlor, *Martyrology*, 27; *AASS*, Iun. VI, 175; *DIS*, 462.

[27 March] Sexto Calendas Aprilis Die 27 B

1. Hierosolymis, resurrectio Domini nostri Jesu Christi.
2. Vormatiae, sancti Ruperti episcopi et confessoris.

1. Molanus is among several *auctaria* of MU that have this entry.
2. Molanus is among the *auctaria* of MU that assign Rupertus to *Wormatia*, 'Worms', where he was born. Others place the saint in Salzburg, where he was first bishop.

Sources: **1.** *AASS*, Iun. VI, 177; Overgaauw, *Martyrologes*, 671. **2.** *AASS*, Iun. VI, 177; Overgaauw, *Martyrologes*, 672; *BiblSS*, xi, 506–7.

[28 March] C Quinto Calendas Aprilis Die 28

1. Romae, sancti Syxti papae.
2. Eodem die, sancti Stephani thaumaturgi.
3. Et sancti Hilarionis iunioris.

1. Molanus, together with several other *auctaria*, follows MA in commemorating Sixtus on this day.
2. Despite the assertions of J.-M. Sauget, the cult of this Stephen did not remain entirely unknown in the West. Although falling a few days later in the East, the feast is on this day in Molanus, with similar wording.

3. This feast may commemorate Hilarion of Pelecete in Bithynia. Molanus, alone of the *auctaria* of MU, also notices it on this day.

Sources: **1**. *AASS*, Iun. VI, 179; Overgaauw, *Martyrologes*, 672–3; Dubois and Renaud, *Martyrologes*, 114. **2**. *AASS*, Iun. VI, 179; J.-M. Sauget in *BiblSS*, xii, 14–15. **3**. *AASS*, Iun. VI, 179; *BiblSS*, vii, 736–7.

[29 March] Quarto Calendas Aprilis Die 29 D

1. Nicomediae, passio sanctorum Pastoris et Uictorini.
2. Ipso die, sancti Bertholdi confessoris, ordinis Carmeli sancti.
3. Depositio sancti Gregorii Nazianzeni.
4. **In Hybernia**, sanctarum uirginum filiarum Baitae.

[4] *Battae* MS; *La líth ingen mBaiti*, 'With the feast of the daughters of Baoide', MO.

1. MU 3, with the omission here, as in several *auctaria*, not including Molanus, of Usuard's description of Nicomedia as a *civitas*.
2. Alone of the *auctaria* of MU, Molanus also has this entry, in much the same words. Bertholdus of Lombardy is supposed to have been the first prior general of the Carmelites, but this is surrounded by doubt. His name was excised from the revised breviary of 1585 but later reintroduced.
3. The presence of this feast in both MO and MT on this day led the editors of MH to declare that they were at a loss as to what source it came from. Here it may have derived from MO. On the other hand, it is also in Grevenus.
4. The daughters are identified as Eithne and Soidhealbh *quae nutriebant Christum*. They were attached to a church named Teach Inghean mBaoide, 'House/church of the daughters of Baoide', near Swords in Co. Dublin.

Sources: **1**. Dubois, *Martyrologe*, 202; *AASS*, Iun. VI, 180–1. **2**. *AASS*, Iun. VI, 181; *BiblSS*, iii, 106–8. **3**. Stokes, *Martyrology*, 84; Best and Lawlor, *Martyrology*, 28; *AASS*, Iun. VI, 181. **4**. Stokes, *Martyrology*, 84, 102; Best and Lawlor, *Martyrology*, 28; Stokes, *Martyrology of Gorman*, 64; *DIS*, 293.

[30 March] E Tertio Calendas April Die 30

1. Romae, uia Appia, natalis beati Quirini martyris et tribuni.
2. **In Hybernia**, sanctorum abbatum et confessorum Mochua, Colmani et Tolani.

2 *Colamani et Totani* MS; *Mochuani, Colmani, Tolani* T; *mo Chuae Ballae... Colmán ó Laind ... Tolai*, 'Mochua of Balla, Colmán of Linns, Tola', MO.

1. MU 1, with transposition here of *martyr* and *tribunus*, as in Molanus. A second feast of Quirinus is listed at 30 April.
2. The first two saints were respectively attached to Balla in the Mayo barony of Claremorris and Linns in the Louth barony of Ardee. Tola's church is now Dysert O Dea in the Clare barony of Inchiquin.

Sources: **1**. Dubois, *Martyrologe*, 203; *AASS*, Iun. VI, 181. **2**. Stokes, *Martyrology*, 85; Best and Lawlor, *Martyrology*, 28; *DIS*, 195, 467–8, 575–6.

[31 March] Pridie Calendas Aprilis 31 F

1. Amos prophetae, quem Ozias, rex Israel, uecte per tempora confixum necauit.
2. Eodem die, Faelicis papae et martyris.

1. MU 1. MReg reads *confixum* for Usuard's *transfixum*.
2. Molanus is one of the very few *auctaria* to have the feast of Pope Felix on this day, which is nowhere else assigned to a pope and martyr of this name.

Sources: **1**. Dubois, *Martyrologe*, 204; *AASS*, Iun. VI, 183. **2**. *AASS*, Iun. VI, 184.

[1 April] G Calendis Aprilis Die 1

1. Romae, passio beatissimae Theodorae, sororis illustrissimi martyris Hermetis.
2. In Aegypto, sanctorum Uictoris et Stephani.

1, 2. MU 1, 3.

Sources: **1, 2**. Dubois, *Martyrologe*, 205.

[2 April] Quarto Nonas Aprilis Die 2 A

1. Francisci de Paula confessoris et Ordinis Minimorum fundatoris.
2. Apud Palestinam, depositio beatae Mariae Aegyptiacae, cuius actus ualde mirabiles inueniuntur.

1   *minorum* MS.

1. Alone of the *auctaria* of MU, Molanus also contains this entry, with slightly different wording. Francis, founder of the Minim friars, was canonized in 1519.
2. MU 3, with the final part of the entry in words similar to those used by Molanus and some other *auctaria*.

Sources: **1**. *AASS*, Iun. VI, 189; *BiblSS*, v, 1163–75. **2**. Dubois, *Martyrologe*, 205; *AASS*, Iun. VI, 189; Overgaauw, *Martyrologes*, 679.

[3 April] B Tertio Nonas Aprilis Die 3

1. In Scythia, ciuitate Thomis, natalis sanctorum Euagrii et Benigni.
2. In Anglia, sancti Ricardi episcopi Cicestriensis et confessoris.

1   *Schythia* MS.

1. MU 1.
2. This feast is in several *auctaria* but only Molanus and Grevenus agree with MReg's wording. Richard of Chichester died in 1253 and was canonized in 1262.

Sources: **1**. Dubois, *Martyrologe*, 206. **2**. *AASS*, Iun. VI, 189; Farmer, *Dictionary*, 342–3.

[4 April] Pridie Nonas Aprilis Die 4 C

1. Depositio beati Ambrosii episcopi et confessoris.
2. **In Hybernia**, natalis Tigernachi episcopi et confessoris.

² *Tigernaci* (in marg.) T; *Tigernach ... Clúana ... hEuis*, 'Tighearnach of Clones', MO.

1. MU 1, with omission here of the location (*Mediolanum*).
2. Tighearnach was patron of the church of Clones in the Monaghan barony of Dartree. Grevenus (*In Scotia, Tigernagi episcopi et confessoris*) places the feast on the following day (*secundum alios die sequenti*), as do the *auctarium* known as Bruxellensis and the text known as Florarium, which was completed in 1486 at Eindhoven in Brabant.

Sources: **1.** Dubois, *Martyrologe*, 206. **2.** Stokes, *Martyrology*, 104; Best and Lawlor, *Martyrology*, 29; *AASS*, Iun. VI, 192, 194; Grosjean, *Catalogus*, 341, 390; *DIS*, 572–4.

[5 April] D Nonis Aprilis Die 5

1. Apud Aegyptum, natalis sanctorum martyrum Martiani, Nicanoris et Apollonii.
2. **In Hybernia**, natalis sancti Becani heremitae et confessoris.

² *Becani* (in marg.) T; *féil ... maicc Cula Béccáin*, 'feast of Beagán son of Cúla', MO.

1. MU 1, with variation in spelling, as also in Molanus. In line with the first recension of MU, these martyrs are again remembered at 5 June.
2. Beagán son of Cúla was patron of Emlagh in the Meath barony of Lower Kells. Grevenus reads on the previous day: *In Hibernia Beghani abbatis*.

Sources: **1.** Dubois, *Martyrologe*, 207, 241–2. **2.** Stokes, *Martyrology*, 6, 104; Best and Lawlor, *Martyrology*, 30; Stokes, *Martyrology of Gorman*, 70; *DIS*, 92.

[6 April] Octauo Idus Aprilis Die 6 E

1. Romae, natalis beati Syxti papae et martyris.
2. In Macedonia, sanctorum Timothei et Diogenis.

1, 2. MU 1, 2. In his first edition, but not in later editions, Molanus adds an entry here on Celsus of Armagh, which reads: *In Hybernia, sancti Celsi Ardinarchensis* [sic] *archiepiscopi et confessoris. De quo B. Bernardus in vita Malachiae.*

Sources: **1, 2.** Dubois, *Martyrologe*, 207; *AASS*, Iun. VI, 196.

[7 April] F Septimo Idus Aprilis Die 7

1. Apud Africam, natalis sanctorum martyrum Epiphanii episcopi, Donati et aliorum tredecim.
2. **In Hybernia**, sancti Finani abbatis et confessoris.

[2] *In Scotia, Finani confessoris* CSOW; *Finani* T; *Fínan camm Cinn Etig*, 'Fíonán the squinting of Kinnity', MO.

1. MU 1.
2. Fíonán Cam ,'of the squint', was patron of Kinnity in the Offaly barony of Ballybrit. His feast is already in Notker, which may have served as the source of CSOW. Grevenus fails to notice this feast but lists that of Brendan (*Brandani episcopi et confessoris*).

Sources: **1.** Dubois, *Martyrologe*, 208. **2.** Stokes, *Martyrology*, 105; Best and Lawlor, *Martyrology*, 30; *AASS*, Iun. VI, 198; *DIS*, 327–30.

[8 April] Sexto Idus Aprilis Die 8 G

1. Apud Corinthum, beati Dionisii episcopi.
2. Item, beati Alberti patris ordinis Carmeli.
3. **In Hybernia**, sancti Kenfelaidi abbatis et confessoris.

[3] *Cenn-faelad abb Bennchuir*, 'Ceann Faoladh, abbot of Bangor', MO.

1. MU 1.

2. Molanus likewise has this entry, in much the same words. The feast of Albert, founder of the Carmelites, began to be celebrated in 1504.
3. Ceann Faoladh, who died in 705, is one of a long list of early abbots of Bangor commemorated in the Irish martyrologies.

Sources: **1**. Dubois, *Martyrologe*, 208. **2**. *AASS*, Iun. VI, 199; *BiblSS*, i, 686–90. **3**. Stokes, *Martyrology*, 105; Best and Lawlor, *Martyrology*, 31; *DIS*, 164.

[9 April] A Quinto Idus Aprilis Die 9

1. Sancti martyris Eutichii.
2. Eodem die, translatio corporis sanctae Monicae, matris sancti Augustini.

1. Molanus, which uses the same words, is the only other version of MU to contain this entry. Sollerius thought that the name was a mistake for Eupsychius. However, although an exile rather than a martyr, Eutichius, patriarch of Constantinople, whose feast fell about this time, may be intended here.
2. Several *auctaria*, including Molanus, contain this entry. The translation of Monica's remains from Ostia to Rome took place in 1430.

Sources: **1**. *AASS*, Iun. VI, 201; *BiblSS*, v, 323–4. **2**. *AASS*, Iun. VI, 201; *BiblSS*, ix, 548–58, at 557.

[10 April] Quarto Idus Aprilis Die 10 B

1. Ezechielis prophetae, qui a iudice populi Israel est interfectus.
2. In Gandauo, depositio beati Macarii episcopi et confessoris.
3. In Hybernia, sancti Cuanni abbatis et confessoris.

3   *ó Russ Eo ... Cuannae*, 'Cuana from Ros Eo', MO.

1. MU 1.
2. Of the *auctaria* that have an entry on Macarius, only Molanus agrees with the text of MReg. The saint is Macarius of Armenia, who died of the plague in Ghent on 10 April 1012. He was greatly venerated in Flanders.

3. Despite MReg, Cuana was a virgin. She may have given name to Cloncowan (perhaps from Cluain Cuana) in the parish of Rathmolyon, barony of Lower Moyfenrath, Co. Meath. The first edition of Molanus has an entry for this day on Malchus of Lismore (*Malachi episcopi Lesmorinensis ... de quo in vita sancti Malachiae*), which MReg appears to have ignored.

Sources: **1**. Dubois, *Martyrologe*, 209. **2**. *AASS*, Iun. VI, 203; *BiblSS*, viii, 417–20. **3**. Stokes, *Martyrology*, 105; Best and Lawlor, *Martyrology*, 31; *AASS*, Iun. VI, 203; *DIS*, 241–2.

[11 April] C Tertio Idus Aprilis Die 11

1. Romae, natalis beati Leonis papae et confessoris.
2. In Britannia, sancti Guthlaci confessoris et anachoritae.
3. In Hybernia, sancti Medoch abbatis et confessoris.

[3] *Maedóc ... haue ... do Dunlang*, 'Maodhóg grandson of Dúnlang', MO.

1. MU 1, with *et confessoris* added here.
2. Several *auctaria*, including the similarly worded Molanus, notice the feast of the celebrated anchorite, Guthlac of Crowland, who died in 714.
3. Maodhóg, alias Aodh, was patron of the church of Clonmore in the Carlow barony of Rathvilly.

Sources: **1**. Dubois, *Martyrologe*, 210. **2**. *AASS*, Iun. VI, 204–5; Overgaauw, *Martryologes*, 687; *EncASE*, 222–3. **3**. Stokes, *Martyrology*, 106; Best and Lawlor, *Martyrology*, 32; *DIS*, 431–2.

[12 April] Pridie Idus Aprilis Die 12 D

1. Romae, uia Aurelia, natalis beati Julii papae et confessoris.
2. Eodem die, sancti Basilii episcopi et confessoris.

1. MU 1, with *et confessoris* added here.
2. Of the *auctaria* of MU only Molanus contains this entry. Basil of Parios was venerated by the Greek Church on this day.

Sources: **1**. Dubois, *Martyrologe*, 211. **2**. *AASS*, Iun. VI, 207; *BiblSS*, ii, 946.

[13 April] E Idibus Aprilis Die 13

1. In Hispania, sancti Hermenigildi martyris.
2. Eodem die, sancti Justini philosophi et martyris.

1. MU 2, with the spelling here of the saint's name as in Molanus and Grevenus.
2. MU 1. Justinus *philosophus* is one of several martyrs located by Usuard *apud Pergamum*.

Sources: **1**. Dubois, *Martyrologe*, 212; *AASS*, Iun. VI, 207. **2**. Dubois, *Martyrologe*, 211.

[14 April] Decimo Octauo Calendas Mai Die 14 F

1. Romae, uia Appia, natalis beatorum martyrum Tiburtii et Ualeriani et Maximi.
2. Apud Alexandriam, sancti Frontonis abbatis.
3. **In Hybernia**, sancti Tassachi episcopi et confessoris.

3 *In Hibernia, sancti Tassach episcopi et confessoris* EF, *Tessani* T; *In rígepscop t'Assach*, 'The royal bishop Tasach', MO.

1, 2. MU 1, 2, with *et* added here, as in Molanus, before *Ualeriani*.
3. Tasach was given the privilege of providing St Patrick with his last communion. He was attached to the church of Raholp in the Down barony of Lecale Lower.

Sources: **1, 2**. Dubois, *Martyrologe*, 212. **3**. Stokes, *Martyrology*, 106; Best and Lawlor, *Martyrology*, 32; Stokes, *Martyrology of Gorman*, 76; Hochholzer, *Martyrologfragment*, 55, 62; *DIS*, 570–1.

[15 April] G Decimo Septimo Calendas Maii Die 15

1. Apud Persidem, in ciuitate Corduba, natalis sanctorum Olimpiadis et Maximi nobilium.
2. In Reomago, depositio sancti Siluestri confessoris.
3. **In Hybernia,** sancti Ruadani abbatis et confessoris.

3 *In Hibernia, sancti Ruadani abbatis et confessoris* EF, *Ruadani* (corrected from *Roadani*) T; *Ródan ... Lothrai*, 'Ruadhán of Lorrha', MO.

1. MU 1. MReg reads *Corduba* with, among others, Molanus in place of Usuard's *Cordula*.
2. Silvester of Réome is commemorated in almost all *auctaria* of MU, including Molanus.
3. Ruadhán was patron of the church of Lorrha in the Tipperary barony of Lower Ormond. Grevenus (*Candani episcopi in Hybernia*) also noticed the feast, albeit corruptly.

Sources: **1.** Dubois, *Martyrologe*, 212. **2.** *AASS*, Iun. VI, 212–13; *BiblSS*, xi, 1071. **3.** Stokes, *Martyrology*, 106; Best and Lawlor, *Martyrology*, 32; *AASS*, Iun. VI, 212; Hochholzer, *Martyrologfragment*, 55–6, 62; *DIS*, 541–4.

[16 April] Decimo Sexto Calendas Maii Die 16 A

1. Coloniae, translatio sancti Albini martyris, huius reliquiae de Britannia per beatum Germanum episcopum primo Romam, deinde Coloniam, ad monasterium sancti Pantaleonis martyris.
2. **In Hybernia**, sanctorum martyrum Donnani cum sociis.

2 *In Hibernia, sanctorum martyrum Donnani cum sociis suis, passi a piratis in insula Alasina* EF; *Donnavi* T; *Donnán Eca*, 'Donnán of Eig', MO.

1. Of the *auctaria* of MU, only the Cologne martyrologies (Grevenus and Lübeck/Cologne) and Molanus notice this translation. The wording here is closest to Molanus.
2. This feast is more commonly on the following day, as also in EF. The reference in EF to *insula Alasina* corresponds to an account of the martyrdom preserved in the Book of Leinster, where *Aldasain* is said to be the name of a well. The place in question is likely to be Ailsa Craig in the Firth of Clyde. Donnán was patron of Eig, an island

in Inverness-shire (Scotland), and his martyrdom through burning is dated to 617.

Sources: **1**. *AASS*, Iun. VI, 214–15. **2**. Hochholzer, *Martyrologfragment*, 56–7, 62–3; Stokes, *Martyrology*, 107; Best and Lawlor, *Martyrology*, 33; Ó Riain, *Corpus* §717; *HDGP*, i, 52; *AASS*, Iun. VI, 209; *DIS*, 273.

[17 April] B Decimo Quinto Calendas Mai[i] Die 17

1. Romae, natalis beati Aniceti pape et martyris.
2. **In Hybernia**, depositio sancti Lasreani abbatis et confessoris, qui fuit pater mille quingentorum et quinquaginta trium monachorum.
3. Ratisbonae, dedicatio ecclesiae sancti Petri extra muros.

¹ *Anniceti* MS.
² *Casreani* MS; *In Hibernia, sancti Lasreani abbatis et confessoris, qui fuit pater mille quingentorum et quinquaginta trium monachorum* EF; *Lasreani* (in marg.) T; *Laisrén ... abb Lethglinne*, 'Laisréan, abbot of Leighlin', MO.
³ *In Ratispona, dedicatio ecclesie sancti Petri extra murum* EF.

1. Absent from MU, the feast of Anicetus, tenth in line of succession to the papacy, is in several *auctaria* of MU, including Molanus, which reads *Anacleti*.
2. Most Irish martyrologies place this feast on the following day, as does EF. Laisréan, alias Molaise, was patron of the church and diocesan see of Leighlin in the Carlow barony of Idrone West. The claim that he had 1553 monks under him, which is also in EF, may be compared to a passage in the Life of Fiontan of Taghmon, where the number is 1500. The two Cologne martyrologies (Grevenus and Lübeck/Cologne) likewise noticed the saint on the following day: Grevenus (*In Hibernia, Lasriani abbatis et confessoris*), Lübeck/Cologne ((*Laceriani episcopi et confessoris*). Uniquely, except for a calendar copied at Aquileia in northern Italy from a south German source, T added to its list for this day the names *Cheren* and *Cholunchille* (Ciarán and Colum Cille).
3. The dedication of the church of St Peter 'ouside the walls', Weih Sankt Peter, is otherwise attested only in EF, which places it on the

following day, and stresses its importance by assigning to it twelve lessons.

Sources: **1**. *AASS*, Iun. VI, 216–17; Overgaauw, *Martyrologes*, 692; Kelly, *Dictionary*, 10–11. **2**. Stokes, *Martyrology*, 107; Best and Lawlor, *Martyrology*, 33; Hochholzer, *Martyrologfragment*, 57, 63; *AASS*, Iun. VI, 218; Heist, *Vitae*, 254 §25; Plummer, *Vitae*, ii, 236 §26; *DIS*, 486–7; *FSHIM* 245. **3**. Hochholzer, *Martyrologfragment*, 46, 63.

[18 April] Decimo Quarto Calendas Mai[i] Die 18 C

1. Romae, beati Apollonii senatoris.
2. Cordubae, passio sancti Perfecti praesbiteri et martyris.

1, 2. MU 2, 3, with the addition here in 2 of the word *passio*.

Sources: **1, 2**. Dubois, *Martyrologe*, 214.

[19 April] D Decimo tertio calendas Mai[i] die 19

1. Romae, depositio beati Leonis papae noni.
2. In Anglia, sancti Elphegi, episcopi Cantuariensis et martyris.

1. Most *auctaria* of MU, including Molanus, include the feast of Leo IX, who died on this day in 1054.
2. Molanus, which has much the same words, is among the *auctaria* that contain the feast of Alphege, archbishop of Canterbury; he was martyred by Danes in 1012.

Sources: **1**. *AASS*, Iun. VI, 220; Overgaauw, *Martyrologes*, 694; Kelly, *Dictionary*, 147–8. **2**. *AASS*, Iun. VI, 220; Overgaauw, *Martyrologes*, 694; *EncASE*, 7.

[20 April] Duodecimo Calendas Maii Die 20 E

1. Romae, sanctorum martyrum Sulpitii et Seruiliani.
2. In Galliis, ciuitate Ebredunensi, sancti Marcellini eiusdem urbis episcopi et confessoris.

Heading   *Quarto* crossed out after *Duodecimo*.

1, 2. MU 2, 3, subject to the use here, as otherwise in Molanus only, of the form *Marcellini* for Usuard's (less correct, according to Sollerius) *Marcelli*.

Sources: **1, 2**. Dubois, *Martyrologe*, 214; *AASS*, Iun. VI, 221.

[21 April] F Undecimo Calendas Mai[i] Die 21

1. Apud Persiden, natalis beati Simeonis episcopi et martyris.
2. **In Hybernia**, sancti Melrubi abbatis et confessoris.
3. In Anglia, sancti Anselmi episcopi Cantuariensis.

[2] *In Hibernia, sancti Melrubi abbatis et confessoris* EF, *Melrubini* T; *I n-Albain … Máelrubai*, 'In Scotland, Maol Rubha', MO.

1. MU 1.
2. Maol Rubha (†722) was abbot of both Bangor in Ireland and Applecross in Scotland. An office Life is preserved in the Breviary of Aberdeen.
3. Of the *auctaria* of MU, only the Cologne martyrologies (Grevenus and Lübeck/Cologne) and Molanus, which has the same words, notice the feast of Anselm (†1109), the Benedictine archbishop of Canterbury.

Sources: **1**. Dubois, *Martyrologe*, 216. **2**. Stokes, *Martyrology*, 107; Best and Lawlor, *Martyrology*, 35; Hochholzer, *Martyrologfragment*, 58, 63; *DIS*, 446–7; *LegSS*, 196–9, 382–4. **3**. *AASS*, Iun. VI, 224–5; Farmer, *Dictionary*, 18–19.

[22 April] Decimo Calendas Mai[i] Die 22 G

1. Romae, uia Appia, natalis beati Caii papae.
2. Ipso die, sancti Sotheris papae et martyris.
3. Item, inuentio beatorum corporum Dionisii, Rustici et Eleutherii martyrum.

1. MU 1, with *Caii* here, as in Molanus, for Usuard's *Gai*.
2. The feast of this pope is in a number of *auctaria*, but not in Molanus.

3. Molanus, which uses much the same wording, is among the many *auctaria* to contain this entry on the celebrated, if legendary, discovery of the relics of St Denis and his companions at Saint-Denis in Paris.

Sources: **1**. Dubois, *Martyrologe*, 216. **2**. *AASS*, Iun. VI, 226–7; Overgaauw, *Martyrologes*, 699. **3**. *AASS*, Iun. VI, 226–7; Overgaauw, *Martyrologes*, 699; *BiblSS*, iv, 650–3.

[23 April] A Nono Calendas Maii Die 23

1. Passio sancti Georgii martyris.
2. Eodem die, Prussiae, natalis sancti Adalberti episcopi et martyris.
3. **In Hybernia**, sancti Ybarii episcopi et confessoris.

³ *In Hibernia, sancti Ybari episcopi et confessoris* EF; *Ibari* T; *epscoip Ibair ... in Hérinn Bicc*, 'Bishop Iobhar in Begerin', MO.

1. MU 1, with the omission here of the location of the martyrdom (*Diospolis*).
2. This feast is in many *auctaria* of MU, including Molanus, whose text is very close to MReg. Adalbert of Prague (†997) was the subject of a widespread cult, especially in Germany.
3. Iobhar was patron of the church on Begerin Island in the Wexford barony of Shelmaliere.

Sources: **1**. Dubois, *Martyrologe*, 217. **2**. *AASS*, Iun. VI, 229; Overgaauw, *Martyrologes*, 700; *BiblSS*, i, 185–9. **3**. Stokes, *Martyrology*, 108; Best and Lawlor, *Martyrology*, 35; Hochholzer, *Martyrologfragment*, 58–9, 64; *DIS*, 381–2.

[24 April] Octauo Calendas Maii Die 24 B

1. Lugduno Galliae, natalis sancti Alexandri martyris.
2. **In Hybernia**, beati Egberti monachi, presbiteri et confessoris.

1. MU 1. See note to **2** of the following day.
2. Only Grevenus and Molanus of the *auctaria* of MU have this entry, and the wording of the latter text agrees closely with that of MReg.

Egbert, who died on Iona in 729, is among the Anglo-Saxon saints commemorated in MT.

Sources: **1**. Dubois, *Martyrologe*, 218. **2**. *AASS*, Iun. VI, 231–2; Best and Lawlor, *Martyrology*, 36; Ó Riain, *Anglo-Saxon Ireland*, 10; Farmer, *Dictionary*, 127.

[25 April] C Septimo Calendas Mai[i] Die 25

1. Romae, Litania maior, ad sanctum Petrum.
2. Apud Alexandriam, natalis beati Marci euangelistae.
3. **In Hybernia**, sancti Maccaille episcopi et confessoris.

3   *Macchaillini* T; *epscop ... Macc caille*, 'bishop Mac Caille', MO.

1. MU 1, with *Litania* here, as in Molanus, for Usuard's *L(a)etania*.
2. MU 2. MReg had first assigned this entry to the previous day, before crossing it out.
3. Mac Caille, who was noted for his role in placing the veil on St Brighid of Kildare, was patron of the church at Croghan Hill in the Offaly barony of Lower Phillipstown.

Sources: **1, 2**. Dubois, *Martyrologe*, 218. **3**. Stokes, *Martyrology*, 108, 118; Best and Lawlor, *Martyrology*, 36; *DIS*, 412–13.

[26 April] Sexto Calendas Mai[i] Die 26 D

1. Romae, natalis sancti Cleti papae et martyyris.
2. Item, Romae, sancti Marcellini pontificis.
3. Trecas, sanctae Exuperantiae uirginis.

2   *Marcellani* MS.

1. MU 1, with *Cleti* for Usuard's *Anacleti*, as in Molanus. See also 13 July.
2. MU 2.
3. The feast of the little known Exsuperantia of Troyes is in a number of *auctaria* of MU, including Molanus, which has the same wording as MReg.

Sources: **1, 2**. Dubois, *Martyrologe*, 219; *AASS*, Iun. VI, 234. **3**. *AASS*, Iun. VI, 236; *BiblSS*, v, 97–8.

[27 April] E Quinto Calendas Maii Die 27

1. Romae, depositio beati Anastasii papae.
2. Tarso Ciliciae, sancti Castoris et Stephani martyrum.

1, 2. MU 1, 3. The addition here in 2 of *et Stephani martyrum* corresponds to the text of several *auctaria*, including Molanus.

Sources: **1, 2**. Dubois, *Martyrologe*, 219; *AASS*, Iun. VI, 237–8.

[28 April] Quarto Calendas Maii Die 28 F

1. Apud Rauennam, natalis sancti Uitalis martyris.
2. Eodem die, egressio Noe de Arca.
3. **In Hybernia**, sancti Cronani confessoris.
4. In Pannonia, sancti Pollionis martyris.

[3] *Crunani* MS. *Cronani* T; *la Cronan Roiss Chree*, 'with Crónán of Roscrea', MO.

1, 4. MU 1, 4.
2. This is the last of the italicized added entries in Molanus, which is the only *auctarium* to have the feast.
3. Crónán was attached to the church of Roscrea in the Tipperary barony of Ikerrin.

Sources: **1, 4**. Dubois, *Martyrologe*, 220. **2**. *AASS* Iunii, VI, 240. **3**. Stokes, *Martyrology*, 109; Best and Lawlor, *Martyrology*, 37; *DIS*, 234–5.

[29 April] G Tertio Calendas Maii Die 29

1. Apud Mediolanum, sancti Petri martyris.
2. Romae, sanctae Katarinae Senensis.

3. In Anglia, in territorio Lingonensi, beati Roberti confessoris.
4. In Hybernia, sancti Fiachra confessoris et sanctae Cuachae uirginis.

⁴ *Fiacrani* T; *Fiachnae* MO.

1. Most *auctaria*, including Molanus, notice the feast of Peter of Verona, the first Dominican martyr, who was killed on 6 April 1252. His
feast was later fixed on 29 April.
2. As in the previous entry, most *auctaria*, including Molanus, commemorate Catherine of Siena, who died in Rome on 29 April 1380.
3. Molanus and most other *auctaria* record the feast of Robert of
Molesme, founder of the abbey of Cîteaux, who died in 1110 and was
canonized in 1222. Nowhere else, to my knowledge, is he placed *in
Anglia*.
4. Fiachra, alias Fiachna, was attached to Lismore, Co. Waterford,
whereas the virgin Cuach, who is mentioned in the notes to MO, was
attached to the church of 'Killynee', in Bogland, in the Wicklow parish and barony of Arklow.

Sources: **1, 2, 3**. *AASS* Iunii, VI, 241–2; Overgaauw, *Martyrologes*,
709–11; *BiblSS*, x, 746–54; ibid., iii, 996–1045; ibid., xi, 238–45. **4**,
Stokes, *Martyrology*, 109, 120; Best and Lawlor, *Martyrology*, 37,
217; *DIS*, 238, 316–17.

[30 April] Pridie Calendas Maii Die 30 April A

1. Romae, sancti Quirini tribuni et martyris.
2. In Britannia, ciuitate Londoniae, sancti Erconualdi episcopi et confessoris.
3. In Hybernia, sancti Ronani confessoris.
4. Item, uigilia apostolorum Philippi et Jacobi.

³ Rodiciani T; *Rónán líath Roiss*, 'Rónán of Liathros', MO.

1. This feast of Quirinus, Roman tribune and martyr, whose relics
were kept in Neuss in Germany, is in most *auctaria* of MU, including,
in the same words, Molanus; Usuard placed the feast on 30 March,
where it is also noticed in MReg.

2. MReg again follows Molanus's text closely here. Earconwald, bishop of London, who died in 693, founded two monasteries, at Chertsey in Surrey and at Barking in Essex.

3. Rónán was attached to the church of Liathros, an unidentified site in Conaille Muirtheimhne, now the northern part of Co. Louth.

4. This is not in any of Usuard's *auctaria*.

Sources: **1**. *AASS* Iunii, VI, 244; Overgaauw, *Martyrologes*, 712; Dubois, *Martyrologe*, 203; *BiblSS*, x, 1329–31. **2**. *AASS* Iunii, VI, 244; *EncASE* 153–4. **3**. Stokes, *Martyrology*, 109, 120; Best and Lawlor, *Martyrology*, 38; *DIS*, 540.

[1 May] B Calendis Mai[i] Die 1 Maii

1. Natalis beatorum apostolorum Philippi et Jacobi.
2. In Britannia, sancti Chorentini episcopi et confessoris.
3. In **Scotia**, sancti Asaphi episcopi.
4. In Hybernia, sancti Nechtani confessoris.
5. In minori Britannia, sancti Brioci episcopi et confessoris.

[2] *Saphi* MS. **4**. *Nectani* T; *Nechtáin daltai Pátric*, 'Neachtan, disciple of Patrick', MO.

1. MU 2.

2. The Cologne martyrologies (Grevenus and Lübeck/Cologne) and Molanus, which agrees with MReg in dropping *minori* after *Britannia*, likewise notice Corentinus, bishop of Quimper, on this day, although his feast usually falls in December.

3. Molanus likewise places Asaph, who gave name to the diocese of St Asaph in Wales, *in Scotia*. His office Life is preserved in the Breviary of Aberdeen.

4. Neachtan is assigned to the unidentified church of Cell Uinche in North Louth; he belongs more properly in the list for the following day.

5. Of the *auctaria* of MU only Molanus notices this feast. Briocus (Brieuc) was patron of Saint-Brieuc in Brittany.

Sources: **1**. Dubois, *Martyrologe*, 221. **2**. *AASS* Iunii, VI, 247; *BiblSS*, iv, 178–9. **3**. *AASS* Iunii, VI, 247; Forbes, *Kalendars*, 271–2; Farmer, *Dictionary*, 23; *LegSS*, 115–17, 324. **4**. Stokes, *Martyrology*, 122; Best and Lawlor, *Martyrology*, 38; *DIS*, 512–13. **5**. *AASS* Iunii, VI, 247; *BiblSS*, iii, 534–6.

[2 May] Sexto Nonas Maii Die 2 C

1. Natalis sancti Athanasii, Alexandriae urbis episcopi et confessoris.
2. In **Hybernia**, sancti Conlaidi episcopi et martyris.

² *Conlathi* T; *Conláid* MO.

1. MU 1, with the omission here of (*patris*) *nostri* and the change of *Alexandrinae* to *Alexandriae*, as in Molanus.
2. Conlaodh, bishop at Kildare, who was already mentioned by Cogitosus in his seventh-century Life of Brighid, belongs more properly in the list for the following day. His description as martyr may be due to the tradition that he was devoured by wolves.

Sources: **1**. Dubois, *Martyrologe*, 222; *AASS* Iunii, VI, 248. **2**. Stokes, *Martyrology*, 122; Best and Lawlor, *Martyrology*, 39; Colgan, *Triadis*, 523, 525; *DIS*, 223–4.

[3 May] D Quinto Nonas Maii Die 3

1. Hierosolymis, inuentio sanctae Crucis ab Helena regina, sub Constantino principe.
2. Romae, uia Numentana, passio sanctorum Alexandri, Euentii et Theoduli martyrum.
3. Ipso die, sancti Juuenalis episcopi et confessoris.

1, 2. MU 1, 2.
3. Although not in MU, the feast is noted on this day in MA and Molanus. Iuvenalis was bishop of Narni in Italy.

Sources: **1, 2**. Dubois, *Martyrologe*, 223. **3**. Dubois and Renaud, *Martyrologes*, 146; *BiblSS*, vi, 1069–70.

[4 May] Quarto Nonas Maii Die 4 E

1. Apud Ostiam Tiberinam, natalis sanctae Monicae uiduae.
2. In Hybernia, natalis sancti Mochua confessoris.

² *Mochua* T; *mo Chuae ... macc Cummíni*, 'Mochua son of Cuimín', MO.

1. The feast of the mother of St Augustine is in several *auctaria*, in-cluding Molanus which places it first. At 9 April, MReg also com-memorated the translation of her relics from Ostia to Rome.
2. Mochua was assigned to the Slieve Felim mountains on Limerick's border with Tipperary. He may be the same as Crónán of Roscrea who was remembered a week earlier (28 April); Mochua is a hypochoristic form of Crónán.

Sources: **1**. *AASS* Iunii, VI, 254; Overgaauw, *Martyrologe*, 721. **2**. Stokes, *Martyrology*, 122; Best and Lawlor, *Martyrology*, 39; *DIS*, 235.

[5 May] F Tertio Nonas Maii Die 5

1. In Monte Oliueti, ascensio Domini nostri Jesu Christi ad caelos.
2. Mediolani, conuersio sancti Augustini episcopi per beatum Ambro-sium.

¹ *assensio* MS.

1. Several *auctaria* contain this entry, and Molanus has the same text.
2. Molanus, together with several other *auctaria* of MU, likewise re-fers here to the conversion in Milan of St Augustine by St Ambrose.

Sources: **1**. *AASS* Iunii, VI, 255–6; Overgaauw, *Martyrologe*, 722. **2**. *AASS* Iunii, VI, 255–6.

[6 May] Pridie Nonas Maii die 6 G

1. Romae, dedicatio sancti Joannis apostoli.
2. In Anglia, sancti Edberti episcopi Lindisfarnensis et confessoris.

1. MU 1, with *dedicatio sancti* here for Usuard's *beati*.

2. Of the *auctaria* of MU only Grevenus and Molanus contain this entry. MReg omits the alternative name-form *Eadbrechti*, which is cited in the other two sources.

Sources: **1**. Dubois, *Martyrologe*, 224. **2**. *AASS* Iunii, VI, 258.

[7 May] A Nonis Maii Die 7

1. Natalis sancti Stanislai episcopi et martyris.
2. Beuerlaci, depositio sancti Joannis episcopi Eboracensis.

1. In line with the Polish calendar, the Cologne *auctaria* (Grevenus and Lübeck/Cologne) and Molanus notice Stanislaus of Cracow (canonized in 1253) on the following day. However, MReg agrees with MR, which likewise places him on this day.
2. The feast of John of Beverley, bishop of York (†721), is recorded in several *auctaria*, including Molanus, whose text is very close to that of MReg.

Sources: **1**. *AASS* Iunii, VI, 262; *AASS* Dec., Propyleum, 176; *BiblSS*, xi, 1362–6. **2**. *AASS* Iunii, VI, 259–60; Farmer, *Dictionary*, 216.

[8 May] Octauo Idus Maii Die 8 B

1. Mediolani, sancti Uictoris martyris.
2. In Monte Gargano, apparitio beati Michaelis archangeli.

1. MU 1.
2. Most *auctaria*, including Molanus, notice this feast of Michael the Archangel.

Sources: **1**. Dubois, *Martyrologe*, 226. **2**. *AASS* Iunii, VI, 261–2; Overgaauw, *Martyrologes*, 726–7.

[9 May] C Septimo Idus Maii Die 9

1. Natalis sancti Gregorii Nazianzani.
2. In Hybernia, beati Sanctani episcopi.
3. In Hybernia, sancti Comgalli abbatis mille monachorum.

2 *Sanctani* T; *epscop Sanctain*, 'Bishop Santán.', MO. **3**. *Congilli* (in main text); *Comgalli* T; *Comgall ... Bennchuir*, 'Comhghall of Bangor', MO.

1. MU 3.
2. Santán was attached to the church of Killalish in the parish of Kilranelagh, Co. Wicklow.
3. The feast of Comgall of Bangor more properly belongs on the following day, where Grevenus (*In Hibernia, Congallionis abbatis*) also places it.

Sources: **1**. Dubois, *Martyrologe*, 226. **2**. Stokes, *Martyrology*, 123; Best and Lawlor, *Martyrology*, 41; Price, *Placenames*, 466; *DIS*, 546–7. **3**. Stokes, *Martyrology*, 123; Best and Lawlor, *Martyrology*, 41; *AASS* Iunii, VI, 266; *DIS*, 217–19.

[10 May] Sexto Idus Maii Die 10 D

1. In terra Hus, depositio Job prophetae.
2. Romae, natalis sanctorum martyrum Gordiani et Epimachi.
3. Eodem die, depositio uenerabilis Bedae presbiteri.

1. MU 1, with the addition here of *In terra Hus, depositio*, exactly as in Molanus.
2. MU 2, with the omission here of the exact location (*via Latina*).
3. Molanus is the only other version of MU to notice the Venerable Bede on this day. The saint is said by his disciple Cuthbert to have died on Ascension Day, which is usually taken to represent 26 May. The feast was later moved, as also below in MReg, to 27 May or, according to a St Gall version of Cuthbert's witness, to 9/10 May, as here. Confusion between the two feasts led to the assignment of 10 May to another Bede, associated with Lindisfarne and mentioned in the Life of St Cuthbert.

Sources: **1**. Dubois, *Martyrologe*, 227; *AASS* Iunii, VI, 266. **2**. Dubois, *Martyrologe*, 227. **3**. *AASS* Iunii, VI, 266; *EncASE*, 57–9; Farmer, *Dictionary*, 33–4; Plummer, *Venerabilis Baedae*, lxxiii; *BiblSS*, ii, 1006.

[11 May] E Quinto Idus Maii Die 11

1. Romae, uia Salaria, natalis beati Anthymi presbiteri.
2. In Hybernia, sanctorum confessorum Mochritochi et Cormaci.

² *mo Chritóc ... cruimther Cormacc*, 'Mochriotóg, the priest Cormac', MO.

1. MU 1.
2. Both Cormac and Mochriodóg were assigned to churches on the island of Aran, off the coast of Co. Galway.

Sources: **1.** Dubois, *Martyrologe*, 228. **2.** Stokes, *Martyrology*, 123; Best and Lawlor, *Martyrology*, 42; *DIS*, 231.

[12 May] Quarto Idus Maii Die 12 F

1. Romae, natalis sanctorum martyrum Nerei et Achillei fratrum.
2. Item, uia Aurelia, sancti Pancratii martyris.
3. Eodem die, sanctae Domitillae uirginis.
4. In Hybernia, sanctorum Ailitheri et Herci abbatum et confessorum.

⁴ *Ailithir ... la hErc ... Nascai*, 'Oilithir, with Earc Nasca', MO.

1, 2. MU 1, 2, with the omission in 1 of the exact location (*via Ardiatina*).
3. MA and some *auctaria*, not including Molanus, which reads *Octauilla*, mention Domitilla in connexion with Nereus and Achilleus (1 above).
4. Oilithir was attached to the church of Muckinish in Lough Derg on the river Shannon, whereas Earc was assigned to Tullylish in the Down barony of Iveagh Lower.

Sources: **1, 2.** Dubois, *Martyrologe*, 228. **3.** *AASS* Iunii, VI, 269–70; Overgaauw, *Martyrologes*, 732; Dubois and Renaud, *Martyrologes*, 157. **4.** Stokes, *Martyrology*, 124; Best and Lawlor, *Martyrology*, 42; Stokes, *Martyrology of Gorman*, 94; *DIS*, 164 (Cearc).

[13 May] G Tertio Idus Maii Die 13

1. Dedicatio sanctae Mariae ad martyres.
2. Eodem die, sanctae Glyceriae martyris.
3. Item, sancti Alexandri martyris sub Maximiano imperatore.

1. MU 1, with *Dedicatio* here in place of Usuard's *Natalis*.
2, 3. Of the *auctaria* of MU only Molanus notices these feasts, approximately in the same words as MReg. Alexander may have been a martyred Roman legionary of that name, whereas Glyceria suffered martyrdom at Heraclea in Thracian Propontis.

Sources: **1.** Dubois, *Martyrologe*, 229. **2, 3.** *AASS* Iunii, VI, 272; *BiblSS*, i, 778–80; ibid., vii, 57–8.

[14 May] Pridie Idus Maii Die 14 A

1. Passio sancti Bonifacii martyris.
2. Eodem die, sancti Pachomii.
3. In Hybernia, sancti Karthagi episcopi et confessoris.
4. Item, sancti Seruatii episcopi.

³ *Cartagi* T; *féil ... Charthaig Rathin*, 'feast of Carthach of Rahan', MO.

1. This martyr, whose feast is on this day in several *auctaria*, including Molanus which places it first, was also commemorated by Usuard, following Ado, at 5 June. Ado states that the martyrdom took place in Tarsus on 14 May but that the burial of the saint was in Rome.
2. MU 3, with the omission here of Usuard's *patris nostri*.
3. Carthach, alias Mochuda, was the founder-patron of Rahan in Co. Offaly, and of Lismore in Co. Waterford. Grevenus (*In Hibernia, Karthagii episcopi*) switched his feast to the previous day, and the same source placed here the feast of Maol Dóid of Muckno in Co. Monaghan (*In Hybernia, Maldod confessoris*), which more properly belongs on 13 May.
4. This feast is more usually on the previous day (MU 3).

Sources: **1**, *AASS* Iunii, VI, 274–5; Overgaauw, *Martyrologes*, 735; Dubois, *Martyrologe*, 241; Dubois and Renaud, *Martyrologes*, 184–5.

2. Dubois, *Martyrologe*, 229. **3**. Stokes, *Martyrology*, 124; Best and Lawlor, *Martyrology*, 42; *DIS*, 439, 470–3. **4**. Dubois, *Martyrologe*, 229.

[15 May] B Idibus Maii Die 15

1. Hierosolimis, aduentus Spiritus sancti.
2. In Hybernia, sanctorum confessorum [Sarani] et Dubliterani.

2. *Dublictani* MS; *Saran ... Duiblitir* MO.

1. Several *auctaria*, including Molanus, which also specifies Jerusalem, notice this feast.
2. MReg's use of the plural *sanctorum confessorum* would suggest that MO's Sárán was also intended for mention here. Sárán was associated with Inis Mór, now possibly Great Island in the Cork barony of Imokilly. Duibhlitir (†796) was abbot of Finglas in Co. Dublin.

Sources: **1**. *AASS* Iunii, VI, 276–7. **2**. Stokes, *Martyrology*, 124; Best and Lawlor, *Martyrology*, 43; *DIS*, 547.

[16 May] Decimo Septimo Calendis Junii Die 16 C

1. In Scotia, sancti Brendani abbatis.
2. Eodem die, sanctorum Carnachi et Huasunachi episcopi et confessoris.
3. In Galliis, ciuitate Ambianis, sancti Honorati episcopi et confessoris.

1 *Brandani* T. **2**. *Wasuagenii* T; *bás ... Carnig ... féil ... haui Súanaig*, 'Cairneach's death, feast of the grandson of Suanach', MO.

1. Of the *auctaria* of MU, Bruxellensis, the two Cologne versions (Grevenus and Lübeck/Cologne) and Molanus, which also specifies *Scotia*, notice the feast of Brendan the Navigator. His principal Irish church was Clonfert in the Galway barony of Longford.
2. Cairneach was attached to the church of Dulane in the Meath barony of Upper Kells. Ua Suanaigh, named Fiodhmhaine, was one of three brothers associated with the Offaly church of Rahan who were made the subject of a vernacular Life.

3. Honoratus, supposedly the third bishop of Amiens, is noticed by some *auctaria* of MU, including Molanus, which has the same words.

Sources: **1.** *AASS* Iunii, VI, 278–9; *DIS*, 115–17. **2.** Stokes, *Martyrology*, 124; Best and Lawlor, *Martyrology*, 43; Plummer, *Bethada*, i, 312–16; *DIS*, 145–6, 324–5. **3.** *AASS* Iunii, VI, 278–9; *BiblSS*, ix, 1201–2.

[17 May] D Decimo 6 Calendas Junii 17

1. In Tuscia, sancti Torpeti martyris et aliorum nouem.
2. Eodem die, translatio corporis sancti Montani monachi.

¹ *Tussia* MS.

1. MU 1, with the addition here of *et aliorum nouem*.
2. The translation of Montanus, who was venerated in Laon, among other places, is noticed in a few *auctaria*. Of those cited by Sollerius, however, only the similarly worded Molanus has this feast.

Sources: **1.** Dubois, *Martyrologe*, 229. **2.** *AASS* Iunii, VI, 280; Overgaauw, *Martyrologes*, 740; *BiblSS*, ix, 569–70.

[18 May] Decimo Quinto Calendas Junii Die 18 E

1. In Aegypto, sancti Dioscori lectoris et martyris.
2. In Suecia, sancti Erici regis et martyris.
3. In Hybernia, sanctorum confessorum Momedochi, Modomnochii et Braini.

² *Suetia* MS. **3.** *moMáedóc ... moDomnóc ... féil Brain bicc ó Chláined*, 'Momhaodhóg, Modhomhnóg, the feast of little Bran from Clane', MO.

1. MU 1.
2. The Cologne *auctaria* (Grevenus and Lübeck/Cologne) and Molanus, which uses the same words, likewise contain this entry. Eric 'the Lawgiver', who, according to tradition, was killed in 1161, became Sweden's principal patron.

3. These constitute a cluster of Leinster saints, belonging respectively to Fiddown in the Kilkenny barony of Iverk, Tibberaghny in the same barony, and Clane in Co. Kildare. Curiously, Grevenus (*In Hibernia, Saran confessoris*) has an entry here concerning an otherwise unattested saint Sárán, but his *Sa-* is possibly an error for *B-*.

Sources: **1**. Dubois, *Martyrologe*, 231. **2**. *AASS* Iunii, VI, 281–2; *BiblSS*, iv, 1322–5. **3**. Stokes, *Martyrology*, 125; Best and Lawlor, *Martyrology*, 44; *AASS* Iunii, VI, 282; *DIS*, 109, 477–8, 494–5.

[19 May] F Decimo Quarto Calendas Junii Die Decimo Nono

1. Romae, sanctae Pudentianae uirginis.
2. In Britannia minori, sancti Juonis praesbiteri et confessoris.
3. Item, sancti Hirlahei confessoris.

1. MU 2, with *Pudentianae* for Usuard's *Potentianae*.
2. This feast is noticed by several *auctaria* of MU, including the similarly worded Molanus. Yves, alias Yves Hélory, of Tréguier and Kermartin in Brittany, the patron saint of lawyers, died in 1303 and was canonized in 1347.
3. This saint has not been identified, but the Reichenau Confraternity Book has an entry which reads: *Sedulius sive Ilarleh* in reference to a ninth-century monk from the Bavarian abbey of Niederaltaich. Several necrological entries in MReg relate to Niederaltaich (Appendix 1).

Sources: **1**. Dubois, *Martyrologe*, 232. **2**. *AASS* Iunii, VI, 283–4; Overgaauw, *Martyrologes*, 742–3; *BiblSS*, vii, 997–1001.

[20 May] Decimo Tertio Calendas Junii Die 20 G

1. Romae, uia Salaria, natalis beatae Basillae uirginis et martyris.
2. Papiae, sancti Theodori episcopi et confessoris.
3. Eodem die, sancti Bernardini Senensis.
4. Herefordiae, sancti Athelberti regis Angliae et martyris.

1. MU 1.

2. Molanus, which has the same wording, is one of a few *auctaria* to notice the feast of Theodore, bishop and patron of Pavia, who flourished in the mid to late eighth century.

3. The Franciscan monk Bernardine of Siena (†1444) was canonized in 1450. His feast is in several *auctaria*, including Molanus which places the entry immediately after that on Theodore.

4. The Cologne martyrologies (Grevenus and Lübeck/Cologne) and Molanus notice the feast of Æthelberht, king of East Anglia, who was assassinated in 794.

Sources: **1**. Dubois, *Martyrologe*, 232. **2**. *AASS* Iunii, VI, 286; *BiblSS*, xii, 259–60. **3**. *AASS* Iunii, VI, 285–6; Overgaauw, *Martyrologes*, 744–5; *BiblSS*, ii, 1294–1316. **4**. *AASS* Iunii, VI, 286; Farmer, *Dictionary*, 137.

[21 May] A Duodecimo Calendas Junii Die 21

1. Translatio beati Pauli martyris.
2. In Anglia, depositio beati Godrici eremitae et confessoris.
3. In Hybernia, sanctorum Colmani et Barrinni.

¹ *Petri* MS. **3**. *Bartinni* MS; *Colmán lobor ... Barrfhind Drommo Cuilinn*, 'Colmán the leper, Bairrfhionn of Drumcullen', MO.

1. Several *auctaria*, including Molanus, likewise commemorate the translation c. 1226 of the relics of the martyr Paul from Constantinople to the church of St George in Venice. The manuscript *Petri* in place of *Pauli* is a natural error.

2. Godric, a celebrated hermit of Finchale in Co. Durham, died in 1170. Of the *auctaria* of MU, only Molanus otherwise notices his feast, in similar wording.

3. Bairrfhionn was the patron of Drumcullen in the Offaly barony of Eglish. Colmán Lobhar was attached to the church of Moynoe in the Clare barony of Tulla Upper.

Sources: **1**. *AASS* Iunii, VI, 287; *BiblSS*, x, 286–93. **2**. *AASS* Iunii, VI, 287; Farmer, *Dictionary*, 174–5. **3**. Stokes, *Martyrology*, 125; Best and Lawlor, *Martyrology*, 45; *DIS*, 83–4, 206.

[22 May] Undecimo Calendas Junii Die 22 B

1. Antisiodori, sanctae Helenae uirginis.
2. In Galliis, sancti Romani abbatis, alumni sancti patris Benedicti.
3. In Hybernia, sanctorum confessorum Baitheni et Ronani.

[3] *Battheni* MS; *Ronani* T; *animm Rónáin Find ... Báithéne macc Findach,* 'the soul of Rónán Fionn, Baoithín son of Fionna(ch)', MO.

1. MU 3, with *Antisiodori* for Usuard's *Autisiodoro*, as in Molanus.
2. Romanus, of Font-Rouge near Auxerre, appears to be intended here; he is commemorated on this day in most *auctaria*, including Molanus which has the same words. Some *auctaria* place his feast on the previous day.
3. Rónán was patron of Magheralin in the Down barony of Iveagh Lower. Baoithín was attached to the church of Ennisboyne in Dunganstown parish in the Wicklow barony of Arklow.

Sources: **1**. Dubois, *Martyrologe*, 233. **2**. *AASS*, Iun. VI, 289; Overgaauw, *Martyrologes*, 745; *BiblSS*, xi, 318–19. **3**. Stokes, *Martyrology*, 125; Best and Lawlor, *Martyrology*, 45; *DIS*, 88, 538–40.

[23 May] C Decimo Calendas Junii Die 23

1. Apud Lingones, passio sancti Desiderii episcopi.
2. In Anglia, ciuitate Rossensi, passio sancti Gulielmi.

1. MU 1.
2. Together with Grevenus only of the *auctaria* of MU, Molanus commemorates this saint, using the same wording as here. William of Rochester (†1201) was a native of Perth (Scotland), but was buried in Rochester (Kent), where his cult flourished.

Sources: **1**. Dubois, *Martyrologe*, 233. **2**. *AASS*, Iun. VI, 289; Farmer, *Dictionary*, 405–6.

[24 May] Nono Calendas Junii die 24 D

1. In portu Romano, natalis sancti Uincentii martyris.
2. In Affrica, natalis sancti Saturnini martyris.
3. In Hybernia, sanctorum Colmani et Adbei abbatum et confessorum.

Heading   The scribe had first written Ap, presumably for Aprilis.
3   *Colmán ... Aidbe ... Tíre*, 'Colmán, Aidhbhe of Terryglass', MO.

1. MU 3.
2. Although commemorated on this day in MH, Saturninus is not noticed in any of MU's *auctaria*.
3. Of this Colmán nothing further is known. Aoidhbhe was thought to
be an abbot of Terryglass in the Tipperary barony of Lower Ormond
but the Irish annals have no record of him.

Sources: **1.** Dubois, *Martyrologe*, 234. **2.** *AASS*, Nov. II/2, 269. **3.**
Stokes, *Martyrology*, 126; Best and Lawlor, *Martyrology*, 45; *DIS*, 76.

[25 May] E Octauo Calendas. Junii Die 25

1. Romae, natalis beati Urbani papae et martyris.
2. In Hybernia, sancti Dunchadi abbatis et confessoris.
3. Leodiae, translatio sancti Lamberti.
4. Bononiae, translatio sancti Dominici confessoris.

2   *Doncadi* T; *Dunchad Híae*, 'Dúnchadh of Iona', MO.

1. MU 1, with omission here of the precise location (*via Numentana*).
2. Dúnchadh, abbot of Iona, died in 717.
3. Molanus (24 May) is otherwise the only *auctarium* to notice this
feast of Lambertus, bishop of Maastricht-Tongerloo, who was assassinated in Liège c. 715. The more usual day of the translation, which
took place in 1141, is 28 April, and there may have been some confusion here with the feast of Lambertus of Vence, who died on this day
in 1154.

4. The *auctaria* of MU, including Molanus, commemorate the feast of the translation of the relics of Dominic, founder of the Dominican order, on the previous day.

Sources: **1**. Dubois, *Martyrologe*, 234. **2**. Stokes, *Martyrology*, 126; Best and Lawlor, *Martyrology*, 46; *DIS*, 277. **3**. *AASS* Iunii, VI, 293; Overgaauw, *Martyrologes*, 708; *BiblSS*, vii, 1079–80; ibid., 1085. **4**. *AASS* Iunii, VI, 292–3; Overgaauw, *Martyrologes*, 748.

[26 May] Septimo Calendas Junii Die 26 F

1. In Britannia, sancti Aldelmi episcopi et confessoris.
2. Ibidem, depositio sancti Augustini, primi Anglorum episcopi.
3. In Hybernia, sanctorum Colmani et Becani abbatum et confessorum.
4. Eodem die, sancti Eleutherii papae et martyris.

[3] *Beocani* T; *Airitiu ... Cholmáin Stelláin ... Béccán ... hi Clúain aird*, 'The reception of Colmán Steallán, Beagán in Peakaun', MO.

1. Several *auctaria* of MU, including Molanus, commemorate Aldhelm, abbot of Malmesbury, on the previous day.
2. MU 6, with slightly different wording.
3. Colmán Steallán was attached to Terryglass in Co. Tipperary and may thus represent Colum, the patron of this church, whose principal feast fell on 13 December. Beagán was patron of Peakaun, alias Toureen, parish of Killardry, in the Tipperary barony of Clanwilliam.
4. Most *auctaria*, including the similarly worded Molanus, record the feast of the late second-century Pope Eleutherius on this day.

Sources: **1**. *AASS*, Iun. VI, 295–6; Overgaauw, *Martyrologes*, 750; *EncASE*, 25–7. **2**. Dubois, *Martyrologe*, 235. **3**. Stokes, *Martyrology*, 126; Best and Lawlor, *Martyrology*, 46; *DIS*, 93–4, 208. **4**. *AASS* Iunii, VI, 297–8; Overgaauw, *Martyrologes*, 752.

[27 May] G Sexto Calendas Junii Die 27

1. In territorio Antisioderensi, passio beati Prisci martyris.
2. Item, depositio Bede presbiteri.
3. Eodem die, natalis beati Joannis papae et martyris.

1. MU 5 (26 May), with *Antisioderensi* here, as in Molanus, for Usuard's *Autisiodorensi*.

2. The feast of the Venerable Bede is in many *auctaria* on this day. See also at 10 May.

3. Pope John I, whom Usuard placed on the following day, is also noticed here by some *auctaria*, including Molanus. John's main feast fell on 18 May.

Sources: **1**. Dubois, *Martyrologe*, 235. **2**. *AASS*, Iun. VI, 299–300; Overgaauw, *Martyrologes*, 753. **3**. Dubois, *Martyrologe*, 235; *AASS* Iunii, VI, 299–300; Overgaauw, *Martyrologes*, 754; Kelly, *Dictionary*, 54–5.

[28 May] Quinto Calendas Junii Die 28 A

1. Parisiis, transitus sancti Germani confessoris.
2. In Sardinia, sanctorum Emilii, Faelicis, Primi et Luciani martyrum.
3. Padebornae, translatio sancti Liborii episcopi Caenomanensis.

1, 2. MU 2, 3, with *Parisiis* here for Usuard's *Parisius civitate*, as otherwise only in Molanus.

3. The Cologne martyrologies (Grevenus and Lübeck/Cologne) and Molanus, which has the same words, contain this entry. The relics of Liborius, bishop of Le Mans, were translated to Paderborn in the ninth century.

Sources: **1, 2**. Dubois, *Martyrologe*, 236. **3**. *AASS*, Iun. VI, 302; *BiblSS*, viii, 32.

[29 May] B Quarto Calendas Junii Die 29

1. Treuiris, beati Maximi episcopi et confessoris.
2. Romae, uia Aurelia, natalis sancti Restituti.
3. In **Hybernia**, sancti Cummeni confessoris.

---

3   *Cummeni* T; *la Cummain ... ingen Allén*, 'with Cuman daughter of Oilléan', MO.

1, 2. MU 3, 4. For Maxim[in]us, see also below at 12 September.

3. Both T and MReg wrongly transmuted into a male this female saint Cuman, who was attached to a church in the Ards peninsula, in Co. Down.

Sources: **1, 2**. Dubois, *Martyrologe*, 237. **3**. Stokes, *Martyrology*, 126; Best and Lawlor, *Martyrology*, 46; *DIS*, 248.

[30 May] Tertio Calendas Junii Die 30 C

1. Romae, natalis beati Faelicis papae et martyris.
2. Eodem die, sancti patris Isaaci.
3. Item, sancti Huberti episcopi Tungrensis ecclesiae.

1. MU 1, with omission here of the precise location (*via Aurelia*).
2. Molanus, which places the saint in Dalmatia, is the only other version of MU to record Isaac's feast on this day.
3. MU 3, which does not cite the placename. Molanus is among the few *auctaria* to place the saint in Tongern, which Hubertus left in favour of Liège.

Sources: **1**. Dubois, *Martyrologe*, 237. **2**. *AASS*, Iun. VI, 306; *BiblSS*, vii, 920–1. **3**. *AASS*, Iun. VI, 306; Overgaauw, *Martyrologes*, 757.

[31 May] D Pridie Calendas Junii Die 31

1. Romae, sanctae Petronillae uirginis.
2. Apud urbem Aquileiam, sanctorum martyrum Cantii et Cantiani fratrum.
3. Eodem die, sancti Crescentiani martyris.

1, 2, 3. MU 1, 2, 3, with omission in MReg (2) of a personal name (*Cantianilla*) and in MReg (3) of a placename (*Turres Sardiniae*).

Sources: **1, 2, 3**. Dubois, *Martyrologe*, 237–8.

[1 June] Calendis Junii Die 1 E

1. Treuiris, depositio beati Symeonis monachi.
2. Item, sancti Jouini abbatis.
3. Romae, sancti Uiuentii martyris.

1. Most *auctaria*, including Molanus, notice Simeon (†1035), a recluse in Trier's *Porta Nigra*, on this day.
2. A small number of *auctaria*, including Molanus, commemorate Yves of *Pictavis* (Poitiers) on this day. He may be the same as Ivo of Chartres.
3. The Cologne martyrologies (Grevenus and Lübeck/Cologne) and Molanus are among the *auctaria* that notice Viventius (recte Iuventius) of Rome on this day in an entry originally drawn from MH.

Sources: **1.** *AASS*, Iun. VI, 310–11; Overgaauw, *Martyrologes*, 760; *BiblSS*, xi, 1157–60. **2.** *AASS*, Iun. VI, 311; *BiblSS*, vii, 994–7. **3.** *AASS*, Iun. VI, 311; Overgaauw, *Martyrologes*, 759–60.

[2 June] F Quarto Nonas Junii Die 2

1. In Campania, natalis sancti Erasmi episcopi et martyris.
2. Eodem die, sancti patris Nicephori, patriarchae Constantinopolis.
3. Romae, sanctorum Marcellini et Petri martyrum.

1. MU has this feast on the following day, but several *auctaria*, including Molanus, place it here in accordance with Franciscan usage.
2. Of the *auctaria* of MU, this is only in Molanus, which has similar wording. Nicephorus, arguably the principal Byzantine historian of the eighth and early ninth centuries, died on 2 June 828/9.
3. MU 1, with altered wording here.

Sources: **1.** Dubois, *Martyrologe*, 240; *AASS*, Iun. VI, 313; Overgaauw, *Martyrologes*, 761. **2.** *AASS*, Iun. VI, 313; *BiblSS*, ix, 871–84. **3.** Dubois, *Martyrologe*, 239.

[3 June] Tertio Nonas Junii Die 3 G

1. In territorio Aurelianensium, sancti Liphardi praesbiteri.
2. Item, sancti Morandi confessoris, discipuli sancti Hugonis.
3. Et sanctae Crotildis reginae.
4. In Hybernia, sancti Coemgeni abbatis et confessoris.

[3] *Cortidis*, MS. **4.** *In Hybernia, sancti Coemgeni abbatis* (*episcopi* C) *et confessoris* COW; *Coemgeni* T; *Cóemgen ... i nGlinn*, 'Caoimhghin (Kevin) in Glendalough', MO.

1. MU 4.

2. Some *auctaria*, including Molanus, which has much the same wording as MReg, notice Morandus (†1115). He was a Cluniac monk, whence the reference here to Hugo, and was buried at Altkirch in Alsace.

3. Molanus is the only other version of MU to notice the feast of Clotilde, wife of Clovis, on this day.

4. The feast of Caoimhghin (Kevin), patron of the church and diocese of Glendalough, is also recorded on this day by Grevenus, in two forms of the saint's name: *In Hibernia, Kevini abbatis Coeemgini confessoris*.

Sources: **1**. Dubois, *Martyrologe*, 240. **2**. *AASS* Iunii, VI, 316; *BiblSS*, ix, 586–8. **3**. *AASS* Iunii, VI, 315; *BiblSS*, iv, 64–5. **4**. Stokes, *Martyrology*, 138; Best and Lawlor, *Martyrology*, 47; *AASS* Iunii, VI, 315; *DIS*, 148–50.

[4 June] A Pridie Nonas Junii Die 4

1. Apud Illiricum, natalis sancti Quirini episcopi.
2. Item, Romae, sanctorum Aretii et Datiani martyrum.

1. MU 1, with the omission here of the exact location (*Siscia*).

2. This feast, originally from MH, is in almost all *auctaria* of MU.

Sources: **1**. Dubois, *Martyrologe*, 240. **2**. *AASS*, Iun. VI, 317; Overgaauw, *Martyrologes*, 763–4.

[5 June] Nonis Junii Die 5 B

1. Apud Aegyptum, natalis sanctorum martyrum Martiani, Nicandri et Apollonii.
2. Item, sancti Bonifacii, qui de Britanniis veniens fidem Christi gentilibus euangelizauit.

1, 2. MU 1, 3. The Egyptian martyrs have already been remembered at 5 April, and Usuard suppressed the present entry in his second recension.

Sources: **1**. Dubois, *Martyrologe*, 241–2.

[6 June] C Octauo Idus Junii Die 6

1. Natalis sancti Philippi, qui fuit unus de septem diaconibus.
2. **In Hybernia** sancti Maelaithgen confessoris.
3. Ciuitate Niueduno, sanctorum Amantii et Alexandri martyrum.

2   *Maelanghen* MS; *Máelaithgin* MO.

1. MU 1.
2. Maol Aithghin is variously assigned to Teach Maoil Aithghin, an unidentified church in what is now the Kildare barony of Carbury, and Moylagh in the Meath barony of Fore.
3. MU 4, with the addition here of *martyrum*.

Sources: **1.** Dubois, *Martyrologe*, 242. **2.** Stokes, *Martyrology*, 139; Best and Lawlor, *Martyrology*, 48; Stokes, *Martyrology of Gorman*, 110. **3.** Dubois, *Martyrologe*, 242.

[7 June] Septimo Idus Junii Die 7 D

1. Constantinopoli, natalis beati Pauli eiusdem ciuitatis episcopi.
2. In Anglia, sancti Roberti abbatis ordinis Cistertiensis.
3. **In Hybernia**, sancti Columbi abbatis.

2   *Cistertcensis* MS. **3.** *Columbi* (corrected from *Columbe*) T; *féil Choluimb ... maccu-Artai*, 'feast of Colum of the Maca Arta', MO.

1. MU 1.
2. Molanus, also with the words *in Anglia*, is the only *auctarium* to notice the feast of Robert of Newminster, who died in 1159.
3. Colum was patron of the church and diocesan see of Dromore in the Down barony of Iveagh. The saint is also noticed by both Grevenus and Molanus (*In Hibernia, Colmanni episcopi et confessoris*), to which the latter mistakenly added *de quo Beda in historia gentis suae*; Colmán of Dromore does not figure in Bede's work.

Sources: **1.** Dubois, *Martyrologe*, 242. **2.** *AASS*, Iun. VI, 323; Farmer, *Dictionary*, 345. **3.** Stokes, *Martyrology*, 139; Best and Lawlor, *Martyrology*, 48; *AASS*, Iun. VI, 323; *DIS*, 187–8.

85

[8 June] E Sexto Idus Junii Die 8

1. In Anglia, sancti Wilhelmi episcopi Eboracensis.
2. **In Hybernia**, sanctorum confessorum et abbatum Medrani et Murconi.

2 *féil Medráin ... féil Murchon*, 'feast of Meadhrán, feast of Muirchú'. MO.

1. Of the *auctaria* of MU only Grevenus and Molanus recorded the feast of William of York, more accurately describing him as an archbishop. William died in 1154.
2. Nothing further is known of this Meadhrán, but he may represent a hibernicized version of Medardus of Soissons, whose feast likewise fell on this day. Muirchú is taken to be one of Patrick's seventh-century biographers.

Sources: **1.** *AASS*, Iun. VI, 325; Farmer, *Dictionary*, 406. **2.** Stokes, *Martyrology*, 139; Best and Lawlor, *Martyrology*, 48; Bieler, *Patrician Texts*, 1–2; *DIS*, 503.

[9 June] Quinto Idus Junii Die 9 F

1. Romae, sanctorum martyrum Primi et Faeliciani.
2. **In Scotia**, beati Columkille abbatis.
3. Eodem die, sancti Baitheni abbatis et confessoris.

2 *Columbe* T; *Colomb cille* MO. **3.** *Baltheni* MS; *Baetheni* T; *Báethíne* MO.

1. MU 1, with omission here of the precise location (*in monte Caelio*) and with the spelling *Faeliciani* for *Feliciani*.
2. Despite its presence in MU among Usuard's handful of Irish saints, Columba's feast is likely to have been drawn here from MO which, as here, uses the vernacular form of the name.
3. Baoithín was Colum Cille's immediate successor as abbot of Iona.

Sources: **1.** Dubois, *Martyrologe*, 244; *AASS*, Iun. VI, 325. **2.** Dubois, *Martyrologe*, 244; Stokes, *Martyrology*, 139; Best and Lawlor, *Martyrology*, 49; *DIS*, 211–14. **3.** Stokes, *Martyrology*, 139; Best and Lawlor, *Martyrology*, 49; *DIS*, 88–9.

[10 June] G Quarto Idus Junii Die 10

1. Apud Nicomediam, sancti Zachariae prophetae.
2. **In Scotia, sanctae Margarethae reginae**.
3. Eodem die, translatio sancti Juonis episcopi.

1. MU 3, with the addition here of *prophetae*.
2. Highlighted here by the use of red letters, the feast of Margaret (†1093), queen of Scotland, is also in Molanus on this day. The more usual day (19 June), on which the Breviary of Aberdeen preserves her office Life, relates to the translation of the saint's remains in 1250. The queen is provided with a second feast here at 16 November.
3. This feast is noticed by some *auctaria*, among them Molanus which adds *de Perside*. The saint, allegedly a Persian bishop, was attached to St Ives, Huntingdonshire. His other feast fell on 24 April.

Sources: **1**. Dubois, *Martyrologe*, 245. **2**. *AASS*, Iun. VI, 329; Farmer, *Dictionary*, 262; *LegSS*, 144–7, 387. **3**. *AASS*, Iun. VI, 329; *BiblSS*, vii, 997; Farmer, *Dictionary*, 206.

[11 June] Tertio Idus Junii Die 11 A

1. Natalis sancti Barnabae apostoli.
2. Bremae, sancti Ramberti archiepiscopi et confessoris.
3. **In Hybernia**, sancti Mactaili episcopi et confessoris.

3   *Meictalini* T; *féil Maicc tháil*, 'feast of Mac Táil', MO.

1. MU 1.
2. Grevenus and Molanus likewise commemorate Rambert (Ragnobert), archbishop of Bremen, who is supposed to have been martyred between Bourg and Belley (Ain) on 13 June 680.
3. Mac Táil, who was first known as Eoghan, was attached to the church of Oldkilcullen in the Kildare barony of Kilcullen.

Sources: **1**. Dubois, *Martyrologe*, 245. **2**. *AASS*, Iun. VI, 331; *BiblSS*, xi, 34–5. **3**. Stokes, *Martyrology*, 140; Best and Lawlor, *Martyrology*, 49; *DIS*, 423–4.

[12 June] B Pridie Idus Junii Die 12

1. Romae, sanctorum martyrum Basilidis, Cirini et Naboris et Nazarii martyrum.
2. **In Hybernia**, sanctorum abbatum et confessorum Coemani et Toronani.

2   *Toronnani, Coemani* T; *Féil ... Chóemáin ... Torannán ... tar Ier*, 'Feast of Caomhán, Torannán across the sea', MO.

1. MU 2. Here as in several other versions of MU, including Molanus, *et Nazarii* is added to Usuard's entry which, more correctly, placed the martyrs in Milan.
2. Caomhán Santleathan was patron of the church of Ardcavan in the Wexford barony of Shelmaliere, whereas Torannán, alias Mothoiréan, was abbot of Bangor, alias Banchory-Ternan (*Beannchor Torannáin*), on the river Dee, near Aberdeen. MReg's *In Hybernia* should not, therefore, apply to Torannán, whose feast is also recorded by Grevenus (*In Scotia, Termani archiepiscopi et confessoris*).

Sources: **1**. Dubois, *Martyrologe*, 245–6. **2**. Stokes, *Martyrology*, 140; Best and Lawlor, *Martyrology*, 49; *AASS*, Iun. VI, 333; *BiblSS*, xii, 430; *DIS*, 157, 501.

[13 June] Idibus Junii 13 C

1. In ciuitate Padua, beati Antonii confessoris.
2. Romae, sanctae Faeliculae uirginis.
3. In **Hybernia**, sancti Maicnisi abbatis et confessoris.

3   *Maichnili* MS; *Meicnisini* T; *Macc nisi ... Clúana*, 'Mac Nise of Clonmacnoise', MO.

1. Almost all *auctaria* of MU commemorate Anthony of Padua, including Molanus which has the same wording as here.
2. MU 1, with the omission here of the precise location (*via Ardiatina*).
3. Mac Nise was attached to Clonmacnoise in the Offaly barony of Garrycastle.

Sources: **1**. *AASS*, Iun. VI, 335; Overgaauw, *Martyrologes*, 777. **2**. Dubois, *Martyrologe*, 246. **3**. Stokes, *Martyrology*, 140; Best and Lawlor, *Martyrology*, 50; *DIS*, 419.

[14 June] D Decimo 8 Calendas Julii Die 14

1. Apud Samariam Palestinae, Elisei prophetae.
2. Syracusis, sancti Martiani episcopi.
3. Apud Caesaream Cappadociae, sancti Basilii episcopi et confessoris.

1, 3. MU 1, 2, with the prepositioning here of *Apud Samariam Palestinae*.
2. Molanus is the only other *auctarium* to commemorate Martianus of Syracuse on this day.

Sources: **1, 3**. Dubois, *Martyrologe*, 246. **2**. *AASS*, Iun. VI, 337; *BiblSS*, viii, 693–5.

[15 June] Decimo Septimo Calendas Julii Die 15 E

1. In Cicilia, sanctorum martyrum Uiti, Modesti et Crescentiae.
2. Monasterio Scithiu, eleuatio pretiosi corporis sancti Bertini.

1. MU 1, with the addition here of *martyrum*.
2. The feast of Bertinus (†c. 709), founder of a monastery at Sithiu, falls on 5 September. The elevation of his remains at Sithiu does not appear to be attested in any other martyrology on this day, but there is a similar entry, with more detail, in Molanus on the following day.

Sources: **1**. Dubois, *Martyrologe*, 247. **2**. *AASS*, Iun. VI, 342; *BiblSS*, iii, 101–2.

[16 June] F Decimo Sexto Calendas Julii Die 16

1. Apud Viennam, sancti Domnolii episcopi.
2. Cremonae, sancti Hemerii episcopi.
3. Eodem die, sanctorum martyrum Manuelis, Sabelis et Ismaelis.

1, 2, 3. All three entries derive from Molanus's list of the following day. Domnolus, bishop of Vienne, was already commemorated by Ado on this day (MA 197.5). Himerius of Amelia, whose remains were translated to Cremona, is supposed to have lived in the twelfth century. Apart from Molanus and Baronius's Roman Martyrology, Manuel and his martyred companions are commemorated only in eastern synaxaries.

Sources: **1, 2, 3**. *AASS*, Iun. VI, 344; *BiblSS*, iv, 770–1; ibid., viii, 637–8, 785–6.

[17 June] Decimo Quinto Calendas Julii Die 17 G

1. Romae, natalis sanctorum Quiriaci, Blasii et Nicandri martyrum.
2. Eodem die, sancti Wolffmari confessoris.
3. In **Hybernia**, sancti Mollingi episcopi et confessoris.

3   *Molingini* T; *Moling Lúachair*, 'Moling of Luachair', MO.

1. Ultimately, this entry derives from MH, but its form here, which includes *Blasii* for *Blasti*, I have failed to find elsewhere. Quiriacus and Nicander are in several *auctaria* but nowhere else together.
2. MU 4.
3. Moling of Luachair was patron of St Mullins in the Carlow barony of the same name. His feast is also in Grevenus, albeit corruptly (*In Hybernia, Enolich confessoris*).

Sources: **1**. *AASS*, Nov. II/2, 322; Overgaauw, *Martyrologes*, 784; *AASS*, Iun. VI, 343–4. **2**. Dubois, *Martyrologe*, 248. **3**. Stokes, *Martyrology*, 141; *AASS*, Iun. VI, 344; *DIS*, 487–90.

[18 June] A Decimo Quarto Calendas Julii Die 18

1. Romae, natalis sanctorum Marci et Martelliani fratrum martyrum.
2. Eodem die, sancti Leontii martyris.
3. In Hybernia, sancti Baitheni et Furudrani abbatum et confessorum.

3   *Battheni* MS; *Báithín ... Furudrán ... maicc Móináin ... ó Laind ... Léri*, 'Baoithín, Furodhrán son of Maonán from Dunleer', MO.

1. MU 1, with omission here of the precise location (*via Ardiatina*).
2. Molanus, the only other *auctarium* to commemorate the saint, locates Leontius *in portu Tripolis*. He was one of the most renowned saints of North Africa.
3. Baodán and Furodhrán were attached to the church of Dunleer in the Louth barony of Ferrard.

Sources: **1**. Dubois, *Martyrologe*, 249. **2**. *AASS*, Iun. VI, 346; *BiblSS*, vii, 1325–7. **3**. Stokes, *Martyrology*, 141; Best and Lawlor, *Martyrology*, 51; *DIS*, 87, 356–7.

[19 June] Decimo Tertio Calendas Julii Die 19 B

1. Mediolani, natalis sanctorum Geruasii et Protasii fratrum et martyrum.
2. Romae, sancti Syluerii papae.

1. MU 1.
2. Almost all *auctaria* of MU, including Molanus, place Silverius, whose reign lasted one year only, on the following day.

Sources: **1**. Dubois, *Martyrologe*, 250. **2**. *AASS*, Iun. VI, 349–50; Overgaauw, *Martyrologes*, 786; *BiblSS*, vii, 1069–71.

[20 June] C Duodecimo Calendas Julii Die 20

1. Romae, depositio sancti Nouati, fratris Timothei presbiteri.
2. **In Hybernia**, sancti Faelani abbatis et confessoris.

² *Foelani* T; *Fáelán ... in t- amlabar*, 'Faolán the mute', MO.

1. MU 1.
2. Despite MReg's *in Hibernia*, Faolán was located in Strathearn, the name of a province in Scotland, between Tay and Forth.

Sources: **1**. Dubois, *Martyrologe*, 250. **2**. Stokes, *Martyrology*, 141; Best and Lawlor, *Martyrology*, 51; *DIS*, 304–5.

[21 June] Undecimo Calendas Julii Die 21 D

1. Romae, sanctae Demetriae uirginis.
2. In Hybernia, sancti Cormaci abbatis et martyris.
3. Eodem die, sancti Albani martyris.

² *Cormaci* T; *Cormacc* ... *haue Liathain*, 'Cormac of the Uí Liatháin', MO.

1. MU 3.
2. Cormac was attached to Durrow in the Offaly barony of Ballycowan. Adhamhnán mentions the saint several times in his Life of Columba.
3. The feast of Albanus of Mainz is noticed by almost all *auctaria* of MU, including Molanus.

Sources: **1.** Dubois, *Martyrologe*, 251. **2.** Stokes, *Martyrology*, 141; Best and Lawlor, *Martyrology*, 51; Anderson and Anderson, *Adomnan's Life of Columba*; *DIS*, 226–7. **3.** *AASS*, Iun. VI, 352; Overgaauw, *Martyrologes*, 790; *BiblSS*, i, 659–60.

[22 June] E Decimo Calendas Julii Die 22

1. In Britannia, sancti Albini martyris, quo in tempore [Diocletiani] persecutio crudelis ociani littus transgressa, etiam Aaron et Juliani Britanniae cum aliis pluribus viris ac faeminis.
2. In Hybernia, sancti Cronani abbatis et confessoris.
3. Eodem die sancti Achatii et sociorum martyrum.

² *Cronán* ... *Fernae*, 'Crónán of Ferns', MO.

1. MU 1. The wording here, which is quite different to that otherwise found in Usuard and his *auctaria*, is also in Molanus. Aaron and Julian were normally commemorated on 1 July. Moreover, a reference to Diocletian, whose persecution made martyrs of all three, seems to have been inadvertently omitted here after *in tempore*.
2. Crónán, alias Mochua Luachra, was abbot of Ferns in Co. Wexford. According to the *vita* of Maodhóg, patron of Ferns, Mochua became his disciple before being elevated to the status of bishop.
3. The feast of Achatius of Armenia was introduced by Baronius to the Roman Martyrology.

Sources: **1**. Dubois, *Martyrologe*, 252. **2**. Stokes, *Martyrology*, 141, 158; Best and Lawlor, *Martyrology*, 51; Plummer, *Vitae* ii, 154; *DIS*, 470. **3**. *BiblSS*, i, 134–8.

[23 June] Nono Calendas Julii Die 23 F

1. Vigilia sancti Joannis Baptistae.
2. **In Britannia**, natalis sanctae Ediltrudis uirginis et reginae.
3. In **Hybernia**, sancti Mochua abbatis et confessoris.

³   *mo Choe ... ó Óendruimm*, 'Mochaoi from Nendrum', MO.

1. MU 1.
2. MU 4, with the addition here, as in many *auctaria*, including Molanus, of *et reginae*.
3. Mochaoi was patron of Nendrum in the parish of Tullynakill, in the Down barony of Lower Castlereagh. Also known as Caolán, Mochaoi is reputed to have died in 497.

Sources: **1, 2**. Dubois, *Martyrologe*, 253; *AASS*, Iun. VI, 352. **3**. Stokes, *Martyrology*, 142; Best and Lawlor, *Martyrology*, 51; Mac Airt and Mac Niocaill, *Annals of Ulster*, 58; *DIS*, 152–3.

[24 June] G Octaua Calendas Julii 24

1. Natiuitas **sancti Joannis Baptistae** et Praecursoris Domini.
2. In Epheso, dormitio beati Joannis apostoli et euangelistae.
3. In ciuitate Augustoduno, depositio sancti Simplicii episcopi et confessoris.

1. MU 1.
2. Of the *auctaria* listed by Sollerius, only Pulsanensis and Bruxellensis contain this feast.
3. MU 3, with the addition here of *in ciuitate*, as in Pulsanensis.

Sources: **1, 3**. Dubois, *Martyrologe*, 253. **2**. *AASS*, Iun. VI, 358.

[25 June] Septimo Calendas Julii 25 A

1. In Alexandria, sancti Gallicani martyris.
2. In Hybernia, sanctorum abbatum Sinchilli, Tellii et Moliui.

2   *Féil Sinchill ... Telli ... la m'Luóc ... Liss móir de Albae*, 'Feast of Sincheall, Teille, Moluóg of Lismore in Scotland', MO.

1. MU 2. Before *Alexandria*, the manuscript has *H.*, probably in anticipation of the next entry.
2. Moluóg was patron of the church of Lismore, on an island in Argyllshire off the west coast of Scotland. His office Life is in the Breviary of Aberdeen and his feast was noticed by the Cologne martyrologies (Grevenus and Lübeck/Cologne) which read: *Moloci episcopi et confessoris*. Teille, alias Oilioll, gave name to the church of Tihelly (Teach Teille) in the parish of Durrow, in the Offaly barony of Ballycowan. Sincheall was patron of Killeigh in Co. Offaly.

Sources: **1.** Dubois, *Martyrologe*, 254. **2.** Stokes, *Martyrology*, 142; Best and Lawlor, *Martyrology*, 52; *LegSS*, 149–59, 395 *DIS*, 494, 562–3, 571.

[26 June] B Sexto Calendas Julii Die 26

1. Romae, natalis sanctorum Joannis et Pauli martyrum et fratrum.
2. Legionensi ciuitate, sancti Pelagii martyris.
3. Eodem die, sanctae Perseuerandae uirginis.

1. MU 1.
2. The Cologne *auctaria* (Grevenus and Lübeck/Cologne) and Molanus likewise commemorate Pelagius on this day. Molanus also refers to *Legionensi civitate*, now León in north-western Spain, where Pelagius's relics were transferred in the tenth century.
3. MU 4.

Sources: **1, 3.** Dubois, *Martyrologe*, 254–5. **2.** *AASS*, Iun. VI, 363; *BiblSS*, x, 441–2.

[27 June] Quinto Calendas Julii 27 C

1. In Gallatia, sancti Cressentis, discipuli sancti Pauli apostoli.
2. Hoya insula, natalis uel potius translatio sancti Florentii confessoris.

1. MU 1.
2. Most *auctaria*, including Molanus, notice the feast of the translation of Florentius's relics. Jean Evenou describes as 'inexplicable' the reference to *Oia* (l'Île d'Yeu); the saint founded the abbey of Saint-Florent-le-Vieil in the diocese of Angers.

Sources: **1**. Dubois, *Martyrologe*, 253. **2**. *AASS*, Iun. VI, 365–6; Overgaauw, *Martyrologes*, 801; J. Evenou in *BiblSS*, v, 854–5.

[28 June] D Quarto Calendas Julii 28

1. Vigilia apostolorum **Petri et Pauli**.
2. Et natalis beati Leonis papae.
3. In Hybernia, sancti Crumeni abbatis et confessoris.

³   *I l-Lecain ... Midi Crummíne*, 'Cruimín in Lacken of Midhe', MO.

1, 2. MU 1, 2.
3. Cruimín was patron of Lacken in the Westmeath barony of Corkaree.

Sources: **1, 2**. Dubois, *Martyrologe*, 256. **2**. Stokes, *Martyrology*, 143; Best and Lawlor, *Martyrology*, 52; *DIS*, 237.

[29 June] Tertio Calendas Julii 29 E

1. **Romae, natalis beatorum apostolorum Petri et Pauli**.
2. Eodem die, sancti Marcelli martyris.
3. In territorio Senonico, Beatae Benedictae uirginis.

1, 2, 3. MU 1, 2, 3. In 3, Usuard appears to have written *Beatae* only but so often was *Benedictae* either added to it or substituted for it that, as Sollerius pointed out, the correct name is in doubt.

Sources: **1, 2, 3**. Dubois, *Martyrologe*, 257; *AASS*, Iun. VI, 369.

[30 June] F Pridie Calendas Julii 30

1. Commemoratio sancti Pauli apostoli.
2. Eodem die, sancti Theobaldi confessoris.
3. Et sanctae Erentrudis uirginis.

³ *Frintrudis* MS.

1. MU 1.

2. Despite the fact that he died on 30 June, Molanus and most other *auctaria* commemorate Theobaldus of Vicenza, who was canonized in 1073, on the following day.

3. Grevenus is the only *auctarium* of MU, in Sollerius's edition, to have Erentrudis, first abbess of Nonnberg, near Salzburg, on this day.

Sources: **1.** Dubois, *Martyrologe*, 258. **2.** *AASS*, Iun. VII, 374–5; Overgaauw, *Martyrologes*, 809; *BiblSS*, xii, 196–7. **3.** *AASS*, Iun. VI, 372; *BiblSS*, iv, 1313.

[1 July] Calendis Julii Die 1 G

1. Octaua sancti Joannis Baptistae.
2. Mechliniae, passio sancti Rumoldi gloriosi martiris, Scotorum regis filii.
3. In Britannia, sancti Leonorii episcopi et confessoris.

1. This feast is noticed in several *auctaria* of MU, including Molanus, which places it first.

2. A small number of *auctaria*, including the Cologne martyrologies (Grevenus and Lübeck/Cologne) and Molanus, whose text is very close to MReg, commemorate Rumoldus of Mechelen/Malines on this day. In Molanus, the entry follows immediately after 1 above.

3. Leonorius (Lunaire), who was said to be Welsh, is said to have founded a church near Saint-Malo in Brittany. His feast, which falls here on the day usually observed in Coutances, is in a small number of *auctaria*, including, in the same words, Molanus.

Sources: **1.** *AASS*, Iun. VII, 374–5; Overgaauw, *Martyrologes*, 809. **2.** *AASS*, Iun. VII, 374–5; Overgaauw, *Martyrologes*, 810; *BiblSS*, xi, 497–501. **3.** *AASS*, Iun. VII, 374–5; *BiblSS*, vii, 1311–13.

[2 July] A Sexto Nonas Julii Die 2

1. Uisitatio gloriosae **Uirginis Mariae**.
2. In Britannia, ciuitate Vintonia, sancti Suuithuni episcopi et confessoris.

1. The feast of the visitation of the virgin, which was proclaimed by Pope Boniface IX in 1389, is in several *auctaria* of MU, including, in the same words, Molanus which also places it first.
2. Most *auctaria*, including, in the same words, Molanus, notice the feast of this bishop of Winchester. This day's feast was later superseded in popularity by that of the translation of the saint's relics in 971, which fell on 15 July.

Sources: **1**. *AASS*, Iun. VII, 377; Overgaauw, *Martyrologes*, 811. **2**. *AASS*, Iun. VII, 377; *BiblSS*, xii, 91–2.

[3 July] Quinto Nonas Julii Die 3 B

1. Apud Edessam Mesopotamiae, translatio corporis sancti Thomae apostoli.
2. Eodem die, sancti martyris Hiacinthi.
3. Et sancti Anatholii episcopi Constantinopolis.

1. MU 1.
2. Molanus is the only *auctarium* of MU to commemorate Hiacinthus of Cappadocia here.
3. Molanus is again the only *auctarium* to notice Anatholius, patriarch of Constaninople, on this day. Usuard and his derivatives assign the feast to the homonymous saint of Laodicea in Syria.

Sources: **1**. Dubois, *Martyrologe*, 261. **2**. *AASS*, Iun. VII, 379; *BiblSS*, vi, 325–6. **3**. Dubois, *Martyrologe*, 261; *AASS*, Iun. VII, 379; *BiblSS*, i, 1083–4.

[4 July] C Quarto Nonas Julii Die 4

1. Oseae et Aggaei prophetarum.
2. In Hybernia, sancti Finbarri abbatis.

3. Eodem die, sancti Procopii abbatis et confessoris.
4. Item, sancti Udalrici episcopi et confessoris.

² *Findbarr Inse Doimle*, 'Fionnbharr of Little Island', MO.

1. MU 1, with the addition here, as in all *auctaria*, of Aggeus, who, as Overgaauw argues, may have been in Usuard's original text.
2. Fionnbharr was attached to Little Island in the parish of Ballynakill, in the Waterford barony of Gaultiere.
3. The Cologne versions of MU (Grevenus and Lübeck/Cologne), but not Molanus, likewise commemorate Procopius, abbot of Sázava in Bohemia, on this day. Prior to 975, when the diocese of Prague was instituted, Bohemia formed part of the diocese of Regensburg.
4. Molanus and almost all other *auctaria* notice here the feast of Ulrich of Augsburg, the first saint known to have been solemnly canonized.

Sources: **1.** Dubois, *Martyrologe*, 262; Overgaauw, *Martyrologes*, 815. **2.** Stokes, *Martyrology*, 160; Best and Lawlor, *Martyrology*, 53; *DIS*, 335. **3.** *AASS*, Iun. VII, 381; *BiblSS*, x, 1167–73. **4.** *AASS*, Iun. VII, 381; *BiblSS*, xii, 796–7.

[5 July] Tertio Nonas Julii Die 5 D

1. Apud Syriam, sancti Domitiani martyris.
2. Treuiris, depositio sancti Numeriani archiepiscopi.
3. In Calabria, sanctae Dominicae uirginis et martyris.

² *Numerani* MS. **3.** *Cambria* MS.

1. MU 1, with *Domitiani* here for Usuard's *Domitii*.
2. This commemoration is otherwise only in the Cologne *auctaria* of MU (Grevenus and Lübeck/Cologne), which describe Numerianus as a bishop, and Molanus, which agrees with MReg's description.
3. Of the *auctaria*, only Molanus notices this feast, but on the following day. First mentioned in western martyrologies in the sixteenth century, Dominica's relics were kept at Tropea in Calabria.

Sources: **1.** Dubois, *Martyrologe*, 262. **2.** *AASS*, Iun. VII, 383; *BiblSS*, ix, 1078–9. **3.** *AASS*, Iun. VII, 385; *BiblSS*, iv, 680–1.

[6 July] E Pridie Nonas Julii Die 6

1. Octaua apostolorum Petri et Pauli.
2. Apud Judeam, Isaiae prophetae.
3. In Britannia, depositio sanctae Sexburgae uiduae.
4. Eodem die, sancti Palladii martyris.
5. In Hybernia, sanctae Moninnae uirginis.

5   *In Hibernia, sanctae Moninnae virginis* COW; *Moninnae* T; *Moninne in tslébe Cuilinn*, 'Moninne of Slieve Gullion', MO.

1. MU 2, with the addition here of *Petri et Pauli*.
2. MU 1, with *Is-* for *Es-*, as in some *auctaria* of MU, not including Molanus.
3. Several *auctaria*, including Molanus which has much the same text as MReg, notice the feast of Sexburg, abbess of Ely.
4. Although nowhere recorded in Irish martyrologies, this is the feast of Palladius, precursor of Patrick. The feast figures regularly in Scottish calendars, and an office Life is preserved in the Breviary of Aberdeen. Grevenus is the only *auctarium* to mention it, with the words: *Paladii episcopi et confessoris*.
5. Moninne, alias Darearca, was patron of Killevy, at Slieve Gullion in the Armagh barony of Upper Orior. Grevenus (*In Hibernia, Moninnae virginis*) also notes her feast.

Sources: **1, 2.** Dubois, *Martyrologe*, 262. **3.** *AASS*, Iun. VII, 385; Overgaauw, *Martyrologes*, 818; *BiblSS*, xi, 1007–8. **4.** *AASS*, Iun. VII, 385; *BiblSS*, x, 60–4 (with extensive bibliography); Forbes, *Kalendars*, 427–30; *LegSS*, 168–71, 406; *DIS*, 524–5. **5.** Stokes, *Martyrology*, 161; Best and Lawlor, *Martyrology*, 54; *AASS*, Iun. VII, 385; *DIS*, 495–7.

[7 July] Nonis Julii Die 7 F

1. Apud Cantuariam in Anglia, translatio sancti Thomae episcopi et martyris.
2. In Hybernia, sancti Melruani abbatis et confessoris.

2   *Moelruani* T; *Máel-rúain* MO.

1. Several *auctaria* of MU commemorate the translation of Thomas's relics, which took place in 1220. The text of MReg agreęs with Molanus, subject to the addition here of *in Anglia*.

2. Maol Ruain was founder-patron of the church of Tallaght, near Dublin.

Sources: **1**. *AASS*, Iun. VII, 387. **2**. Stokes, *Martyrology*, 161; Best and Lawlor, *Martyrology*, 54; *DIS*, 445–6.

[8 July] G Octauo Idus Julii Die 8

1. Treuiris, sancti Auspicii episcopi.
2. In Britannia, sancti Grimbaldi abbatis.
3. In ciuitate Herbipoli, sancti Kiliani Scoti et martyris, primi eiusdem ciuitatis episcopi.
4. In Hybernia, sanctorum confessorum Brocani et Diarmetii.

⁴ *Diarmei* MS; *Brocani, Diarmetii* T; *Broccán scríbnid ... Díarmait ...Glinne hUissen*, 'Brocán the scribe, Diarmuid of Killeshin', MO.

1. Only the Cologne *auctaria* of MU (Grevenus and Lübeck/Cologne) and Molanus otherwise notice Auspicius's feast. He was also bishop of Toul, where he died between 487 and 490.

2. Several *auctaria*, including Molanus, notice the feast of Grimbald (†901), formerly of Saint-Bertin, later dean of New Minster in Winchester. MReg's wording differs from all others.

3. MU 4. Usuard's entry was very bare, whereas most *auctaria* provide more detail concerning Kilian, patron of Würzburg, and his associates. However, none agrees with MReg's wording.

4. Brocán was attached to the church of Mothel in the Waterford barony of Upperthird, whereas Diarmuid was patron of the church of Killeshin in the Laois barony of Slievemargy.

Sources: **1**. *AASS*, Iun. VII, 389; *BiblSS*, i, 626–7. **2**. *AASS*, Iun. VII, 389; *BiblSS*, vii, 406–7. **3**. *AASS*, Iun. VII, 389; *BiblSS*, iii, 1235–7. **4**. Stokes, *Martyrology*, 161; Best and Lawlor, *Martyrology*, 54; *DIS*, 128, 264.

[9 July] Septimo Idus Julii Die 9 A

1. Sancti Cirilli episcopi.
2. In Hybernia, sancti Garbani abbatis et confessoris.
3. Eodem die, sancti Blathmethi episcopi et confessoris.

2 *Barbani* MS; *Garbani* T; *Garbán ... Cinn sháli*, 'Garbhán of Kinsaley', MO. **3**. *Blatmetii* T.

1. MU 2, with *sancti* here, as in Molanus, in place of Usuard's *beati*.
2. Garbhán was attached to the church of Kinsaley in the Dublin barony of Coolock. Grevenus's *In Hibernia, Germani confessoris* probably refers to Garbhán.
3. Blathmac, more correctly Onchú son of Blathmac, was attached to the church of Killonaghan in the Clare barony of Burren.

Sources: **1**. Dubois, *Martyrologe*, 264. **2**. Stokes, *Martyrology*, 161; Best and Lawlor, *Martyrology*, 54; *DIS*, 362–3. **3**. Stokes, *Martyrology*, 168; *DIS*, 108.

[10 July] B Sexto Idus Julii Die 10

1. Romae, septem fratrum, filiorum sanctae Faelicitatis.
2. Item, sanctarum uirginum Ruffinae et Secundae.
3. In Hybernia, sancti Cuannani confessoris.

3 *Cúán* MO.

1. MU 1.
2. MU 3, with the omission here of the location (*Roma*).
3. Cúán was attached to a place named Airbhre, now probably the church of Kilcowan (Irish Ceall Chúáin, 'church of Cúán') in the Wexford barony of Bargy.

Sources: **1, 2**. Dubois, *Martyrologe*, 265. **2**. Stokes, *Martyrology*, 161; Best and Lawlor, *Martyrology*, 55; *DIS*, 239.

[11 July] Quinto Idus Julii Die 11 C

1. **Solemnitas sancti Benedicti Abbatis**, siue translatio de Italia in Floriacum Galliarum monasterium, et sanctae Scolasticae sororis eius in partes Cenomanensium.
2. Romae, beati Pii papae et martyris.
3. Ex Britannia, sancti Hidulphi episcopi et confessoris, qui Treuiris uitam finiuit.

1. MU 1, but MReg's more substantial red-letter entry follows most closely the text of the entry in Molanus which, like most other *auctaria*, is likewise rich in detail.
2. The feast of Pope Pius I is in almost every *auctarium*, including Molanus, which uses the same words.
3. A few *auctaria*, but not Molanus, notice the feast of Hidulphus, but *ex Britannia* appears to stem from the pen of the compiler of MReg. A Benedictine saint, and supposedly a brother of Erhard of Regensburg, Hidulphus was regarded as the founder of Moyenmoutier in the Vosges mountains, where, despite MReg, he is said to have ended his life.

Sources: **1**. Dubois, *Martyrologe*, 265; *AASS*, Iun. VII, 394–5; Overgaauw, *Martyrologes*, 826. **2**. *AASS*, Iun. VII, 394–5; Kelly, *Dictionary*, 10. **3**. *AASS*, Iun. VII, 389; *BiblSS*, vii, 645–6.

[12 July] D Quarto Idus Julii Die 12

1. Mediolani, sanctorum martyrum Naboris et Faelicis.
2. In Pompeia ciuitate, passio sancti Vincentii martyris.
3. Apud Antiochiam, sanctae Margaretae uirginis et martyris.

1. This commemoration is in several *auctaria* of MU, including Molanus, which has the same wording as MReg. The wording ultimately comes from Florus, which adds, however, as does Ado, the word *translatio*.
2. Of the *auctaria*, only Grevenus and Molanus, which agrees with the wording of MReg, notice this feast.
3. Several *auctaria* notice this feast, albeit on the following day, as does MA (II).

Sources: **1**. *AASS*, Iun. VII, 397; Overgaauw, *Martyrologes*, 828. **2**. *AASS*, Iun. VII, 397–8. **3**. *AASS*, Iun. VII, 399–400; Overgaauw, *Martyrologes*, 830.

[13 July] Tertio Idus Julii Die 13 E

1. Joel et Esdrae prophetarum.
2. Romae, sancti Anacleti papae et martyris.
3. **In Hybernia**, sancti Mosilochi confessoris.
4. In Britannia minori, sancti Turiani episcopi et confessoris.

³ *lam' Shílóc*, 'with Moshiológ', MO.

1. MU 1, with *Esdrae* here, as in most *auctaria* of MU, including Molanus.
2. Some *auctaria*, including Molanus which, as here, places it second, likewise list Pope Anacletus's feast on this day. A very early pope of whom little is known, he had a second feast on 26 April.
3. Moshíológ, patron of Clonatin, parish of Kilmakilloge, in the Wexford barony of Gorey, is again remembered at 26 July.
4. MU 4, with *Turiani* here, as in Molanus and most other *auctaria*, for Usuard's *Turiavi*.

Sources: **1**. Dubois, *Martyrologe*, 267, *AASS*, Iun. VII, 398. **2**. *AASS*, Iun. VII, 399; Overgaauw, *Martyrologes*, 830; Kelly, *Dictionary*, 7. **3**. Stokes, *Martyrology*, 162; Best and Lawlor, *Martyrology*, 55. **4**. Dubois, *Martyrologe*, 267; *AASS*, Iun. VII, 398; *DIS*, 500.

[14 July] F Pridie Idus Julii Die 14

1. Lugduni, depositio sancti Bonauenturae, cardinalis et episcopi Albanensis.
2. Apud Treuerim, depositio sancti Justi confessoris.

¹ *Lugdunae* MS. **2**. *Justis* (with crossed out final *s*) MS.

1. A few *auctaria* of MU, including Molanus, which uses the same words as MReg, notice this feast. Molanus also places the feast first. Bonaventure (†1274) of Bagnoregio was cardinal-bishop of Albano.

2. Iustus of Trier is otherwise found only in Molanus which has the same wording as MReg. MH also commemorates Iustus on this day, but places him in Lyon, where MReg also places him, albeit on 2 September.

Sources: **1**. *AASS*, Iun. VII, 401–2. **2**. *AASS*, Iun. VII, 402; *AASS*, Nov. II/2, 374–5.

[15 July] Idibus Julii Die 15 G

1. Nisibi, natalis sancti Jacobi episcopi.
2. Eodem die, diuisio apostolorum.
3. Cantuariae in Anglia, depositio sancti Deusdedit archiepiscopi et confessoris.

3   *Cantnariae* MS.

1. MU 1.
2. Molanus and almost all other *auctaria* of MU record the feast of the division of the apostles on this day.
3. Grevenus and Molanus, whose wording resembles that of MReg, likewise notice the feast of Deusdedit, the first Anglo-Saxon to be appointed archbishop.

Sources: **1**. Dubois, *Martyrologe*, 268. **2**. *AASS*, Iun. VII, 403–4; Overgaauw, *Martyrologes*, 834–5. **3**. *AASS*, Iun. VII, 404; Overgaauw, *Martyrologes*, 837; *EncASE*, 140.

[16 July] A Decimo 7 Calendas Augusti Die 16

1. Apud Antiochiam, natalis beati Eustachii episcopi et confessoris.
2. Treuiris, sancti Valentini episcopi et martyris.

1. MU 1.
2. Grevenus and Molanus, whose wording is the same as that of MReg, also have this feast. Despite his place in the Roman Martyrology, Valentinus appears never to have existed.

Sources: **1**. Dubois, *Martyrologe*, 268. **2**. *AASS*, Iun. VII, 406; *BiblSS*, xii, 900.

[17 July] Decimo Sexto Calendas Augusti Die 17 B

1. Natalis sancti Alexii confessoris.
2. Ticini, sancti Enodii episcopi et confessoris.
3. In Anglia, sancti Kenelmi pueri, regis Merciorum et martyris.

1. Molanus and most other *auctaria* of MU locate Alexius in Rome. The saint, of whom there is no trace in Roman tradition prior to the tenth century, became the subject of one of the most widely diffused hagiographical legends.

2. The feast of Ennodius is otherwise in Molanus, which also places him in Ticinum (now Pavia).

3. Several *auctaria*, including Molanus, whose text is very close to that of MReg, commemorate Kenelm; the king is said to have been murdered at the age of seven.

Sources: **1**. *AASS*, Iun. VII, 407–8; Overgaauw, *Martyrologes*, 839; *BiblSS*, i, 814–23. **2**. *AASS*, Iun. VII, 408; *BiblSS*, iv, 1216–20. **3**. *AASS*, Iun. VII, 407–8; *EncASE*, 269.

[18 July] C Decimo Quinto Calendas Augusti Die 18

1. Apud Tiburtinam urbem Italiae, sanctae Symphorosae cum septem filiis.
2. In Nortmannia, sancti Clari monachi et martyris.
3. Et octaua sancti Benedicti.

1. The Cologne martyrologies (Grevenus and Lübeck/Cologne) and Molanus, which places the entry first, likewise commemorate Symphorosa here; her more usual day, as in MU, was 27 June. Overgaauw attributes the switch of day to Franciscan influence.

2. Some *auctaria* of MU, including Molanus which agrees with MReg in specifying Nortmannia, likewise notice Clarus's feast on this day; the more usual day was 4 November. The saint was allegedly a native of Rochester in England, but was later active in Normandy.

3. A small number of *auctaria*, not including Molanus, commemorate the octave of Benedict's translation (11 July). The Regensburg *Schottenkloster* was a Benedictine house.

Sources: **1**. *AASS*, Iun. VII, 410–11; Dubois, *Martyrologe*, 255; Over-gaauw, *Martyrologes*, 843. **2**. *AASS*, Iun. VII, 410–11; *BiblSS*, iii, 1232–3. **3**. *AASS*, Iun. VII, 410.

[19 July] Decimo Quarto Calendas Augusti Die 19 D

1. In Hispaniis, ciuitate [Hispali], passio sanctarum Iustae et Ruffinae virginum et martyrum.
2. Treuiris, passio beati Martini, eiusdem urbis episcopi.

1. MU 3, with *Hispaniis* for *Hispania*, as in Grevenus and Molanus, and inadvertent omission of the name of the *civitas*.
2. The Cologne martyrologies (Grevenus and Lübeck/Cologne) and Molanus likewise commemorate Martinus, who is considered to be one of the twenty-three 'eingeschobene' bishops of Trier.

Sources: **1**. Dubois, *Martyrologe*, 269. **2**. *AASS*, Iun. VII, 413; Mies-ges, *TrierFest*, 70–1.

[20 July] E Decimo Tertio Calendas Augusti Die 20

1. Natalis beati Josephi, qui cognominatus est Iustus.
2. Ciuitate Corduba, sancti Pauli diaconi et martyris.
3. In Hybernia, sancti Curphini abbatis et confessoris.

3   *Curufin* MO.

1, 2. MU 1, 3.
3. This saint was located in Uí Fhidhgheinte, now roughly the area covered by the diocese of Limerick.

Sources: **1, 2**. Dubois, *Martyrologe*, 270. **2**. Stokes, *Martyrology*, 163; Best and Lawlor, *Martyrology*, 56; Stokes, *Martyrology of Gorman*, 140.

[21 July] Duodecimo Calendas Augusti Die 21 F

1. Danielis prophetae.
2. Romae, sanctae Praxedis uirginis.
3. Trecas, sanctae Juliae uirginis.

1, 2, 3. MU 1, 2, 4.

Sources: **1, 2**. Dubois, *Martyrologe*, 270–1.

[22 July] G Undecimo Calendas Augusti Die 22

1. Sanctae Mariae Magdalenae.
2. Papiae, sancti Hieronimi episcopi.
3. **In Hybernia,** sancti Mobiu abbatis et confessoris.

3 *Mobiuani* T; *moBíu Inse Cúscraid*, 'Mobhí of Inch', MO.

1. MU 2.
2. A few *auctaria* of MU, including Molanus, which has the same wording as MReg, likewise notice Hieronymus, an eighth-century bishop of Pavia of whom little is known.
3. Mobhí, alias Bíthe, was attached to the church of Inch in the Down barony of Lecale Lower.

Sources: **1, 2**. Dubois, *Martyrologe*, 271. **2**. *AASS*, Iun. VII, 419; *BiblSS*, vi, 1142. **2**. Stokes, *Martyrology*, 164; Best and Lawlor, *Martyrology*, 57; *DIS*, 106.

[23 July] Decimo Calendas Augusti Die 23 A

1. Apud Rauennam, natalis beati Apollinaris episcopi.
2. Romae, sanctae Brigittae uiduae.
3. Apud Coloniam Agrippinam, translatio trium Regum.

1. MU 1, with the mention here of *Ravenna*, as in Grevenus and Molanus.
2. The feast of Birgitta (here *Brigitta*), patron of Sweden, who died in 1373, is noticed by several *auctaria* of MU, including Molanus.
3. The Cologne martyrologies (Grevenus and Lübeck/Cologne), Molanus and a few other *auctaria* likewise commemorate the translation of the relics of the three kings from Milan to Cologne by Archbishop Reinald von Dassel in 1164.

Sources: **1**. Dubois, *Martyrologe*, 272; *AASS*, Iun. VII, 420. **2**. *AASS*, Iun. VII, 421. **3**. *AASS*, Iun. VII, 421; Overgaauw, *Martyrologes*, 851; Zilliken, *Festkalender*, 84–5.

[24 July] B Nono Calendas Augusti Die 24

1. **Vigilia sancti Jacobi**, fratris Joannis Euangelistae.
2. In Italia, ciuitate Tyro, natalis sanctae Christinae uirginis.

1. Molanus, which places the entry first, and several other *auctaria* note the vigil of St James, who was patron of the Regensburg *Schottenkloster*, whence the red lettering.
2. MU 3.

Sources: **1**. *AASS*, Iun. VII, 423. **2**. Dubois, *Martyrologe*, 272.

[25 July] Octauo Calendas Augusti Die 25 C

1. Natalis **sancti Jacobi apostoli, qui ab Herode rege decollatus est**, huius sacratissima ossa ab Hierosolymis ad Hyspanias translata, celeberrima illarum gentium ueneratione excoluntur.
2. Eodem die, sancti Christophori martyris.

1. MU 1, with the omission here of some of the detail in Usuard, and red lettering because of James's special status as patron of the Regensburg *Schottenkloster*.
2. MU 2, with the omission here of much of Usuard's detail.

Sources: **1, 2**. Dubois, *Martyrologe*, 272–3.

[26 July] D Septimo Calendas Augusti Die 26

1. Natalis sanctae Annae, matris **Virginis Mariae**.
2. In ciuitate Tenremundae, beatae Christianae uirginis, filiae regis Angliae.
3. In **Hybernia**, sanctorum Mocholmok, Mosiloc et Nessani abbatum et confessorum.

---

3   *Mocolmoni, Nessani* T; *Mo Cholmóc, mo Shilóc ... Nessán*, MO.

1. Most *auctaria* of MU, including Molanus, which places the entry first and uses much the same words, commemorate Anna mother of Mary on this day.

2. Molanus is the only other *auctarium* to notice the feast of Christiana (al. Christina) of Dendermonde in Belgium, whose legend, which is of no historical value, attributes an English origin to the saint.

3. These saints are usually on the previous day. Mocholmóg was also known as Mocholmóg of Uí Fhiachrach, whence Tireragh barony in Co. Sligo. Moshíológ, previously remembered on 13 July, was a pupil of Moling, and Neasán was the deacon of that name venerated as patron of Mungret in Co.Limerick.

Sources: **1**. *AASS*, Iun. VII, 427. **2**. *AASS*, Iun. VII, 428; *BiblSS*, iv, 342–3. **3**. Stokes, *Martyrology*, 164; Best and Lawlor, *Martyrology*, 58; *DIS*, 500, 514–15.

[27 July] Sexto Calendas Augusti Die 27 E

1. Apud Nicomediam, passio beati Pantaleonis martyris.
2. Apud Ephesum, natalis septem Dormientium.
3. Eodem die, in Sicilia, beati Simonis monachi.

1. MU 1, on 28 July. Molanus also has the feast in first place on the present day.

2. Molanus and most other *auctaria* of MU commemorate here the feast of the Seven Sleepers of Ephesus, whom Usuard named individually.

3. MU 3.

Sources: **1**. Dubois, *Martyrologe*, 274; *AASS*, Iun. VII, 430. **2**. Dubois, *Martyrologe*, 274; *AASS*, Iun. VII, 429–30. **3**. Dubois, *Martyrologe*, 274.

[28 July] F Quinto Calendas Augusti Die 28

1. In Britannia minori, sancti Sampsonis episcopi et confessoris.
2. Mediolani, natalis beati Nazarii martyris.
3. Eodem die, Romae, sancti Victoris papae.

109

1. MU 2, with omission here of the precise monastery (*Dolum*). Like MReg, Molanus places the entry first.

2. Most of the *auctaria*, including Molanus, commemorate Nazarius of Milan on this day, whereas MU placed his feast at 12 June.

3. Again, Molanus and most other *auctaria* commemorate Pope Victor on this day.

Sources: **1.** Dubois, *Martyrologe*, 274. **2.** *AASS*, Iun. VII, 431–2; Dubois, *Martyrologe*, 245. **3.** *AASS*, Iun. VII, 431–2; Kelly, *Dictionary*, 12.

[29 July] Quarto Calendas Augusti Die 29 G

1. Romae, uia Aurelia, natalis sancti Faelicis papae et martyris.
2. Eodem die, beatae Marthae, sororis Lazari.
3. Aurelianis, depositio beati Prosperi episcopi.

1. MU 1, with *sancti* here, as in Molanus, for Usuard's *beati*.

2. Molanus and most other *auctaria* commemorate Martha here.

3. Some *auctaria*, including Molanus, which likewise specifies *Aurelianis*, notice Prosperus's feast. The saint is little known, but his feast is already in MH.

Sources: **1.** Dubois, *Martyrologe*, 275. **2.** *AASS*, Iun. VII, 434. **3.** *AASS*, Iun. VII, 434; *BiblSS*, x, 1206–7.

[30 July] A Tertio Calendas Augusti Die 30

1. Romae, natalis sanctorum Abdon et Sennen.
2. In Suecia, beatae Helenae uirginis.
3. Apud Africam, sanctarum uirginum Maximae, Donatillae, et Secundae.

¹ *Abbon* corrected to *Abdon* MS.

1. MU 1, with *Sennen* here for *Sennis* (*Sennes*) of the Usuardian tradition.

2. Otherwise only Grevenus and Molanus notice the feast of Helena (†1160) of Västergötland in Sweden.

3. MU 2, with omission of the precise location (*Lucernaria*).

Sources: **1**. Dubois, *Martyrologe*, 275; *AASS*, Iun. VII, 435. **2**. *AASS*, Iun. VII, 436; *BiblSS*, iv, 996–7. **3**. Dubois, *Martyrologe*, 275.

[31 July] Pridie Calendas Augusti Die 31 B

1. Apud Cesaream, passio beati Fabii martyris.
2. In Anglia, beati Neoti sacerdotis.
3. Romae, obiit beatus Ignatius Loiola, fundator Societatis Jesu.
4. In **Hybernia**, sancti Colmani episcopi et confessoris.

4 *Colmani* T; *epscop* ... *Colmán macc Daráne*, 'Bishop Colmán son of Daráine', MO.

1. MU 1.
2. A few *auctaria* of MU, including Molanus whose text agrees with MReg, likewise commemorate the Cornish St Neot.
3. Ignatius of Loyola (†1556), founder of the Jesuit order, is otherwise commemorated on this day only in Molanus, which uses the same words.
4. Colmán was patron of Longfordpass, parish of Kilcooly, in the Tipperary barony of Eliogarty.

Sources: **1**. Dubois, *Martyrologe*, 276. **2**. *AASS*, Iun. VII, 438; *EncASE*, 331. **3**. *AASS*, Iun. VII, 438. **4**. Stokes, *Martyrology*, 165; Best and Lawlor, *Martyrology*, 59; *DIS*, 195–6.

[1 August] C Calendis Augusti Die 1

1. Antiochiae, natalis sanctorum Machabeorum.
2. Romae, **ad sanctum Petrum, sancti Petri ad uincula**.
3. Item, octaua sancti Jacobi.

1. MU 1.
2. MU 2, with retention of Usuard's *ad sanctum Petrum*, followed by the addition, as in Molanus, of the red-lettered, simpler formulation *sancti Petri*. The use of red letters probably stems from the association

of the Regensburg *Schottenkloster* with Weih Sankt Peter. See also above at p. 1.

3. Despite the absence here of red lettering, the monks of the *Schottenkloster* would have had special devotion to their patron, St James, dedicatee of their church, whose octave is commemorated in no other version of MU.

Sources: **1, 2**. Dubois, *Martyrologe*, 276; Overgaauw, *Martyrologes*, 866.

[2 August] Quarto Nonas Augusti Die 2 D

1. Romae, in cemeterio Calixti, natalis beati Stephani papae.
2. Ciuitate Padua, sancti Maximi.
3. Carnoti, sancti Betharii eiusdem ciuitatis episcopi.

1. MU 1.

2. Molanus is among the few *auctaria* to notice the feast of Maximus, whose relics were discovered, following a dream, in the basilica of Padua on 2 August 1053.

3. Molanus, which has the same text as MReg, is the only other version of MU to notice Betharius. Despite the reference here to Chartres, where 14 August was the saint's more usual day, 2 August was Betharius's day in Blois.

Sources: **1**. Dubois, *Martyrologe*, 277. **2**. *AASS*, Iun. VII, 443–4; *BiblSS*, ix, 62–4. **3**. *AASS*, Iun. VII, 444; *BiblSS*, ii, 143–4.

[3 August] E Tertio Nonas Augusti Die 3

1. Hierosolimis, inuentio corporis beatissimi Stephani protomartyris.
2. Apud Nouaram, sancti Gaudentii episcopi.

2   *Nonariam* MS.

1. MU 1.

2. Most *auctaria*, including Molanus, commemorate Gaudentius of Novara on this day, despite the fact that the day of his death was 22 January.

Sources: **1**. Dubois, *Martyrologe*, 278. **2**. *AASS*, Iun. VII, 445–6; *BiblSS*, vi, 56–7.

[4 August] Pridie Nonas Augusti Die 4 F

1. Ciuitate Bononia, sancti Dominici confessoris, fundatoris ordinis fratrum praedicatorum.
2. Turonis, sancti Euphronii episcopi et confessoris.
3. In Hybernia, sancti Molua abbatis et confessoris.

3   *Moluani* T; *moLua Macc oche*, 'Molua of the Maca Oiche.', MO.

1. Most *auctaria* commemorate Dominic, founder of the Dominican order, on the following day. However, Molanus, which likewise places it first, has the feast on this day, in the same words as MReg.
2. Molanus is the only *auctarium* to notice Euphronius on this day, with most other versions of MU commemorating the sixth-century bishop of Tours on the previous day.
3. Molua was patron of Clonfertmulloe, alias Kyle, in the Laois barony of Clandonagh.

Sources: **1**. *AASS*, Iun. VII, 438; Overgaauw, *Martyrologes*, 872. **2**. *AASS*, Iun. VII, 438; Overgaauw, *Martyrologes*, 869; *BiblSS*, v, 173. **3**. *AASS*, Iun. VII, 438. **4**. Stokes, *Martyrology*, 174; Best and Lawlor, *Martyrology*, 60; *DIS*, 490–92.

[5 August] G Nonis Augusti Die 5

1. Romae, **sancte Mariae matris Dei ad Niues**.
2. Eodem die, sancti Osualdi regis Anglorum.
3. Augustoduni, beati Cassiani episcopi et confessoris.

1. Molanus, which places it first, and most other *auctaria* have this feast of Mary which, having been introduced in the thirteenth century by Pope Honorius III, was made popular by the Franciscans.
2, 3. MU 2, 3.

Sources: **1**. *AASS*, Iun. VII, 449–50; Overgaauw, *Martyrologes*, 873–4. **2, 3**. Dubois, *Martyrologe*, 278.

[6 August] Octauo Idus Augusti Die 6 A

1. In monte Tabor, transfiguratio Domini nostri Jesu Christi.
2. Romae, uia Appia, natalis beati Syxti papae et martyris.
3. In Hybernia, sancti Mochua abbatis.

³ *Mochua ... ó Chluain Dolcain,* 'Mochua of Clondalkin', MO.

1. Molanus, which likewise places it first, and almost all other *auctaria* notice this feast; it was officially promulgated by Pope Calixtus III in 1457.
2. MU 1, with *papae* here, as in Molanus, for *episcopi*.
3. Mochua was patron of Clondalkin in the Dublin barony of Uppercross.

Sources: **1.** *AASS*, Iun. VII, 449–50; Overgaauw, *Martyrologes*, 876. **2.** Dubois, *Martyrologe*, 279. **3.** Stokes, *Martyrology*, 175; Best and Lawlor, *Martyrology*, 60; *DIS*, 233–4.

[7 August] B Septimo Idus Augusti Die 7

1. Apud Tusciam, natalis beati Donati episcopi et martyris.
2. In Galliis, ciuitate Rothomagensi, depositio beati Victricii, praefatae urbis episcopi et confessoris.

1. MU 1, with omission here of the precise location (*Aretium*).
2. Molanus, which has the same wording, likewise commemorates Victricius, bishop of Rouen.

Sources: **1.** Dubois, *Martyrologe*, 279. **2.** *AASS*, Iun. VII, 454; *BiblSS*, xii, 1313.

[8 August] Sexto Idus Augusti Die 8 C

1. Romae, natalis beati Ciriaci diaconi, et sanctorum martyrum Largi et Smaragdi.
2. In **Hybernia,** sancti Columbani episcopi.
3. Et sancti Beani abbatis.

2 *In Hibernia, sancti Columbani episcopi et confessoris* COW; *Beani* T; *Féil Beóáin maicc Nessáin ... Colmán ... ó Inis Bó Finde*, 'Beoán son of Neasán, Colmán from Inishboffin', MO.

1. MU 1, with omission here of the exact location (*via Ostiensis*).
2, 3. Beóán was patron of Feighcullen in the Kildare baronies of Offaly and Connell, whereas Colmán was attached to the church on Inishboffin island, off the coast of Mayo.

Sources: **1**. Dubois, *Martyrologe*, 280. **2, 3**. Stokes, *Martyrology*, 175; Best and Lawlor, *Martyrology*, 61; *DIS*, 104, 190.

[9 August] D Quinto Idus Augusti Die 9

1. Vigilia sancti Laurentii martyris.
2. Romae, sancti Romani militis.
3. In Hybernia, sancti Nathi abbatis et confessoris.

3 *i nAchud ... Nathí*, 'Nathí in Achonry', MO.

1, 2. MU 1, 3.
3. Nathí was patron of Achonry in the Sligo barony of Leyny.

Sources: **1**. Dubois, *Martyrologe*, 280. **2, 3**. Stokes, *Martyrology*, 175; Best and Lawlor, *Martyrology*, 61; *DIS*, 511.

[10 August] Quarto Idus Augusti Die 10 E

1. Romae, uia Tiburtina, natalis beati Laurentii archidiaconi.
2. Eodem die, Romae, centum sexaginta quinque militum.
3. Metis, depositio sancti Auctoris episcopi.

1, 2. MU 1, 2.
3. Several *auctaria*, including Molanus, likewise commemorate Auctor, the thirteenth bishop of Metz on this day.

Sources: **1, 2**. Dubois, *Martyrologe*, 281. **3**. *AASS*, Iun. VII, 459; Overgaauw, *Martyrologes*, 880; *BiblSS*, ii, 634–5.

[11 August] F Tertio Idus Augusti Die 11

1. Romae, natalis sancti Tiburtii martyris.
2. Item, Romae, sanctae Susannae virginis.
3. In Hybernia, sancti Aererani abbatis et confessoris.

³ *Elerani* T; *Airerán n-ecnai*, 'Oireannán of the wisdom', MO.

1, 2. MU 1, 2, with omission in 1 of the precise location (*inter duas lauros*).
3. Oirearán (alias Oireannán) 'of the wisdom' was abbot of Tallaght after Maol Ruain.

Sources: **1, 2.** Dubois, *Martyrologe*, 280. **3.** Stokes, *Martyrology*, 175; Best and Lawlor, *Martyrology*, 62; *DIS*, 521.

[12 August] Pridie Idus Augusti Die 12 G

1. In ciuitate Assisio, sanctae Clarae uirginis.
2. In Syria, sanctorum martyrum Macarii et Juliani.
3. **In Hybernia,** sanctorum Lasreani, Mochtei et Segeni abbatum et confessorum.

³ *Lasreni, Sageni* T; *Togairm Lassréin Inse Muredaig móir, mochtai ...féil Segéni*, 'The calling of Laisréan of great and glorified Inishmurray, the feast of Séighín', MO.

1. The feast of Clare (†1253), founder of the Poor Clares, who was canonized two years after her death, is in almost every *auctarium*, including Molanus, which places it first.
2. MU 5, with the addition here of *martyrum*.
3. Laisréan, alias Molaise, was patron of the church on Inishmurray island, off the Sligo coast. Séighín (†652) was abbot of Iona, whereas *Mochtei* is a ghost name, based on a misunderstanding of the word *mochtai*, 'glorified' in the corresponding quatrain of MO. For another example of this, see 18 March above. The martyrologist may have been conscious of the fact that the feast of Mochta of Louth fell precisely seven days later, on 19 August.

Sources: **1**. *AASS*, Iun. VII, 463–4; Overgaauw, *Martyrologes*, 883–4. **2**. Dubois, *Martyrologe*, 282. **3**. Stokes, *Martyrology*, 176; Best and Lawlor, *Martyrology*, 62; *DIS*, 465–7, 482–3.

[13 August] A Idibus Augusti Die 13

1. Romae, beati Hyppoliti martyris. Passa est etiam, eodem die, Concordia nutrix eius.
2. **In** Hybernia, sancti Momedoch abbatis et confessoris.

2   *moMáedóc* MO.

1. MU 1.
2. Momhaodhóg was patron of Fiddown in the Kilkenny barony of Iverk.

Sources: **1**. Dubois, *Martyrologe*, 283. **2**. Stokes, *Martyrology*, 176; Best and Lawlor, *Martyrology*, 63; *DIS*, 494–5.

[14 August] Decimo Nono Calendas Septembris Die 14 B

1. Vigilia assumptionis **Dei genetricis Mariae**.
2. Romae, natalis beati Eusebii praesbiteri et confessoris.
3. In Africa, sancti Demetri confessoris.
4. In **Hybernia**, sancti Fachneani abbatis et confessoris.

4   *Farniani* MS; *Factnani* T; *féil Fachtnai maicc Mongaig*, 'feast of Fachtna son of Mongach', MO.

1. MU 1, with red-lettered *Dei genetricis* here, as in Molanus, in place of MU's *sanctae*.
2. MU 2, with omission here of the precise location (*via Appia*).
3. The feast of Demetrius of Africa, originally taken from MH, is found in almost every *auctarium*, including Molanus.
4. Fachtna was patron of the church of Ross in the Cork barony of East Carbery. Grevenus (*In Hibernia, Fachna episcopi*) also notices the feast.

Sources: **1, 2**. Dubois, *Martyrologe*, 283. **3**. *AASS*, Iun. VII, 463–4; Overgaauw, *Martyrologes*, 885. **4**. Stokes, *Martyrology*, 176; Best and Lawlor, *Martyrology*, 63; *DIS*, 300–1.

[15 August] C Decimo Octauo Calendas Septembris Die 15

1. **Assumptio beatae genetricis Dei Mariae**.
2. **Romae**, natalis sancti Tharsitii acolyti et martyris.
3. **In Hybernia**, sancti Macharthini episcopi et confessoris.

³ *Fer dá chrích* MO.

1. MU 1, with *assumptio* here, as in the margin of Molanus, for MU's *dormitio*.
2. MU 2, with characteristic omission here of the precise location (*via Appia*).
3. Mac Caorthainn was patron of the church and diocese of Clogher. A note in MO equates Mac Caorthainn with Fear Dá Chríoch, 'man of two districts'.

Sources: **1, 2**. Dubois, *Martyrologe*, 284. **3**. Stokes, *Martyrology*, 176; Best and Lawlor, *Martyrology*, 63; *DIS*, 413–14.

[16 August] Decimo 7 Calendas Septembris Die 16 D

1. In Nicea Bithyniae, natalis beati Vrsacii confessoris.
2. In Galliis, depositio beati Rochi confessoris.

1. MU 1.
2. Molanus, which uses the same words as MReg, is among the few *auctaria* to notice the feast of Roch, patron of those suffering from plague. The saint's cult began to spread throughout Christendom in the second half of the fifteenth century.

Sources: **1**. Dubois, *Martyrologe*, 284. **2**. *AASS*, Iun. VII, 471–2; *BiblSS*, xi, 264–73.

[17 August] E Decimo Sexto Calendas Septembris Die 17

1. Apud Affricam, sanctorum martyrum Liberati abbatis, Bonifacii diaconi, Rogati et Septimi monachorum.
2. Eodem die, sancti Myronis martyris.

1. MU 1, with omission here of some of Usuard's names.
2. Molanus is the only other *auctarium* to commemorate the Byzantine saint Myron.

Sources: **1.** Dubois, *Martyrologe*, 285. **2.** *AASS*, Iun. VII, 474; *BiblSS*, ix, 502–3.

[18 August] Decimo Quinto Calendas Septembris Die 18 F

1. Apud Praenestinam ciuitatem, sancti Agapiti martyris.
2. Romae, beatorum presbiterorum Joannis et Crispi.
3. **In Hybernia**, sanctorum Daigei mac Karill et Mernok abbatum et confessorum.

3 *Macc Cresséni m'Ernóc ... Daig ... macc Cairill*, 'Mearnóg son of Creisín, Daigh son of Coireall', MO.

1. MU 1, with the omission here, as so very often, of the precise topographical detail (*miliario ab urbe tricesimo tertio*).
2. MU 2.
3. Mearnóg was attached to the church of Rathnew in the Wicklow barony of Newcastle. Daigh was patron of Inishkeen in the Monaghan barony of Farney. The use of *mac* 'son' here, the only example in the text, probably stems from its occurrence in MO.

Sources: **1, 2.** Dubois, *Martyrologe*, 285. **3.** Stokes, *Martyrology*, 177; Best and Lawlor, *Martyrology*, 64; *DIS*, 252–3, 292.

[19 August] G Decimo Quarto Calendas Septembris Die 19

1. Romae, natalis sancti Julii senatoris et martyris.
2. In territorio Bituricensi, sancti Mariani confessoris.
3. Norembergae, sancti Sebaldi confessoris.

4. **In Hybernia**, sanctoru*m* abbatum et confessorum Mochtani et Aenani.

⁴ *Mochtae ... Enán Dromma Ráthe*, 'Mochta, Éanán of Drumraney', MO.

1, 2. MU 3, 4.

3. The Cologne martyrologies (Grevenus and Lübeck/Cologne) and Molanus likewise commemorate Sebald, whose remains are said to have been temporarily translated to the Nuremberg *Schottenkloster*. The cult began to spread in the thirteenth century.

4. Mochta was patron of the church and diocesan see of Louth in the county and barony of the same name. Éanán's church was at Drumraney in the Westmeath barony of Kilkenny West. For a second feast of this saint, see below at 18 September.

Sources: **1, 2.** Dubois, *Martyrologe*, 286. **3.** *AASS*, Iun. VII, 477; A. Borst, *Die Sebaldslegenden*. **4.** Stokes, *Martyrology*, 177; Best and Lawlor, *Martyrology*, 64; *DIS*, 280–1, 465–7.

[20 August] Decimo Tertio Calendas Septembris Die 20 A

1. Samuelis prophetae.
2. In territorio Lingonensi, depositio beati Bernardi primi Clarauallis abbatis.
3. In Anglia, sancti Osuini martyris.

1. MU 1.

2. Molanus and almost every other *auctarium* notice Bernard's feast, which was introduced to the Cistercian liturgy in 1175.

3. Some *auctaria*, including, in the same words, Molanus, likewise commemorate Oswiu (†670), king of Northumbria. Placed on the previous day in both MT and Willibrord's calendar, the date of the feast here accords with Bede's testimony (*Historia* III.14), which Molanus cites as its source.

Sources: **1.** Dubois, *Martyrologe*, 286. **2.** *AASS*, Iun. VII, 478–9; Overgaauw, *Martyrologes*, 893. **3.** *AASS*, Iun. VII, 479–80; *EncASE*, 349; Ó Riain, *Anglo-Saxon Ireland*, 7–8.

[21 August] B Duodecimo Calendas Septembris Die 21

1. Romae, sanctae Cyriacae martyris, quae in Vesalia translata quiescit.
2. In ciuitate Salona, sancti Anastasii martyris.
3. In **Hybernia**, sancti Senachi confessoris.

---

1   *sancti Cyriaci ... qui ... translatus* MS.
3   *Senaci* T; *epscop Senach ... Clúana hIraird*, 'bishop Seanach of Clonard', MO.

1. Both Grevenus and Molanus commemorate a martyred Roman named Cyriaca, whose relics were translated to Wesel (*Vesalia, Uuesalia* (Molanus)) in the Rheinland. The wording here, although corrupt in the manuscript, is close to that of Molanus.
2. MU 3.
3. Seanach (†588) was a bishop at Clonard in the Meath barony of Moyfenrath Upper.

Sources: **1**. *AASS*, Iun. VII, 481; *BiblSS*, iii, 1290–1. **2**. Dubois, *Martyrologe*, 287. **3**. Stokes, *Martyrology*, 177; Best and Lawlor, *Martyrology*, 65; *DIS*, 555.

[22 August] Undecimo Calendas Septembris Die 22 C

1. Octaua **Assumptionis Beatae Virginis Mariae**.
2. Romae, natalis beati Timothei martyris.
3. Item, sancti Hyppoliti, qui dicitur Nonus, et sociorum.
4. Eodem die, Romae, sancti Antonini martyris.

1. Most *auctaria*, including, in first place, Molanus, notice the octave of the feast of the Assumption, which was proclaimed by Leo IV about the middle of the ninth century.
2. MU 1, with typical omission here of the precise location (*via Ostiensis*).
3. Although on the following day in MU, with quite different wording, the Roman Hippolytus is commemorated on this day by some *auctaria*, including Molanus, which likewise specifies the alias (*Non[n]us*) and companions of the saint.
4. MU 4.

Sources: **1**. *AASS*, Iun. VII, 483. **2**. Dubois, *Martyrologe*, 288. **3**. *AASS*, Iun. VII, 483–4; Dubois, *Martyrologe*, 288; Overgaauw, *Martyrologes*, 898. **4**. Dubois, *Martyrologe*, 288.

[23 August] D Decimo Calendas Septembris Die 23

1. Vigilia sancti Bartholomei apostoli.
2. Eodem die, natalis sanctorum Timothei et Appollinaris.
3. Aruernis, sancti Sidonii episcopi et confessoris.
4. **In Hybernia, sancti Eogani episcopi** et confessoris.

4 *Logani* MS; *Eugenii* T; *féil Eogain Aird Shratha*, 'feast of Eoghan of Ard-straw', MO.

1. The vigil of the apostle's feast is in several *auctaria*, including Molanus.
2. MU 6.
3. This feast is in some *auctaria*, among them Molanus, which likewise locates Sidonius of Clermont in *Aruernis*. The saint has been identified with Cedd of Lindisfarne, which may explain the *Schottenkloster* interest in him.
4. Eoghan was patron of Ardstraw, later a diocesan see, in the Tyrone barony of Strabane Lower.

Sources: **1**. *AASS*, Iun. VII, 485–6. **2**. Dubois, *Martyrologe*, 288. **3**. *AASS*, Iun. VII, 485–6; *BiblSS*, xi, 1023–4. **4**. Stokes, *Martyrology*, 178; Best and Lawlor, *Martyrology*, 65; *DIS*, 295–6.

[24 August] Nono Calendas Septembris Die 24 E

1. Natalis beati **Bartholomei apostoli**.
2. Eodem die, passio apud Carthaginem trecentorum martyrum, qui passi sunt tempore Valeriani et Gallieni.
3. **In Hybernia**, sancti Patricii abbatis et confessoris.

3 *sen-Phátraic*, 'Old Patrick', MO.

1, 2. MU 1, 2.

3. Two Patricks were remembered on this day, one at Armagh, the other in Ros Deala. As Paul Grosjean has shown, the cult was also attested outside Ireland.

Sources: **1, 2**. Dubois, *Martyrologe*, 289. **3**. Stokes, *Martyrology*, 178; Best and Lawlor, *Martyrology*, 65; Grosjean, *S. Patrice d'Irlande*.

[25 August] F Octauo Calendas Septembris Die 25

1. Romae, sancti Genesii martyris.
2. Parisiis, sancti Ludouici regis Franciae.
3. Eodem die, sancti Gregorii Traiectaensis episcopi.

1. MU 2.
2. Molanus and almost all other *auctaria* commemorate Louis, king of France, who died on crusade in 1270. He was canonized in 1297.
3. A small number of *auctaria*, including Molanus, likewise notice the feast of Gregory, a disciple of Boniface, who, although administrator of the diocese of Utrecht, was never elected bishop.

Sources **1**. Dubois, *Martyrologe*, 290. **2**. *AASS*, Iun. VII, 489–90. **3**. *AASS*, Iun. VII, 490–1; Overgaauw, *Martyrologes*, 904; *BiblSS*, vii, 222.

[26 August] Septimo Calendas Septembris Die 26 G

1. Romae, natalis sancti Zepherini papae et martyris.
2. In ciuitate Pergamis, sancti Alexandri martyris.
3. In Hybernia, translatio sancti Flannani episcopi et confessoris.

1. MU 1, with the addition here, as in Molanus, of *et martyris*.
2. MU 4, with *Pergamis* for *Bergamis*, as in Molanus.
3. This feast is not recorded in any Irish record. Flannán was a popular saint in the Regensburg *Schottenkloster*, where his Life may also have been written. His regular feast is at 15 December.

Sources: **1**. Dubois, *Martyrologe*, 290; *AASS*, Iun. VII, 493. **2**. Dubois, *Martyrologe*, 291. **3**. Ó Riain-Raedel, 'Cashel and Germany', 202, 211–12; *DIS*, 346–9.

[27 August] A Sexto Calendas Septembris 27

1. Apud Capuam, natalis sancti Rufi martyris.
2. Tomis ciuitate, sanctorum martyrum Marcellini tribuni et uxoris eius Manneae.

1, 2. MU 1, 2.

Sources: **1, 2**. Dubois, *Martyrologe*, 291.

[28 August] Quinto Calendas Septembris Die 28 B

1. In Africa, depositio sancti Augustini episcopi.
2. Romae, natalis beati Hermetis.
3. Apud Santonas, natalis sancti Bibiani episcopi et confessoris.

1. MU 3. Although placed third by Usuard, Augustine is placed first in many later versions of MU, including Molanus.
2. MU 1.
3. MU 5, with the common *Bibianus* for *Vivianus*, as also in Molanus.

Sources: **1, 2, 3**. Dubois, *Martyrologe*, 292; *AASS*, Iun. VII, 495; Overgaauw, *Martyrologes*, 908.

[29 August] C Quarto Calendas Septembris Die 29

1. Decollatio sancti Joannis Baptistae.
2. Romae, natalis sanctae Sabinae martyris.
3. Ipso die, sanctae Candidae virginis.
4. Apud Louanium, sancte Veronae virginis.

1,2, 3. MU 1, 2, 5, with the omission here in 1 and 2 of several words contained in MU.
4. Of the *auctaria*, only Molanus otherwise commemorates Verona on this day. Supposedly a sister of Verono of Lembeek, the saint is first heard of in the writings of Olbertus (Albert), abbot of Gembloux, whose floruit was in the first half of the eleventh century.

Sources: **1, 2, 3**. Dubois, *Martyrologe*, 293. **4**. *AASS*, Iun. VII, 500; *BiblSS*, xii, 1056–7.

[30 August] Tertio Calendas Septembris Die 30 D

1. Romae, beati Faelicis praesbiteri.
2. Item, Romae, sanctae Gaudentiae uirginis.
3. In territorio Meldensi, **sancti Fiacrii confessoris regis Scotorum filii**, magnae uirtutis uiri.

1. MU 1, with typical omission here of the precise location (*via Ostiensis*).
2. MU 2.
3. Several *auctaria*, including Molanus, commemorate Fiachra here. The reference to *rex Scotorum* is peculiar to MReg.

Sources: **1, 2**. Dubois, *Martyrologe*, 294. **3**. *AASS*, Iun. VII, 501–2. **3**. *DIS*, 316.

[31 August] E Pridie Calendas Septembris Die 31

1. Treueris, natalis sancti Paulini episcopi et confessoris.
2. In Anglia, sanctae Cuthburgae virginis et reginae.
3. Autisiodoro, sancti Optati episcopi et confessoris.

² *Cuthburgis* ? MS. **3**. *Antisiodoro* MS.

1. MU 1.
2. Molanus and several other *auctaria* notice the feast of Cuthburga, wife of Aldfrith, king of Northumbria. She founded Wimborne (Dorset), where Lioba, abbess of Bischofsheim in Baden and allegedly a 'Scota' (see below at 28 September), received her formation.
3. MU 3.

Sources: **1, 3**. Dubois, *Martyrologe*, 294. **3**. *AASS*, Iun. VII, 501–2; *EncASE*, 133.

[1 September] Calendis Septembris Die 1 F

1. Jesu Naue et Gedeon prophetarum.
2. Item, natalis beatissimae Annae prophetissae.
3. Eodem die, sancti Aegidii abbatis.
4. Item, Beneuenti, sanctorum martyrum duodecim fratrum.

1, 2, 3. MU 1, 2, 7.
4. Several *auctaria*, including, in the same words, Molanus, commemorate here the twelve brothers of Benevento whose origins lay in four groups of African martyrs commemorated on this day in MH.

Sources: **1, 2, 3**. Dubois, *Martyrologe*, 295. **4**. *AASS*, Iun. VII, 506–8; *BiblSS*, iv, 669–70.

[2 September] G Quarto Nonas Septembris Die 2

1. Lugduno Galliae, natalis sancti Justi episcopi et confessoris.
2. Eodem die, sancti Cosmae confessoris et eremitae.
3. Item, translatio sanctae Agnetis virginis.
4. **In Hybernia**, sancti Nessani abbatis et confessoris.

2   *eodie die* MS. **4**. *Nessani* MS; *Senán* MO.

1. MU 1. See also 14 July above.
2. This feast is in some *auctaria*, including Molanus. The relics of the hermit were translated in 1058 from Crete to Venice, which became the centre of his cult in the West.
3. Some *auctaria*, including Molanus, likewise commemorate the translation to Utrecht in 964 of the relics of Agnes. According to Overgaauw, the day is more properly that of the elevation of the relics which took place in the early fifteenth century.
4. Since no feast of Neasán is known on this day, the more usual Seanán of Laraghbryan was probably intended.

Sources: **1**. Dubois, *Martyrologe*, 295. **2**. *AASS*, Iun. VII, 510; *BiblSS*, iv, 219. **3**. *AASS*, Iun. VII, 510; Overgaauw, *Martyrologes*, 920. **4**. Stokes, *Martyrology*, 192; *DIS*, 514–15, 557–60.

[3 September] Tertio Nonas Septembris Die 3 A

1. Romae, beatae Serapiae virginis.
2. Apud Aquileiam, sanctarum Euphemiae, Dorotheae, Teclae et Erasmae, quae tempore Neronis capitae plexae sunt.

1. MU 2, with omission here of *passio*, as in the main text of Molanus.
2. This feast is otherwise only in Grevenus and Molanus, whose wording is very similar to that of MReg. The cult of Euphemia of Chalcedon put down firm roots in northern Italy, among other places in Aquileia, where the companions named here became attached to her.

Sources: **1**. Dubois, *Martyrologe*, 296. **2**. *AASS*, Iun. VII, 512; *BiblSS*, v, 154–60, at 158; ibid., 163–4.

[4 September] B Pridie Nonas Septembris Die 4

1. Romae, beati Victorini martyris.
2. **In Hybernia**, sancti Maicnisie episcopi et confessoris.
3. Ipso die, ordinatio sancti Gregorii papae.
4. Eodem die, sancti Marcelli martyris.
5. **In Hybernia**, sancti Ultani episcopi et confessoris.

2. *Macc nisse ... ó Chonderib*, 'Mac Nise from Connor', MO. **5**. *Ultan Aird Breccáin*, 'Ultán of Ardbraccan', MO.

1. MU 1 (5 September).
2. Mac Nise, whose feast in MO fell on the previous day, was patron of Connor, later a diocesan see in the Antrim barony of Lower Antrim.
3. As with the previous entry, this belongs to feasts of 3 September, where it is recorded by most *auctaria*, including Molanus.
4. The Cologne martyrologies (Grevenus and Lübeck/Cologne) and Molanus likewise commemorate Marcellus. His name may have been interpolated into the list of bishops of Trier from the Tongres bishoplist.
5. Ultán was patron of Ardbraccan in the Meath barony of Navan Lower. Grevenus (*Vulcani abbatis in Hybernia*) also lists the feast.

Sources: **1**. Dubois, *Martyrologe*, 297. **2**. Stokes, *Martyrology*, 192. **3**. *AASS*, Iun. VII, 511–12; *BiblSS*, vii, 222–78, at 237; *DIS*, 419. **4**. *AASS*, Iun. VII, 514; *BiblSS*, viii, 671–2. **4**. Stokes, *Martyrology*, 192; Best and Lawlor, *Martyrology*, 68; *DIS*, 580–1.

[5 September] Nonis Septembris Die 5 C

1. Romae, in portu, sancti Herculani martyris.
2. **In Hybernia**, sanctorum confessorum atque abbatum Brechani et Eolangi.
3. Eodem die, Zachariae prophetae.

² *Colanigi* MS; *La Brecc ... Eolang ... Achid Bó*, 'With Breac, Eolang of Aghaboe', MO.

1. MU 2, with the addition here of *martyris*.
2. Eolang was patron of Aghabulloge in the Cork barony of Muskerry East. Brechanus, alias Bricín, was attached to the church of Tomregan in the Cavan barony of Loughtee Lower.
3. MU 1 (6 September).

Sources: **1, 3**. Dubois, *Martyrologe*, 297. **2**. Stokes, *Martyrology*, 192, 202; Best and Lawlor, *Martyrology*, 68; *DIS*, 118, 297–8.

[6 September] D Octauo Idus Septembris Die 6

1. In Africa, beatorum episcoporum et confessorum Donatiani, Mansueti et Germani.
2. Eodem die, natalis sancti Magni abbatis et confessoris, Scoti et discipuli beati Galli confessoris.

1. MU 2, with transposition here of *episcoporum* and *confessorum*.
2. Magnus, patron of Füssen in the Bavarian Allgäu, is commemorated in most *auctaria*, including Molanus. However, none of these alludes to his supposed Irish origins.

Sources: **1**. Dubois, *Martyrologe*, 298. **2**. *AASS*, Iun. VII, 518; Overgaauw, *Martyrologes*, 928; *BiblSS*, viii, 542–5.

[7 September] Septimo idus Septembris die 7 E

1. Apud Nicomediam, natalis beati Joannis martyris.
2. **In Hybernia**, sancti Mecculini episcopi et confessoris.
3. Item, sancti Columbi abbatis et confessoris et sanctae Scethae uirginis.

2,3 *Meicculini* T; *Lusca la Macc cuilinn ... féil Scéthe ... Coluimb Roiss ... Glandai*, 'Mac Cuilinn of Lusk, feast of Sciath, Colum of Ros Glanda', MO.

1. MU 1.
2, 3. These three Irish saints more properly belong on the previous day. Mac Cuilinn was patron of Lusk in the Dublin barony of Balrothery East, whereas Colum was attached to Donaghmore in the Tyrone barony of Dungannon Middle. Sciath gave name to Ardskeagh in the Cork barony of Fermoy.

Sources: **1, 3**. Dubois, *Martyrologe*, 298. **2, 3**. Stokes, *Martyrology*, 193; Best and Lawlor, *Martyrology*, 68; *DIS*, 415, 550–1.

[8 September] F Sexto Idus Septembris Die 8

1. **Natiuitas gloriosae Uirginis Mariae**.
2. Apud Nicomediam, natalis sancti Adriani martyris cum aliis uiginti tribus.
3. Frisingae, depositio sancti Corbiniani episcopi et confessoris.

3 *Corbiani* MS.

1. MU 1, with some differences in the wording.
2. MU 2.
3. Corbinianus, patron of Freising in Bavaria, who was held to be of insular origin, is in most *auctaria*, including, with much the same wording, Molanus.

Sources: **1**. Dubois, *Martyrologe*, 299. **2**. *AASS*, Iun. VII, 522; Overgaauw, *Martyrologes*, 931; *BiblSS*, iv, 169–71.

[9 September] Quinto Idus Septembris Die 9 G

1. Apud Nicomediam, passio sanctorum martyrum Dorothei et Gorgonii.
2. **In Scotia, sancti Cuaerani abbatis**.
3. Eodem die, sancti Seueriani martyris.

[2] *In Hibernia, sancti Cherani abbatis* COW; *Querani, Kyarani* T; *Ciaráin* MO.

1. MU 1.
2. MU 4. Ciarán of Clonmacnoise was one of the Irish saints introduced to the Continental tradition by Usuard, who spelt the name *Quaerani*, whence the odd spelling here.
3. The feast of this saint, from Sebaste in Armenia Minor, is otherwise only in Molanus, which adds a note regarding his forty companions.

Sources: **1, 2**. Dubois, *Martyrologe*, 300; Stokes, *Martyrology*, 193; *DIS*, 169–71. **3**. *AASS*, Iun. VII, 524; *AASS*, Sep. III, 355–64.

[10 September] A Quarto Idus Septembris Die 10

1. Romae, beati Hilarii papae.
2. Tolentini, depositio beati Nicolai episcopi et confessoris.
3. **In Scotia**, sancti Finbarri episcopi et confessoris.
4. **In Britannia, sancti Otgeri** confessoris et diaconi.

[3] *In Hibernia, sancti Findbarri* (*Vindibarri* O) *episcopi et confessoris* COW; *Finbarrini* T; *Findbarr Maige Bili*, 'Fionnbharr of Movilla', MO.

1. MU 1.
2. A number of *auctaria*, including Molanus, commemorate Nicholas of Tolentino, an Augustinian monk who died in 1305.
3. Fionnbharr, better known as Finnian, was patron of Movilla in the Down parish of Newtownards, barony of Ards Lower.
4. A number of *auctaria*, including Molanus, likewise commemorate Otgerus (Odger). English in origin, the saint preached among the inhabitants of the eastern part of the Low Countries. He was buried in

Sint-Odilienberg, near Roermond, but some relics were transferred to Utrecht in 858.

Sources: **1**. Dubois, *Martyrologe*, 301. **2**. *AASS*, Iun. VII, 526; *BiblSS*, ix, 953–68. **3**. Stokes, *Martyrology*, 193; Best and Lawlor, *Martyrology*, 70; *DIS*, 321–4. **3**. *AASS*, Iun. VII, 526; Overgaauw, *Martyrologes*, 934; *BiblSS*, ix, 1108.

[11 September] B Tertio Idus Septembris Die 11

1. Romae, natalis sanctorum martyrum Prothi et Hiacinthi.
2. Lugduno, depositio sancti Patientis episcopi.
3. **In Scotia, sancti Sylleni** abbatis et confessoris.

2   *Lugduo* MS. **3**. *Sillán ... i nImbliuch*, 'Siollán in Emlagh', MO.

1. MU 1, with typical omission here of the precise location (*via Salaria*).
2. Several *auctaria*, including Molanus, which uses the same words, also note the feast of Patiens, a late fifth-century bishop of Lyon.
3. Siollán, alias Moshiona, was patron of Emlagh in the barony and county of Louth.

Sources: **1**. Dubois, *Martyrologe*, 301. **2**. *AASS*, Iun. VII, 526; Overgaauw, *Martyrologes*, 935; *BiblSS*, x, 426–7. **3**. Stokes, *Martyrology*, 193; Best and Lawlor, *Martyrology*, 70; *DIS*, 500.

[12 September] C Pridie Idus Septembris Die 12

1. Apud urbem Ticinum, sanctorum confessorum Syri et Euentii.
2. **In Hybernia**, sanctorum confessorum Ailbei et Lasreani.
3. **Treuiris, depositio sancti Maximini** episcopi et confessoris.

2   *Lafreani* MS; *Lasreani, Elbini* T; *Celebair féil nAilbi ... hi féil Laissréin ... ó Daminis*, 'Celebrate the feast of Ailbhe on the feast of Laisréan of Devinish', MO. **3**. *Maximi* MS.

1. MU 1, with *Euentii* here for *Yventii*.

2. Laisréan, alias Molaise, was patron of Devenish island on Lough Erne in County Fermanagh, whereas Ailbhe was attached to the church of Emly in the Tipperary barony of Clanwilliam.

3. Molanus and most other *auctaria* record here the feast of Maximinus of Trier, who was a native of Aquitaine. His more usual feast fell on 29 May, where MReg, following MU, again commemorates him.

Sources: **1**. Dubois, *Martyrologe*, 301. **2**. Stokes, *Martyrology*, 194; Best and Lawlor, *Martyrology*, 70; *DIS*, 58–60, 483–5. **3**. *AASS*, Iun. VII, 529–30; Overgaauw, *Martyrologes*, 937; *BiblSS*, ix, 33–4.

[13 September] Idibus Septembris Die 13 D

1. Apud Aegyptum, ciuitate Alexandria, beati Philippi episcopi.
2. Turonis, sancti Lidorii episcopi et confessoris.
3. **In Scotia**, sancti Dagani abbatis et confessoris.

³ *Dagaui* T; *Dagán Indbir Dóile*, 'Daghán of Ennereilly', MO.

1. MU 1.
2. Molanus and most other *auctaria* notice the feast of Lidorius, the second bishop of Tours.
3. Daghán was attached to the church of Ennereilly in the Wicklow barony of Arklow.

Sources: **1**. Dubois, *Martyrologe*, 302. **2**. *AASS*, Iun. VII, 531–2; Overgaauw, *Martyrologes*, 939; *BiblSS*, viii, 68. **3**. Stokes, *Martyrology*, 194; Best and Lawlor, *Martyrology*, 70; *DIS*, 251–2.

[14 September] E Decimo Octauo Calendas Octobris Die 14

1. Exaltatio sanctae Crucis.
2. Romae, beati Cornelii papae.
3. In Africa, sancti Cipriani.
4. Treuiris, sancti Materni episcopi.

⁴ *Martini* MS.

1, 2, 3. MU 1, 2, 4, with omission in 2 of the precise location (*via Appia*).

4. Most *auctaria*, including Molanus, notice this feast. Maternus of Trier, allegedly a disciple of St Peter and probably identical with his namesake, Maternus of Cologne, was one of the earliest bishops of the see.

Sources: **1, 2, 3**.Dubois, *Martyrologe*, 302–3. **4**. *AASS*, Iun. VII, 534; Overgaauw, *Martyrologes*, 941; *BiblSS*, ix, 85–9.

[15 September] Decimo Septimo Calendas Octobris Die 15 F

1. Romae, natalis beati Nicomedis praesbiteri et martyris.
2. Eodem die, sancti Valeriani martyris.
3. Item, octaua natiuitatis **beatae Mariae uirginis**.

1.2. MU 1, 2, with omission here in both entries of the precise locations (*via Numentana* and *in territorio Cabilonensi*).
3. Introduced by Pope Innocent IV in 1243, this octave is in almost every *auctarium*, including Molanus.

Sources: **1, 2**. Dubois, *Martyrologe*, 303. **3**. *AASS*, Iun. VII, 536–7; Overgaauw, *Martyrologes*, 942–3.

[16 September] G Decimo Sexto Calendas Octobris 16

1. Romae, beati Cornelii papae.
2. **In Scotia**, **sancti** Niniani episcopi Candidae Casae et confessoris.
3. **In Hybernia**, sancti Lasreani episcopi et sancti Monenni abbatis et confessoris.

2   *mo Ninn … i nĺ Laissrén*, 'Maoineann, Laisréan in Iona', MO.

1. This corresponds to MU 2 at 14 September, where we have already met Cornelius. However, Molanus also has Cornelius in first place on this day.
2. Molanus likewise notices Ninian here, also with mention of Candida Casa. The saint's office Life is in the Breviary of Aberdeen.
3. Stokes, no doubt conscious of this being Ninnian's day, wrongly emended *Moínenn* to read *Mo Ninn*. The saint in question here is Maoineann of Cloncurry in Co. Kildare. Both Laisréan of Durrow and

Iona and Laisréan of Mundrehid in the Laois parish of Aghaboe are remembered on this day.

Sources: **1**. *AASS*, Iun. VII, 539. **2**. *AASS*, Iun. VII, 539. **3**. Stokes, *Martyrology*, 194; Best and Lawlor, *Martyrology*, 71; *DIS*, 389, 436.

[17 September] Decimo Quinto Calendas Octobris 17 A

1. Apud Leodium, diocesi Tungrensi, beati Lamberti ibidem episcopi.
2. In Britannis, sanctorum Socratis et Stephani.
3. **In Hybernia**, sancti Brocani abbatis et confessoris et sanctae Regulae virginis.

3   *Broceani* MS; *Broccán Roiss Tuirc ...la féil ... Riaglae*, 'Brocán of Ros Tuirc, with the feast of Riaghail', MO.

1, 2. MU 3, 4, with differences here in 1 in wording and spelling. Molanus likewise places Lambert first.
3. Brocán was attached to Ros Tuirc, an unidentified church in Ossory, whereas Riaghail was patron of Muckinish island in Lough Derg on the river Shannon.

Sources: **1, 2**. Dubois, *Martyrologe*, 304. **3**. Stokes, *Martyrology*, 194; Best and Lawlor, *Martyrology*, 71; *DIS*, 128, 535.

[18 September] B Decimo Quarto Calendas Octobris 18

1. Natalis beati Methodii episcopi.
2. In Germania, monasterio Andelaha, depositio sanctae Ricardis imperatricis coniugis Caroli Crassi et uirginis.
3. **In Hybernia**, sancti Enani abbatis.

2   *cong* (crossed out) *coniugis* MS. **3**. *Énán Dromma Ráthe*, 'Éanán of Drumraney', MO.

1. MU 1.
2. Molanus, which uses exactly the same words, is among the few *auctaria* to notice the feast of Richardis, wife of Charles III (the Fat); she founded the monastery of Andlau in Alsace about 880 and retired to it after her husband's death in 888.

134

3. Éanán was patron of Drumraney in the Westmeath barony of Kilkenny West; his feast has previously been noticed at 19 August.

Sources: **1**. Dubois, *Martyrologe*, 304. **2**. *AASS*, Iun. VII, 543; *BiblSS*, xi, 157–8. **3**. Stokes, *Martyrology*, 195; Best and Lawlor, *Martyrology*, 72; *DIS*, 280–1.

[19 September] Decimo Tertio Calendas Octobris 19 C

1. Apud Nuceriam, natalis sanctorum Faelicis et Constantiae martyrum.
2. Treuiris, sancti Mileti episcopi et confessoris.
3. Turonis, sancti Eustachii episcopi, magnarum virtutum viri.

1. MU 3.
2. This feast is otherwise in the Cologne martyrologies (Grevenus and Lübeck/Cologne) and Molanus, which uses the same words. Milet(i) us was a fifth-century bishop of Trier.
3. Most *auctaria*, including Molanus which has the same text, commemorate this fifth-century bishop of Tours.

Sources: **1**. Dubois, *Martyrologe*, 305. **2**. *AASS*, Iun. VII, 545; Overgaauw, *Martyrologes*, 948; *BiblSS*, ix, 484–5. **3**. *AASS*, Iun. VII, 545; Overgaauw, *Martyrologes*, 948; *BiblSS*, v, 307.

[20 September] D Duodecimo Calendas Octobris 20

1. In Phrigia, sanctorum Dionisii et Primati martyrum.
2. Eodem die, vigilia sancti Mathei apostoli et euangelistae.
3. Ciuitate Corduba, passio sancti Eulogii presbiteri et martyris.

1. MU 3, with the addition here of *martyrum*. Molanus spells the latter name *Priuati*.
2. Almost all *auctaria* of MU, including Molanus, note this vigil.
3. MU 2.

Sources: **1, 3**. Dubois, *Martyrologe*, 306. **2**. *AASS*, Iun. VII, 546–7; Overgaauw, *Martyrologes*, 949.

[21 September] Undecimo Calendas Octobris 21 E

1. Natalis **beati Mathei** apostoli et euangelistae.
2. Romae, sancti Pamphili martyris.
3. Apud Constantias inferioris Normanniae, beati Laudi episcopi et confessoris.

1, 2. MU 1, 3.
3. The feast of Laudus (Lo), sixth-century bishop and patron of Coutances in Normandy, is in some *auctaria* for the next day, but in most – including Molanus which likewise specifies town and province – for this day.

Sources: **1, 2.** Dubois, *Martyrologe*, 306. **3.** *AASS*, Iun. VII, 549; Overgaauw, *Martyrologes*, 952–3; *BiblSS*, vii, 1121–2.

[22 September] F Decimo Calendas Octobris 22

1. In Bauaria, apud Ratisbonam, passio sancti Emerami episcopi et martyris.
2. In pago Pictauensi, sancti Florentii episcopi et confessoris.

1. MU 2, with the addition here of the precise location (*Ratisbona*), and with somewhat different wording for this local feast. Surprisingly, red lettering is not used for the feast.
2. MU 3, with incorrect *episcopi*, as in some *auctaria*, not including Molanus.

Sources: **1.** Dubois, *Martyrologe*, 307. **2.** Overgaauw, *Martyrologes*, 952.

[23 September] Nono Calendas Octobris 23 G

1. Romae, natalis beati Lini papae et martyris.
2. Eodem die, sanctae Tecle virginis.
3. In territorio ciuitatis Constanciae, sancti Paterni episcopi et confessoris.

1. The feast of this very early pope, of whom almost nothing is known, is placed first in most *auctaria*, including Molanus.
2, 3. MU 2, 3.

Sources: **1**. *AASS*, Iun. VII, 553–4; Overgaauw, *Martyrologes*, 953–4; Kelly, *Dictionary*, 6–7. **2, 3**. Dubois, *Martyrologe*, 308.

[24 September] A Octauo Calendas Octobris 24

1. Conceptio sancti Joannis Baptistae, praecursoris Domini.
2. Aruernis, depositio sancti Rustici episcopi.
3. In Hungaria, sancti Gerardi episcopi et martyris.

1. MU 1, with the addition here of the final two words; Molanus also adds a reference to *praecursor*.
2. Molanus, which uses the same words, and most other *auctaria*, commemorate Rusticus, bishop of Clermont in Auvergne, on this day.
3. Molanus, which has the same text, and a few other *auctaria*, commemorate this saint. A native of Venice, Gerardus was among those involved in the conversion of Hungary in the eleventh century. He died in Budapest on 24 September 1046 and was elevated to the status of saint by Gregory VII in 1083.

Sources: **1**. Dubois, *Martyrologe*, 308; *AASS*, Iun. VII, 556. **2**. *AASS*, Iun. VII, 555–6; Overgaauw, *Martyrologes*, 955; *BibSS* xi, 511–12. **3**. *AASS*, Iun. VII, 556; *BiblSS*, vi, 184–6.

[25 September] Septimo Calendas Octobris 25 B

1. Natalis beati Cleophae, a Judeis pro Christo occisi.
2. In Glasconia, depositio sancti Ceolfridi episcopi et confessoris.
3. **In Hybernia**, sancti Barri episcopi et confessoris.

---

[3] *In Hibernia, sancti Barri confessoris* COW; *Barri* T; *féil Barri ó Chorc-aig*, 'the feast of Bairre from Cork', MO.

1. MU 1, with the inclusion here, as in Molanus, of a reference to his having beeen slain by Jews.

2. A few *auctaria*, including Molanus, which has the same wording as MReg, commemorate Ceolfrith, abbot of Wearmouth and Jarrow in Northumbria, who died at Langres in Burgundy in 716. The monks of Glastonbury claimed to have received his relics in the tenth century, whence *Glasconia* alias *Glastonia* here.

3. Bairre, otherwise Fionnbharr, was venerated as founder-patron of the church of Cork, later a diocesan see. Grevenus (*In Hibernia, Barre episcopi et confessoris*) also commemorated the saint.

Sources: **1.** Dubois, *Martyrologe*, 308. **2.** *AASS*, Iun. VII, 557–8; Overgaauw, *Martyrologes*, 958; Farmer, *Dictionary*, 73–4. **3.** Stokes, *Martyrology*, 196; Best and Lawlor, *Martyrology*, 74; *AASS*, Iun. VII, 558; *DIS*, 332–4.

[26 September] C Sexto Calendas Octobris 26

1. Natalis sanctorum martyrum Cypriani et Justinae uirginis.
2. Romae, sancti Eusebii episcopi et confessoris.
3. **In Hybernia**, sancti Colmani abbatis et confessoris.

³   *Colmani* T; *Colmán ó Laind Elo*, 'Colmán of Lynally', MO.

1. MU 1, with the omission here of *episcopi* after *Cypriani*.
2. Eusebius's feast is noticed in almost all *auctaria* of MU, including Molanus which has the same text.
3. Colmán was patron of Lynally in the Offaly barony of Ballycowan.

Sources: **1.** Dubois, *Martyrologe*, 309. **2.** *AASS*, Iun. VII, 557–8; Overgaauw, *Martyrologes*, 959. **3.** Stokes, *Martyrology*, 196; Best and Lawlor, *Martyrology*, 74; *DIS*, 203–5.

[27 September] Quinto Calendas Octobris 27 D

1. Apud ciuitatem Aegeam, natalis sanctorum martyrum Cosmae et Damiani.
2. Parisiis, sancti Eleazari confessoris.
3. Laetiis, sanctae Hiltrudis uirginis.

1. MU 1.

2. Several *auctaria*, including Molanus, notice this feast. A member of the Franciscan Third Order, Elzearius, count of Ariano, died in Paris in 1323.

3. Of the *auctaria* of MU, only Molanus otherwise notices the feast of Hiltrude of Liessies, near Waulsort in Belgium.

Sources: **1.** Dubois, *Martyrologe*, 310. **2.** *AASS*, Iun. VII, 561–2; Overgaauw, *Martyrologes*, 960; *BiblSS*, iv, 1155–7. **3.** *AASS*, Iun. VII, 561–2; *BiblSS*, vii, 780.

[28 September] E Quarto Calendas Octobris 28

1. Apud Tolosam, sancti Exuperii episcopi et confessoris.
2. In Germania, **sanctae Liobae uirginis** Scotae, quae de Scotia a beato Bonifacio vocata fuit et postea in monasterio Fulda sepulta.
3. **Ex Scotia**, sancte Gunthildis uirginis.
4. In Hybernia, sanctae Nesenae uirginis.

1. MU 1.
2. The feast of Lioba, abbess of Bischofsheim in Baden, is otherwise recorded in some *auctaria*, including Molanus and Grevenus. *Scotia* is substituted here for *Britannia*, in keeping perhaps with *MenScot* which turns Lioba into Lupita, reputed sister of St Patrick. Lioba received her formation at Wimborne, which had been founded by Cuthburga (31 August above), before responding to Boniface's call for missionaries to Germany.
3. Neither Molanus nor any other *auctarium* notices the feast of the eleventh-century Gunthildis of Suffersheim, near Eichstätt, who was remembered on this day. She is sometimes confused with a much earlier Anglo-Saxon saint of the same name, who is thought to have entered the convent of Wimborne, where she met Lioba, before joining the latter on her mission in Germany. There she was attached both to the church of Ohrdruf in Thüringen, a dependency of Fulda, and to the diocese of Eichstätt where there was a *Schottenkloster*. However, the Anglo-Saxon saint's feast fell on 8 December.
4. There is probably confusion here, involving a change of gender, with Neasán of the Ulstermen, who was usually commemorated on the following day.

Sources: **1**. Dubois, *Martyrologe*, 311. **2**. *AASS*, Iun. VII, 564; Overgaauw, *Martyrologes*, 962; *BiblSS*, viii, 60–1. **3**. *BiblSS*, vii, 532–3. **4**. Best and Lawlor, *Martyrology*, 75; *DIS*, 514–15.

[29 September] Tertio Calendas Octobris 29 F

1. In Monte Gargano, venerabilis memoria **beati Michaelis archangeli**.
2. Treuiris, natalis sancti Loutuini episcopi et confessoris.
3. Trecas, beati Vrsionis monachi et confessoris.

1. MU 1, with transposition here of the last two words.
2. The feast of Loutuinus (more commonly Liutwinus/Liutwin), an early eighth-century bishop of Trier,who died in Reims, is otherwise in most *auctaria*, including Molanus. He was buried in Mettlach near Trier.
3. The Cologne martyrologies (Grevenus and Lübeck/Cologne) and Molanus likewise notice the feast of Ursio, patron of a church named after him in Saint-Lyé, north-west of Troyes.

Sources: **1**. Dubois, *Martyrologe*, 311. **2**. *AASS*, Iun. VII, 565–6; *BiblSS*, viii, 314–15. **3**. *AASS*, Iun. VII, 566; *BiblSS*, xii, 865–6.

[30 September] G Pridie Calendas Octobris 30

1. In Galliis, passio sanctorum martyrum Victoris et Vrsi.
2. Eodem die, apud Bethleem, depositio beati Hieromini presbiteri.
3. In Anglia, sancti Honorii Cantuariensis.

1. MU 1, with omission here of the precise location (*castrum Solodorum*).
2. MU 2, with omission here of *Iudae* after *Bethleem*.
3. A few *auctaria*, including Molanus, likewise notice the feast of Honorius, fifth archbishop of Canterbury, who died in 653.

Sources: **1, 2**. Dubois, *Martyrologe*, 312. **3**. *AASS*, Iun. VII, 568; Overgaauw, *Martyrologes*, 965; *EncASE*, 242.

[1 October] Calendis Octobris 1 A

1. Romae, natalis beati Aretae martyris.
2. Remis, sancti Remigii episcopi et confessoris.
3. In portu Ganda, sancti Bauonis confessoris.
4. Eodem die, sancti Romani Melodi.
5. Treuiris, sancti Nicetii episcopi et confessoris.

1. MU 1.
2. Usuard (MU 5) records here the translation of Remigius's relics, together with those of Germanus whose name is omitted, as in some *auctaria*.
3. MU 6.
4. This feast is otherwise noticed only by Molanus. A Byzantine saint, born in Syria, Romanus became noted as a religious poet.
5. Some *auctaria*, including Molanus, also notice the feast of Nicetius, a sixth-century bishop of Trier, on this day. Usuard has his feast on 5 December.

Sources: **1.** Dubois, *Martyrologe*, 312. **2.** Dubois, *Martyrologe*, 312; *AASS*, Iun. VII, 571–2; Overgaauw, *Martyrologes*, 968. **3.** Dubois, *Martyrologe*, 313. **4.** *AASS*, Iun. VII, 572; *BiblSS*, xi, 319–23. **5.** *AASS*, Iun. VII, 571–2; Dubois, *Martyrologe*, 354; *BiblSS*, ix, 900–02.

[2 October] B Sexto Nonas Octobris 2

1. Apud Nicomediam, natalis sancti Eleutherii martyris cum aliis innumeriis.
2. In Anglia, sancti Thomae Herefordensis episcopi et confessoris.
3. Assisii, translatio sanctae Clarae uirginis.
4. In Hybernia, sancti Oenimi confessoris.

4   *onme* MO.

1. MU 1.
2. The Cologne martyrologies (Grevenus and Lübeck/Cologne) and Molanus, which has the same text, likewise notice the feast of Thomas, bishop of Hereford, who died in 1282.

3. Several *auctaria*, including Molanus, notice the translation of the relics of Clare, whose commemoration became fixed on this day, although the event took place on 3 October 1260.
4. The otherwise unknown name *Onme* was taken by Stokes, the editor of MO, to be non-onomastic. However, a note added to MT identifies him as Giallán, eponym of Ceall Ghialláin, now probably Killelan in the Kildare barony of Kilkea and Moone.

Sources: **1**. Dubois, *Martyrologe*, 313. **2**. *AASS*, Iun. VII, 574; Farmer, *Dictionary*, 379–80. **3**. *AASS*, Iun. VII, 573–4; Overgaauw, *Martyrologes*, 970. **4**. Stokes, *Martyrology*, 214; Best and Lawlor, *Martyrology*, 76, 116; *HDGP*, iv, 2.

[3 October] Quinto Nonas Octobris 3 C

1. In ciuitate Assisii, natale beati Francisci confessoris fundatoris ordinis minorum.
2. Apud Corinthum, sanctorum Crispi et Caii.
3. Eodem die, natalis beati Dionisii Areopagitae.

1 *Assisio* MS.

1. Most *auctaria*, including Molanus, place Francis's feast on the following day.
2. MU 1 (4 October).
3. MU 1, with the addition here, as in Molanus, of *Areopagitae*.

Sources: **1**. *AASS*, Iun. VII, 578–9; Overgaauw, *Martyrologes*, 973–4. **2**. Dubois, *Martyrologe*, 314. **3**. Dubois, *Martyrologe*, 314; *AASS*, Iun. VII, 576.

[4 October] D Quarto Nonas Octobris 4

1. In Aegypto, sanctorum Marci et Marciani fratrum.
2. Ciuitate Parisiis, sanctae Aureae virginis.
3. Item, Treuiris, sancti Tyrsi martyris et sociorum.

1, 2. MU 2, 3, with *Parisiis* for Usuard's *Parisius*, as in Molanus.

3. The Cologne martyrologies (Grevenus and Lübeck/Cologne) and Molanus, which has the same words, likewise notice the feast of Tyrsus and his companions; the feast goes back to the alleged discovery of an inscription in the Trier church of St Paulin in 1071.

Sources: **1, 2**. Dubois, *Martyrologe*, 315; *AASS*, Iun. VII, 577. **3**. *AASS*, Iun. VII, 578–9; Overgaauw, *Martyrologes*, 974; *BiblSS*, xii, 500–1.

[5 October] Tertio Nonas Octobris 5 E

1. Apud Siciliam Messanae, natalis sanctorum martyrum Placidi, discipuli beati patris nostri Benedicti, cum aliis, Eutichii, Victorini et Donati.
2. In Galliis, sancti Apollinaris episcopi.
3. In Hybernia, sanctae Synechae virginis.

3   *Sineche* T; *Sínech ingen Fhergnae Crúachan Maige Abnae*, 'Sineach daughter of Feargna of Crohane', MO.

1. MU 1, with the addition here, as in Molanus, of a reference to Messana, and to Benedict, Victorinus and Donatus. The reference to Benedict is also found in other *auctaria* of MU.
2. MU 3, with the omission here of the precise location (*Valentia*).
3. Sineach was attached to the church of Crohane in the Tipperary barony of Slievardagh.

Sources: **1, 2**. Dubois, *Martyrologe*, 315; *AASS*, Iun. VII, 580–1. **3**. Stokes, *Martyrology*, 214; Best and Lawlor, *Martyrology*, 77; *DIS*, 563.

[6 October] Pridie Nonas Octobris 6 F

1. In Calabria, depositio sancti Brunonis confessoris, primi institutoris ordinis Carthusiensis.
2. Romae, sanctae Balbinae uirginis.
3. In Hybernia, sanctorum confessorum atque abbatum Lucelli et Baitheni, Ferdachrichi et Lugadi episcoporum.

³ *Battheni* MS; *Abb Clúana in Lucell la Baíthine ... Fer dá Chrích ... epscop Lugdach*, 'Luiceall, abbot of Clonmacnoise, with Baodán, Fear Dá Chríoch, bishop Lughaidh', MO.

1. Some *auctaria*, including Molanus which accords it first place, likewise notice the feast of Bruno of Calabria, founder of the Carthusian order, who died on this day in 1101.

2. Many *auctaria*, including Molanus, have this feast which was originally drawn from a copy of MH.

3. Fear Dá Chríoch was attached to the church of Derrynaflan in the townland of Lurgoe, parish of Graystown, barony of Slievardagh, Co. Tipperary. Luiceall is described as abbot of Clonmacnoise, and Baodán was taken to be identical with the patron of Cloney in the Kildare parish of Kilberry, barony of Narragh and Reban West. Finally, Lughach was attached to the church of Coolbanagher in the Laois barony of Portnahinch.

Sources: **1**. *AASS*, Iun. VII, 582–3; *BiblSS*, iii, 561–77. **2**. *AASS*, Iun. VII, 582–3; Overgaauw, *Martyrologes*, 977. **3**. Stokes, *Martyrology*, 215; Best and Lawlor, *Martyrology*, 77; *DIS*, 85–6, 407–8.

[7 October] Nonis Octobris Die 7 G

1. Romae, via Appia, depositio sancti Marci papae.
2. Eodem die, sanctorum Marcelli et Apulei martyrum.
3. Apud Paduam, sanctae Justinae uirginis.
4. Item, canonizatio beatae Brigittae uiduae per Bonifacium nonum.

1, 2. MU 1, 2, with *sancti* for *beati* (1), as in Molanus, and transposition of *martyrum* (2).

3. A few *auctaria*, including Molanus, likewise commemorate Justina of Padua who enjoyed a very widely diffused cult in Italy.

4. The Cologne martyrologies (Grevenus and Lübeck/Cologne) and Molanus also notice here the feast of the canonization of Birgitta, who died on 8 October. Her canonization was proclaimed by Boniface IX on 7 October 1391, and her feast was transferred to the following day by Urban VIII in the seventeenth century.

Sources: **1, 2**. Dubois, *Martyrologe*, 316; *AASS*, Iun. VII, 583. **3**. *AASS*, Iun. VII, 585; *BiblSS*, vi, 1345–7. **4**. *AASS*, Iun. VII, 585; *BiblSS*, iii, 439–530, at 520–1.

[8 October] A Octauo Idus Octobris 8

1. Natalis beati Symeonis, qui Dominum in ulnis suis suscepit.
2. Eodem die, translatio **sancti Erhardi** episcopi et confessoris.
3. In ciuitate Hispali, sancti Petri martyris.

1. MU 1, with slightly different wording here.
2. The Cologne martyrologies (Grevenus and Lübeck/Cologne) likewise commemorate the translation of Erhard's relics, which Leo IX arranged to have elevated on 8 October 1059, before canonizing the saint-bishop of Regensburg. The name is red-lettered in MReg, thus underlining the local importance of the feast. See also below at 15 October.
3. MU 3.

Sources: **1, 3**. Dubois, *Martyrologe*, 316. **3**. *AASS*, Iun. VII, 587; *BiblSS*, iv, 1285–7.

[9 October] Septimo Idus Octobris 9 B

1. Abrahae patriarchae.[1]
2. Apud Parisium, natalis sanctorum martyrum Dionisii episcopi et martyris Rustici et Eleutherii martyrum.

---

[1] *Abraham* MS.

1. MU 1.
2. MU 2, with a superfluous second *martyrum* here.

Sources: **1, 2**. Dubois, *Martyrologe*, 317.

[10 October] C Sexto Idus Octobris 10

1. Loth prophetae.
2. In Britannia, Eboraci, sancti Paulini episcopi et confessoris.
3. Apud ciuitatem Wurtzburg, sancti Burchardi episcopi et confessoris.

4. **In Hibernia**, sancti Fintani abbatis et confessoris.

⁴   *In Britannia* MS; *Fintani* T; *Fintan* ... *Dromma Ing*, 'Fiontan of Dromin', MO.

1. Loth's feast, which is also in MA on this day, is in first place in Molanus, as well as in almost all other *auctaria* of MU.
2. MU 5, with the addition here of *Eboraci*, as in some *auctaria*, including Molanus.
3. No other version of MU has Burchard's feast on this day; it normally falls on the 14 October. However, the saint is commemorated on 11 October in *MenScot*.
4. Fiontan was patron of Dromin in the Louth barony of Ardee, in Ireland and not *in Britannia*, as the manuscript would have it.

Sources: **1**. *AASS*, Iun. VII, 591–2. **2**. Dubois, *Martyrologe*, 318; *AASS*, Iun. VII, 590, 592; Overgaauw, *Martyrologes*, 987. **3**. Forbes, *Kalendars*, 214. **4**. Stokes, *Martyrology*, 215; Best and Lawlor, *Martyrology*, 78; *DIS*, 343–4.

[11 October] Quinto Idus Octobris 11 D

1. **In Scotia**, sancti Canici abbatis.
2. In Anglia, sanctae Ethelburgae uirginis et abbatissae.
3. Coloniae, ad sanctum Pantaleonem, beati Brunonis episcopi.
4. In Hybernia, sancti Kainnici abbatis et confessoris.
5. Item, sanctorum confessorum Fortcherni, Lommani et Fergnani.

⁴   *Kamnechi* MS; *Cainnech maccu Dálan*, 'Cainneach of the Maca Dhálann', MO. **5**. *Forcherni* MS; *Fortchern*, *Lommán* MO.

1. MU 3. Cainnech of Kilkenny, one of the chief saints of the diocese of Ossory, was among a small number of Irish saints, mainly of Midland provenance, commemorated by Usuard. The feast is duplicated here at 4.
2. The Cologne martyrologies (Grevenus and Lübeck/Cologne) and Molanus, which uses the same words as MReg, likewise commemorate Ethelburga, abbess of Barking.

3. The Bruxellensis MU, the Cologne martyrologies (Grevenus and Lübeck/Cologne) and Molanus also commemorate Bruno, archbishop of Cologne, who died in 965.
4. See above at 1.
5. Foirtchearn and Lommán were attached to the church of Trim in the Meath barony of Lower Moyfenrath, whereas the church of Feargna, who is not in MO, but who is described as *cruimhthear*, 'presbyter', in MT on this day, is not known.

Sources: **1**. Dubois, *Martyrologe*, 320. **2**. *AASS*, Iun. VII, 594; Farmer, *Dictionary*, 137. **3**. *AASS*, Iun. VII, 593–4; *BiblSS*, iii, 581–3. **4**. Stokes, *Martyrology*, 215; Best and Lawlor, *Martyrology*, 78; *DIS*, 138–40. **5**. Stokes, *Martyrology*, 215; Best and Lawlor, *Martyrology*, 78; *DIS*, 350–1.

[12 October] E Quarto Idus Octobris 12

1. Romae, beati Faelicis papae.
2. In Syria, sancti Eustachii presbiteri.
3. In Anglia, sancti Uuilfridi episcopi Eboracensis et confessoris.
4. In Hybernia, sanctorum confessorum Fiaci, Fiachraigi, et Mobi abbatum et confessorum.

4   *Mobini, Fiachani, Miacrani* T; *Fíacc ... Fiachraig ... moBíi* MO.

1. No pope named Felix was commemorated on this day but the African bishops Felix and Cyprian are named in MU 2.
2. MU 3.
3. Most *auctaria*, including Molanus which uses the same words, commemorate Wilfrid, abbot of Ripon and bishop of York, who died on this day in 709.
4. Mobí was patron of the church of Glasnevin in the Dublin barony of Coolock. Grevenus (*In Scotia, Movei abbatis*) also notices this feast. Fiac and Fiachra were attached to the church of Sleaty in the Laois barony of Slievemargy. *Miacrani* of T may reflect the form Mo Fhiachra.

Sources: **1**. Dubois, *Martyrologe*, 320. **2**. Dubois, *Martyrologe*, 320.
3. *AASS*, Iun. VII, 596; *EncASE*, 474–6. **4**. Stokes, *Martyrology*, 216;
Best and Lawlor, *Martyrology*, 78–9; Stokes, *Martyrology*, 215; *DIS*,
315–16, 457–8.

[13 October] Tertio Idus Octobris 13 F

1. In Hyspaniis, passio sanctorum Fausti, Januarii et Martialis.
2. In Hybernia, sanctae Finsigae uirginis.
3. Item, Colomanni martyris apud Medelicam.
4. Et sancti Lubentii episcopi et confessoris.

2   *Finsingae* MS; *Uincechae* T; *féil Findsiche*, 'Finnseach's feast', MO.

1. MU 2, with omission here of the precise location (*Corduba*).
2. Later martyrologies place Finnseach, alias Finncheall, in Slieve Gorey in Co. Cavan.
3. The Cologne martyrologies (Grevenus and Lübeck/Cologne,) and
the first edition of Molanus likewise commemorate Colomannus
(Koloman) of Melk who was killed at Stockerau near Vienna in 1012
while on pilgrimage to the Holy Land. Only MReg mentions Melk.
4. Both Cologne martyrologies (Grevenus and Lübeck/Cologne) and
Molanus likewise notice the feast of this saint who had associations
with several churches in the Rhineland, and especially with the see of
Trier.

Sources: **1**. Dubois, *Martyrologe*, 321. **2**. Stokes, *Martyrology*, 216;
Best and Lawlor, *Martyrology*, 79; *DIS*, 318. **3**. *AASS*, Iun. VII, 598;
BiblSS, iv, 96–7. **4**. *AASS*, Iun. VII, 598; *BiblSS*, viii, 185–6.

[14 October] G Pridie Idus Octobris 14

1. Romae, natalis beati Calixti papae et martyris.
2. Item, sanctorum Saturnini et Lupi.
3. Treuiris, sancti Rustici episcopi et confessoris.

1. MU 1, with omission here of the precise location (*via Aurelia*).
2. This feast, originally borrowed from MH, found its way into most
auctaria of MU, including Molanus.

3. The Cologne martyrologies (Grevenus and Lübeck/Cologne) and Molanus likewise commemorate Rusticus, whose name appears to have been interpolated into the list of bishops of Trier.

Sources: **1**. Dubois, *Martyrologe*, 321. **2**. *AASS*, Iun. VII, 599–600; Overgaauw, *Martyrologes*, 995. **3**. *AASS*, Iun. VII, 600; *BiblSS*, xi, 514–15.

[15 October] Idibus Octobris 15 A

1. Romae, uia Aurelia, sancti Fortunati martyris.
2. Ex Britannia, sancti Oswaldi episcopi Vuigorniensis.
3. Apud Veronam, sanctae Placidiae uirginis, Valentiniani imperatoris filiae.
4. Et octaua translationis sancti Erhardi.

2   *episcopo Vuigarniensis* MS.

1. MU 2, with the addition here of *martyris*.
2. The feast of Oswald, bishop of Worcester and York, which normally fell on 28 February, is otherwise recorded in the same words on this day in Molanus, as well as in the Reims group of *auctaria*.
3. Grevenus and Molanus, which has much the same text as MReg, likewise commemorate Placida of Verona here.
4. For the feast, see above at 8 October.

Sources: **1**. Dubois, *Martyrologe*, 322. **2**. *AASS*, Iun. VII, 603; Overgaauw, *Martyrologes*, 997; *EncASE* 348. **3**. *AASS*, Iun. VII, 603; *BiblSS*, x, 941–2.

[16 October] B Decimo Septimo Calendas Nouembris 16

1. In territorio Bituricensi, sancti Ambrosii episcopi Caturcensis.
2. Alemannia, **Sancti Galli** presbiteri et confessoris, qui, Scotus natus, cum Sueuis collocat artus.
3. In Hybernia, sanctarum uirginum Regulae et Kyarae.

3   *Ciar ... Riaguil* MO.

1. MU 2, with the addition here of the name of the see (*Caturcensis*), in line with the second recension of MU and Molanus.
2. Gallus's feast is in most *auctaria* of MU, including Molanus.
3. Despite the claim made here, Ciar, recte Caere (*in Africa*), was not an Irish saint. Riaghail – whom we have already met at 17 September – was patron of Muckinish island.

Sources: **1**. Dubois, *Martyrologe*, 323. **2**. *AASS*, Iun. VII, 604–6; Overgaauw, *Martyrologes*, 999. **3**. Stokes, *Martyrology*, 216; Best and Lawlor, *Martyrology*, 80; *DIS*, 535.

[17 October] Decimo Sexto Calendas [Nouembris] 17 C

1. In Antiochia, sancti Heronis discipuli beati Ignatii episcopi.
2. In Hybernia, sancti Maenachi episcopi et confessoris.
3. Treuiris, sancti Florentini episcopi et martyris.

1. MU 1, with the substitution here, in line with some *auctaria*, including Molanus, of *episcopi* for *martyris*.
2. Although abbot of the church of Dunleer in the Louth barony of Ferrard, Maonach had several associations with south Munster, which may explain his presence here; he is not in MO. Grevenus (*In Hibernia, Monachi confessoris*) likewise commemorates this saint.
3. The Cologne martyrologies (Grevenus and Lübeck/Cologne) and Molanus, which has the same text, also notice this feast.

Sources: **1**. Dubois, *Martyrologe*, 323. **2**. Stokes, *Martyrology of Gorman*, 198; Best and Lawlor, *Martyrology*, 80; *AASS*, Iun. VII, 608; *DIS*, 448–9. **3**. *AASS*, Iun. VII, 608; *BiblSS*, v, 852.

[18 October] D Decimo Quinto Calendas Nouembris 18

1. Natalis sancti Lucae euangelistae, hic fuit etiam arte medicus, Paulum sequutus usque ad confessionem eius.
2. In Nassonia, beati Mononis martyris, qui, angelico monitu, de Scotia Arduennam deuenit, ibique post martyrium in ecclesia quam ipse construxerat sepultus.

1. MU 1, but the wording here is different, as is that of Molanus.
2. The feast of Mono, who is supposed to have been born in Ireland, is otherwise in some *auctaria*, including Molanus, whose text agrees fairly closely with that of MReg.

Sources: **1**. Dubois, *Martyrologe*, 324; *AASS*, Iun. VII, 610. **2**. *AASS*, Iun. VII, 610; *BiblSS*, ix, 563–6.

[19 October] E Decimo Quarto Calendas Nouembris 19

1. Ebroicas, sancti Aquilini episcopi et confessoris.
2. Oxoniae, sanctae Fredesuuidae uirginis.
3. In Britannia, sancti Etbini abbatis Nectensis.

1, 2, 3. Several *auctaria*, including Molanus which has much the same wording as MReg, commemorate these three saints, respectively Aquilin of Évreux, Frideswide of Oxford and Etbin of a church near Dol in Brittany. Grevenus places Etbinus *in Hibernia*.

Sources: **1, 2, 3**. *AASS*, Iun. VII, 612–13; *BiblSS*, ii, 330–1; Farmer, *Dictionary*, 161; *BiblSS*, v, 113–14.

[20 October] F Decimo Tertio Calendas Nouembris 20

1. In Galliis, ciuitate Agenno, sancti Caprasii martyris.
2. Apud Mindam, natalis sancti Feliciani episcopi et martyris.
3. In Hybernia sanctorum confessorum Fintani Meeldubii.

---

[3] *Fintani et* MS; *la Fintan Maeldub ... dend Eoganacht*, 'with Fiontan Mao-ldubh of the Eoghanacht', MO.

1. MU 2.
2. Molanus, which has the same text, and the Cologne martyrologies (Grevenus and Lübeck/Cologne) likewise notice the feast of the Tuscan saint, Felicianus; the saint's relics were translated to Minden in Westphalia in 965.
3. Fiontan Maoldubh – the name of a single saint despite MReg's *confessorum* – was attached to the church of Durrow in the Laois barony of Clarmallagh.

Sources: **1**. Dubois, *Martyrologe*, 325. **2**. *AASS*, Iun. VII, 615; *BiblSS*, v, 597–9. **3**. Stokes, *Martyrology*, 217; Best and Lawlor, *Martyrology*, 81; Ó Riain, *Corpus*, §86; *DIS*, 344.

[21 October] Duodecimo Calendas Nouembris 21 G

1. Natalis sancti Hilarionis confessoris.
2. In Colonia Agrippinensi, sanctorum undecim millium virginum, quae pro virginitatis constantia martyrio uitam consummauerunt.
3. In Hybernia, sancti Mundii abbatis et confessoris.

3   *Munnuni* T; *Fintan ... macc Telcháin*, 'Fiontan son of Tealchán', MO.

1. MU 2, albeit with different wording here.
2. This entry is in almost all *auctaria* of MU, including Molanus which has much the same text as MReg.
3. Munna, alias Fiontan, was patron of Taghmon in the Wexford barony of Shelmaliere West. The hypocoristic form *Munnu* is given in the notes to MO. Grevenus (*In Hibernia, Nummi confessoris*) also records the feast.

Sources: **1**, Dubois, *Martyrologe*, 326. **2**. *AASS*, Iun. VII, 616–18; Levison, *Das Werden der Ursula-Legende*. **3**. Stokes, *Martyrology*, 217, 226; Best and Lawlor, *Martyrology*, 82; *AASS*, Iun. VII, 618; *DIS*, 505–7.

[22 October] A Unodecimo Calendas Nouembris 22

1. Natalis sanctae Salomae, quae in euangelio legitur sollicitam circa Domini sepulturam.
2. Coloniae, sanctae Cordulae uirginis et martyris.

1. MU 3.
2. This feast of one of the 11,000 virgins of Cologne is in most *auctaria* of MU, including Molanus, whose text is very close to MReg.
Sources: **1**. Dubois, *Martyrologe*, 326. **2**. *AASS*, Iun. VII, 619–20; Overgaauw, *Martyrologes*, 1013.

[23 October] Decimo Calendas Nouembris 23 B

1. Ciuitate Colonia, sancti Seuerini episcopi et martyris.
2. In pago Pictauensi, sancti Benedicti confessoris.
3. Eodem die, translatio sancti Galli confessoris.

1, 2. MU 3, 4, with the substitution here in 1 of *martyris* for *confessoris*.
3. No other *auctarium* of MU notices this feast, which falls within the octave of the saint's *natale* on 16 October. The usual day of Gallus's translation was 2 February.

Sources: **1, 2.** Dubois, *Martyrologe*, 327. **3.** *BiblSS*, vi, 15–19.

[24 October] C Nono Calendas Nouembris 24

1. In Britannia, transitus beati Maglorii episcopi et confessoris.
2. In Nicomedia, sancti Seueri et Dorothei martyrum.
3. In Cesarea Cappadoceae, sancti Longini martyris.

³ *Cappadocea* MS.

1. Most *auctaria*, including Molanus, which uses the same words, notice the feast of Maglorius (Magloire); the saint's relics were kept at Lehon near Dinan in Brittany.
2. A small number of *auctaria*, not including Molanus, likewise notice the feast of these two saints which appears to have come originally from the previous day in MH.
3. A few *auctaria* notice the feast of Longinus, albeit on the previous day, where it is also noticed by MO; the latter refers in a note to Caesarea Cappadociae. In line with MU, Longinus has already been provided with a feast at 15 March.

Sources: **1.** *AASS*, Iun. VII, 624–5; *BiblSS*, viii, 534–6. **2.** *AASS*, Iun. VII, 624–5. **3.** *AASS*, Iun. VII, 624–5; Stokes, *Martyrology*, 217, 226; *BiblSS*, viii, 89–95.

[25 October] Octauo Calendas Nouembris 25 D

1. Romae, sanctorum martyrum Chrisanti et Dariae uirginis.
2. Romae, uia Salaria, sancti Bonifacii papae et confessoris.
3. In Hybernia, sancti Lasreani abbatis et confessoris.

3   *Laissrén ... macc Nascai*, 'Laisréan son of Nasca', MO.

1. Placed by MU at 1 December, this feast is displaced to here in a large number of *auctaria*, including Molanus. Like MReg, Molanus places the feast first.
2. Most *auctaria*, including Molanus, which has much the same text as MReg, likewise notice here the feast of Pope Boniface I, although the day appears to be that of Boniface V.
3. Laisréan son of Nasca was patron of Holywood in the Down barony of Castlereagh Lower.

Sources: **1**. Dubois, *Martyrologe*, 351; *AASS*, Iun. VII, 627–8; Overgaauw, *Martyrologes*, 1019. **2**. *AASS*, Iun. VII, 624–5; Overgaauw, *Martyrologes*, 1019; Kelly, *Dictionary*, 40–1, 69–70. **3**. Stokes, *Martyrology*, 218; Best and Lawlor, *Martyrology*, 84; *DIS*, 389–90.

[26 October] E Septimo Calendas Nouembris 26

1. Apud Africam, sanctorum martyrum Rogatiani praesbiteri et Faelicissimi.
2. Romae, sancti Euaristi papae et martyris.

1. MU 1.
2. Most *auctaria*, including Molanus, commemorate Pope Evaristus, who died c. 109.

Sources: **1**. Dubois, *Martyrologe*, 329. **2**. *AASS*, Iun. VII, 629–30; Overgaauw, *Martyrologes*, 1021; Kelly, *Dictionary*, 8.

[27 October] Sexto Calendas Nouembris 27 F

1. In Britannia, translatio sancti Juonis confessoris.
2. In Hybernia, sancti Abbani abbatis et confessoris.

3. Item, sanctorum Odrani et Colmanni confessorum.
4. Eodem die, uigilia sanctorum apostolorum Simonis et Judae.

2 *Albani* T; *Abbán abb,* 'Abán the abbot', MO. **3**. *In Hibernia, sancti Odrani martiris, discipuli magni praedicatoris Patricii* COW; *Odrán ... Colmán haue Fiachrach,* 'Odhrán, Colmán of Uí Fhiachrach', MO.

1. A number of *auctaria*, including Molanus which has much the same text, notice the translation of the relics of St Yves of Tréguier in Brittany; the saint died in 1303.
2. Abán of Adamstown was already remembered above at 16 March.
3. Odhrán was abbot of Iona, whereas Colmán was attached to the church of Templeshanbo in the Wexford barony of Scarawalsh. Grevenus (*In Hibernia, Orani episcopi et confessoris*) also commemorates the feast of Odhrán.
4. Molanus, which has the same text, and most other *auctaria* note the vigil of the feast of the two apostles.

Sources: **1**. *AASS*, Iun. VII, 631–2; Overgaauw, *Martyrologes*, 1023; *BiblSS*, vii, 997–1001. **2**. Stokes, *Martyrology*, 219; Best and Lawlor, *Martyrology*, 84; *DIS*, 51–2. **3**. Stokes, *Martyrology*, 219; Best and Lawlor, *Martyrology*, 84; *DIS*, 200, 518. **4**. *AASS*, Iun. VII, 631–2; Overgaauw, *Martyrologes*, 1022.

[28 October] G Quinto Calendas Nouembris 28

1. Natalis sanctorum apostolorum Simonis Cananei et Thadei, qui et Judas dicitur.
2. Parisiis, translatio sanctae Genouefae uirginis.

1, 2. MU 1, 4, with *Parisiis* for Usuard's *Parisius*, as in Molanus.

Sources: **1, 2**. Dubois, *Martyrologe*, 330; *AASS*, Iun. VII, 634.

[29 October] Quarto Calendas Nouembris 29 A

1. Jerosolimis, natalis sancti Narcissi episcopi.
2. In Gallia, Viennae, depositio sancti Theodarii episcopi et confessoris.

1 *Narcisci* MS.

1. MU 1.

2. Most *auctaria*, including Molanus whose text is close to that of MReg, notice the feast of Theodarius; the saint is also in MA on this day.

Sources: **1, 2**. Dubois, *Martyrologe*, 330. **2**. *AASS*, Iun. VII, 636–7; Dubois and Renaud, *Martyrologes*, 369.

[30 October] B Tertio Calendas Nouembris 30

1. Antiochiae, natalis sancti Serapionis episcopi et confessoris.
2. In Dania, sancti Theodgari confessoris.
3. Xanthis, translatio sancti Victoris.

³ *Zanthis* MS.

1. MU 3, with addition here of *et confessoris*.

2. Molanus, which uses the same words, and Grevenus likewise notice the feast of Theodgarus (Thöger), patron of the diocese of Vendsyssel in Denmark; the saint is said to have come from Thüringen in Germany.

3. Lübeck/Cologne and Molanus also have this feast, which Sollerius took to refer to the Victor (of Xanten) who is commemorated with his companions in MU at 10 October.

Sources: **1**. Dubois, *Martyrologe*, 331. **2**. *AASS*, Iun. VII, 638; *BiblSS*, xii, 217–19. **3**. *AASS*, Iun. VII, 638; Dubois, *Martyrologe*, 318.

[31 October] Pridie Calendas Nouembris 31 C

1. Vigilia omnium sanctorum.
2. Fossis, natalis sancti Foillani episcopi, qui de Scotia ueniens in saltum qui Carbonarias nuncupatur martyrizatus est.
3. Ratisbonae, sancti Wolfgangi episcopi et confessoris.

1. MU 1.

2. This feast of Foillan of Fosses, near Nivelles in Belgium, who was a brother of Fursa, is in numerous *auctaria*, including Molanus. Here the more usual *Hibernia* is replaced by *Scotia*.

3. Most *auctaria*, including Molanus, likewise commemorate the feast of Wolfgang of Regensburg, which, despite its local character, is not written here in red letters.

Sources: **1**. Dubois, *Martyrologe*, 331. **2**. *AASS*, Iun. VII, 640; Overgaauw, *Martyrologes*, 1028–9; *BiblSS*, v, 952–5; *DIS*, 303–4. **3**. *AASS*, Iun. VII, 638; Overgaauw, *Martyrologes*, 1029; *BiblSS*, xii, 134–42.

[1 November] D Calendis Nouembris 1

1. Faestiuitas omnium sanctorum.
2. In Hybernia, natalis sanctorum Lonani, Colmani et Cronani abbatum et confessorum.

² *Lonani, Lommani, Colmani, Cronani* T; *Lonán, Colmán, Crónán* MO.

1. MU 1, MR 1, with the wording here of the latter source.
2. These three saints were patrons, respectively, of Trevet in the Meath barony of Skreen, of Ahamlish in the Sligo barony of Carbury, and of Tomgraney in the Clare barony of Upper Tulla.

Sources: **1**. Dubois, *Martyrologe*, 332. **2**. Stokes, *Martyrology*, 232; Stokes, *Martyrology of Gorman*, 208; *DIS*, 183, 235–6, 403.

[2 November] Quarto Nonas Nouembris 2 E

1. Commemoratio omnium fidelium defunctorum.
2. Ipso die, passio beati Justi martyris.
3. In Hybernia, sancti Hercani episcopi et confessoris.

³ *Ercani* T; *epscop Erc Sláne*, 'Bishop Earc of Slane', MO.

1. This is in most *auctaria*, including Molanus which has the same text and likewise places the feast first.
2. Molanus and a few other *auctaria* likewise commemorate Justus of Trieste.
3. Earc was patron of Slane in the Meath barony of Upper Slane and was also associated with Lullymore in the Kildare barony of East Offaly.

Sources: **1**. *AASS*, Iun. VII, 646–7. **2**. *AASS*, Iun. VII, 646–7; *BiblSS*, vii, 33. **3**. Stokes, *Martyrology*, 232; Stokes, *Martyrology of Gorman*, 208; *DIS*, 285–6.

[3 November] F Tertio Nonas Nouembris 3

1. Natalis beati Quarti, apostolorum discipuli.
2. In Anglia, sanctae Uuenefridae uirginis et martyris, quam Caedocus, filius Alani regis, occidit pro castitate.

1. MU 1.
2. Molanus, which has the same text as MReg, is one of a small number of *auctaria* to note the feast of the Welsh virgin Winefride (Gwenfrewi).

Sources: **1**. Dubois, *Martyrologe*, 335. **2**. *AASS*, Iun. VII, 648–9; Farmer, *Dictionary*, 408–9.

[4 November] Pridie Nonas Nouembris 4 G

1. Apud Bononiensem urbem, natalis sanctorum Agricolae et Uitalis.
2. Eodem die, natalis beatae Perpetuae coniugis sancti Petri apostoli.
3. In Hybernia, sancti Dograni abbatis et confessoris.

1. Some *auctaria*, including Molanus, place the feast of Agricola and Vitalis, which is otherwise at 27 November in MU, on this day. Molanus also accords the feast first place.
2. Molanus, which uses the same words, and most other *auctaria* have this feast. MO was the first to record it.
3. The name refers to Dodhrán of Doora in the Clare barony of Bunratty Upper.

Sources: **1**. *AASS*, Iun. VII, 651–2; Overgaauw, *Martyrologes*, 1039; Dubois, *Martyrologe*, 349. **2**. *AASS*, Iun. VII, 651–2; Overgaauw, *Martyrologes*, 1038; Stokes, *Martyrology*, 232. Ó Riain, 'The Feast of the Dedication'. **3**. Stokes, *Martyrology of Gorman*, 212; *DIS*, 270–1.

[5 November] A Nonis Nouembris 5

1. Natalis sancti Zachariae prophetae, patris beati Joannis Baptistae.
2. In Campania, sanctorum martyrum Faelicis presbiteri et Eusebii monachi.

1, 2. MU 1, 2, with the omission here in 2 of the placename (*Terracina*).

Sources: **1.** Dubois, *Martyrologe*, 336.

[6 November] Octauo Idus Nouembris 6 B

1. In Phrigia, sancti Attici.
2. Eodem die, sancti Leonardi confessoris.
3. Barcinone, natalis sancti Seueri episcopi et martyris, qui a Gothis clauo in capite est confossus.

1. MU 3.
2. The feast of Leonhard of Noblac, whose cult spread in the eleventh century, is in most *auctaria*, including Molanus.
3. Molanus was the first and only *auctarium* of MU to note the feast of Severus of Barcelona.

Sources: **1.** Dubois, *Martyrologe*, 336. **2.** *AASS*, Iun. VII, 655–6; Overgaauw, *Martyrologes*, 1042; *BiblSS*, iv, 958–9. **3.** *AASS*, Iun. VII, 656; *BiblSS*, xi, 988–9.

[7 November] C Septimo Idus Nouembris 7

1. In Frisia, depositio sancti Willibrordi, episcopi Traiecti inferioris et confessoris.
2. Apud Argentinam, sancti Florentii Scoti episcopi et confessoris cum sociis, Arbogasto, Theodato et Hidulpho.

1. MU 4, with an added reference here, as in Molanus, to the saint's see of Utrecht.
2. Molanus, which likewise attributes an Irish origin to the saint, is one of a few other *auctaria* to note the feast of Florentius and his asso-

159

ciates; Florentius is said to have been the seventh bishop of Strasbourg (Strassburg).

Sources: **1**. Dubois, *Martyrologe*, 337; *AASS*, Iun. VII, 659. **2**. *AASS*, Iun. VII, 658–9; Overgaauw, *Martyrologes*, 1045–6; *BiblSS*, v, 858.

[8 November] Sexto Idus Nouembris 8 D

1. Romae, uia Lauicana, natalis quatuor coronatorum Seueri, Seueriani, Carpophori et Uictorini.
2. In Hybernia, sanctorum Barrinni et Meltolini abbatum et confessorum.
3. Item, octaua omnium sanctorum.

² *Bartinni* MS; *Barrini* T; *Barrfind mórmaicc Áeda*, 'of Bairrfhionn, great son of Aodh', MO.

1. MU 2.
2. Bairrfhionn was patron of Aughkiletaun in the Kilkenny parish of Powerstown, barony of Gowran. Although there were several saints named Maol Tuile (Meltolinus), I know of none whose feast fell on this day.
3. Most *auctaria*, including Molanus, note the octave of All Saints.

Sources: **1**. Dubois, *Martyrologe*, 338. **2**. Stokes, *Martyrology*, 233; Stokes, *Martyrology of Gorman*, 214; *DIS*, 83. **3**. *AASS*, Iun. VII, 660–1; Overgaauw, *Martyrologes*, 1046.

[9 November] F Quinto Idus Nouembris 9

1. Apud Amasiam, natalis sancti Theodori martyris.
2. Eodem die, crucifixio imaginis Domini Nostri Jesu Christi a Judeis in Syria, ciuitate Beritho.

1. MU 1, with omission here of the precise location (*civitas Marmaritanorum*).
2. Molanus and a number of other *auctaria* likewise commemorate the feast of the *crucifixio imaginis*. The wording is that of Molanus.

Sources: **1**. Dubois, *Martyrologe*, 339. **2**. *AASS*, Iun. VII, 662–3.

[10 November] Quarto Idus Nouembris 10 F

1. Natale sanctorum martyrum Triphonis, Respicii et Nimphae uirginis.
2. In Britannia, sancti Justi episcopi et confessoris.
3. In Hybernia, sancti Edi episcopi et sancti Kerani abbatis.

3 *Edini* T; *Aed macc Bricc ... sab síl Chuinn*, 'Aodh son of Breac, champion of the descendants of Conn', MO.

1. Most *auctaria*, including Molanus, which accords it first place, notice here the feast of Triphon and his companions. Of the saint's companions, Respicius begins to be mentioned only in the eleventh century, and Nimpha is often commemorated separately.
2. Molanus, which uses the same wording, and the Cologne martyrologies also note this feast.
3. Aodh was remembered at three churches: Rahugh in the Westmeath barony of Moycashel, Killare in the Westmeath barony of Rathconrath, and a church on Slieve League, a mountain range in south-west Donegal. Ciarán was remembered at Tubbrid in the Tipperary barony of Iffa and Offa.

Sources: **1**. *AASS*, Iun. VII, 665–6; Overgaauw, *Martyrologes*, 1049–50; *BiblSS*, xii, 656–7. **3**. Stokes, *Martyrology*, 233; Stokes, *Martyrology of Gorman*, 214; *DIS*, 66–8, 173–4.

[11 November] G Tertio Idus Nouembris 11

1. In Galliis, ciuitate Turonis, natalis beati Martini episcopi et confessoris.
2. Lugduni, sancti Verani episcopi.
3. In Scythia, sancti Mennae martyris.

1, 2, 3. MU 1, 3, 2, with the omission here in 3 of the precise location in Scythia (*metropolis Frigiae Salutariae*).

Sources: **1, 2, 3**. Dubois, *Martyrologe*, 340.

[12 November] Pridie Idus Nouembris 12 A

1. Natalis beati Martini papae et martyris.
2. In portu Gandensi, depositio sancti Liuini episcopi et martyris, qui uenit ibidem ex Scotia.
3. Eodem die, sancti Renati episcopi et confessoris.
4. In Hybernia, sanctorum Cummeni et Fingeni abbatum et confessorum.

4   *Cumeni* T; *dom Chummain ... macc ... Fotae Fiachnai*, 'to my Cuimín Fada son of Fiachna', MO.

1. MU assigns this feast to 10 November. The switch in Molanus, which gives it first place, and other *auctaria*, is thought by Overgaauw to have been due to Franciscan influence.
2. Molanus, one of several *auctaria* to notice this feast, has the same text as MReg, except for the addition here of the reference to Scotic origins.
3. Although rarely attested in martyrologies, the feast of Renatus, supposed bishop of Angers, is otherwise in Grevenus and Molanus.
4. Cuimín Fada was associated with the church of Clonfert, a diocesan see in the Galway barony of Longford. There is otherwise no trace of a Fínghin on this day in Irish martyrologies, but the name may be for Fionnchadh, who was a bishop at Killarga in the Leitrim barony of Drumahaire.

Sources: **1**. Dubois, *Martyrologe*, 339; Overgaauw, *Martyrologes*, 1054. **2**. *AASS*, Iun. VII, 670–1; Overgaauw, *Martyrologes*, 1054; *BiblSS*, viii, 74. **3**. *AASS*, Iun. VII, 670–1; *BiblSS*, xi, 116–17. **4**. Stokes, *Martyrology*, 234; Stokes, *Martyrology of Gorman*, 216; *DIS*, 243–5, 335.

[13 November] B Idibus Nouembris 13

1. Turonis, natalis sancti Brictii episcopi et confessoris.
2. Albiniaci, sancti Kiliani Scoti episcopi et confessoris.
3. Ciuitate Toleto, sancti Eugenii episcopi et confessoris.

1. MU 4, with *Brictius* for Usuard's *Briccius*, as in Molanus.
2. The feast of Kilianus of Aubigny, who was reputedly Irish in origin, is found in several *auctaria* of MU, including Molanus. MReg added the word *Scoti*.
3. MU 5.

Sources: **1**. Dubois, *Martyrologe*, 341; *AASS*, Iun. VII, 671. **2**. *AASS*, Iun. VII, 672–3; Overgaauw, *Martyrologes*, 1055; *BiblSS*, iii, 1235–7. **3**. Dubois, *Martyrologe*, 341.

[14 November] Decimo Octauo Calendas Decembris 14 C

1. Alexandriae, sancti Serapionis martyris.
2. Apud Rothomagum, sancti Laurentii episcopi et confessoris in ciuitate Dublinensi in Hybernia, primus electus ad episcopatum, qui ab
Honorio papa in numerum sanctorum relatus fuit.

1. MU 2.
2. Molanus, together with several other *auctaria*, likewise commemorates Laurence's feast, but not with the same detail as here.

Sources: **1**. Dubois, *Martyrologe*, 342. **2**. *AASS*, Iun. VII, 675; *BiblSS*,
viii, 160–1; *DIS*, 403–5.

[15 November] D Decimo Septimo Calendas Decembris 15

1. Apud Nolam, Campaniae urbem, beati Faelicis episcopi et martyris.
2. Ipso die, Santonas ciuitate, depositio sancti Machuti Scoti.
3. In Austria, sancti Leopoldi eiusdem prouinciae marchionis et confessoris.

1. MU 1.
2. Molanus, which has much the same text, and several other *auctaria* notice the feast of Machutus. In the main text Molanus refers
to the saint under his other name of Maclovius, but glosses this as
Machuti. The description of the saint as *Scotus*, which is found in
no other martyrology, probably derives from his supposed association
with St Brendan.

3. Molanus, which uses the same words, is the only other *auctarium* to contain the feast of Leopold; the saint succeeded his father as margrave of Austria in 1095–6, and founded numerous abbeys, including Melk.

Sources: **1**. Dubois, *Martyrologe*, 342. **2**. *AASS*, Iun. VII, 677; Overgaauw, *Martyrologes*, 1057–8; *BiblSS*, viii, 461–3. **3**. *AASS*, Iun. VII, 677; *BiblSS*, vii, 1340–1.

[16 November] Calendas Decembris 16 E

1. Apud Viennam, depositio sancti Leoniani abbatis.
2. In Alemannia, sancti Othmari abbatis.
3. In Scotia, sanctae Margarethae reginae, sponsae regis Malcolmi tertii.

1. Only Molanus otherwise notes this feast, which is rarely attested outside Vienne. Leonianus is said to have originated in Pannonia before being brought as a prisoner to Gaul.
2. Most *auctaria*, including Molanus, commemorate the feast of Otmar of St Gall.
3. Molanus is otherwise the only *auctarium* to note here the feast of Margaret, queen of Scotland, who died in 1093. Her office Life is in the Breviary of Aberdeen, but the reference here to her husband Malcolm III is peculiar to MReg among the martyrologies. The queen's feast has already been noticed at 10 June.

Sources: **1**. *AASS*, Iun. VII, 679; *BiblSS*, vii, 1307–8. **2**. *AASS*, Iun. VII, 679; Overgaauw, *Martyrologes*, 1060; *BiblSS*, ix, 1300–1. **3**. *AASS*, Iun. VII, 679; *LegSS*, 290–3, 387; *BiblSS*, viii, 781–6.

[17 November] F Decimo Quinto Calendas Decembris 17

1. Apud Neocesaream Ponti, natalis beati Gregorii episcopi et confessoris.
2. Apud Alexandriam, beati Dionisii episcopi.
3. In Britannia, ciuitate Lincolniensi, beati Hugonis episcopi et confessoris.

1. Several *auctaria*, including Molanus which likewise places it first, notice the feast of Gregorius Thaumaturgus, bishop of Neocaesarea in Pontus.
2. MU 1.
3. Molanus and a number of other *auctaria* likewise commemorate Hugh of Lincoln, a Carthusian monk and bishop who died about 1200.

Sources: **1**. *AASS*, Iun. VII, 681–2; Overgaauw, *Martyrologes*, 1060; *BiblSS*, vii, 214–17. **2**. Dubois, *Martyrologe*, 343. **3**. *AASS*, Iun. VII, 681–2; Overgaauw, *Martyrologes*, 1061; Farmer, *Dictionary*, 99–100.

[18 November] Decimo Quarto Calendas Decembris 18 G

1. Apud Antiochiam, natalis sancti Romani martyris.
2. Apud Constantias inferioris Normanniae, beati Rumpharii, praefatae urbis episcopi et confessoris.
3. Insula Lirino, beati Anselmi abbatis et confessoris.

1. MU 1.
2. Grevenus and Molanus, which has much the same text as here, also notice the feast of this sixth-century bishop of Coutances in Normandy.
3. Otherwise only Molanus has the feast of Anselm, abbot of Lérins, on this day; the saint is supposed to have lived in the fifth century.

Sources: **1**. Dubois, *Martyrologe*, 343. **2**. *AASS*, Iun. VII, 684. **3**. *AASS*, Iun. VII, 684; *BiblSS*, ii, 21.

[19 November] A Decimo Tertio Calendas Decembris 19

1. Romae, natalis beati Pontiani papae et martyris.
2. Eodem die, uia Appia, natalis sancti Maximi presbiteri et martyris.
3. In Hybernia, sancti Ronani episcopi et confessoris.

---

3 *In Hibernia, sancti Romani episcopi et confessoris* COW; *Ronani* [corrected from *Romani*]) T; *maicc Beraig ... féil ... Rónáin*, 'feast of Rónán son of Bearach', MO.

1. MU 1 (20 November). Molanus and several other *auctaria* moved this feast from the following day in MU, because of possible Franciscan influence, according to Overgaauw.
2. MU 1, with the omission here of *via Appia*'s location in Rome.
3. This feast is placed on the previous day in MO and MG, and also in T and CSOW. Rónán was patron of Dromiskin in the barony and county of Louth.

Sources: **1**. Dubois, *Martyrologe*, 344; Overgaauw, *Martyrologes*, 1067. **2**. Dubois, *Martyrologe*, 344. **3**. Stokes, *Martyrology*, 235, Stokes, *Martyrology of Gorman*, 220; *DIS*, 538–40.

[20 November] Duodecimo Calendas Decembris 20 B

1. Cabilone, sancti Syluestri episcopi et confessoris.
2. In Scotia, sanctae Maxentiae regis Scotorum filiae et martyris.
3. In Anglia, sancti Eadmundi regis et martyris.

1. MU 2, but first in Molanus.
2. A small number of *auctaria*, but not Molanus, likewise commemorate Maxentia of Pont-Sainte-Maxence, who is here transformed into a 'Scota'. A late legend describes her as a disciple of St Patrick.
3. Most *auctaria*, including Molanus, commemorate here Edmund, king of England, who was killed by Vikings in 869.

Sources: **1**. Dubois, *Martyrologe*, 344. **2**. *AASS*, Iun. VII, 688–9; *BiblSS*, ix, 6. **3**. *AASS*, Iun. VII, 688–9; Farmer, *Dictionary*, 120–2.

[21 November] C Undecimo Calendas Decembris 21

1. Hierosolymis, praesentatio beati Dei genetricis Virginis Mariae in templo.
2. In Italia, monasterio Bobio, depositio sancti Columbani Scoti abbatis, qui innumerabilium extitit pater monachorum.

1. Present in almost all *auctaria*, including Molanus which places it first, this feast did not become popular until the late fourteenth century.

2. MU 4, with less abbreviation here than usual, and the addition of *Scoti*.

Sources: **1**. *AASS*, Iun. VII, 691; Overgaauw, *Martyrologes*, 1070–1.
2. Dubois, *Martyrologe*, 345.

[22 November] Decimo Calendas Decembris 22 D

1. Romae, natalis sanctae Ceciliae uirginis et martyris.
2. Item, Romae, sancti Mauri martyris.
3. Augustoduni, sancti Pragmatii episcopi et confessoris.

1, 2, 3. MU 1, 2, 3.

Sources: **1, 2, 3**. Dubois, *Martyrologe*, 346.

[23 November] E Nono Calendas Decembris 23

1. Natalis sancti Clementis episcopi et martyris, qui quartus a beato Petro pontificatum tenuit.
2. Eodem die, sanctae Faelicitatis matris septem filiorum martyrum.

1, 2. MU 1, 2.

Sources: **1, 2**. Dubois, *Martyrologe*, 346.

[24 November] Octauo Calendas Decembris 24 F

1. Romae, natalis beati Chrisogoni martyris.
2. Mediolani, sancti Prothasii episcopi et confessoris.
3. In Hybernia, sanctorum Kyannani et Meiclenini confessorum.

³ *Kyannani, Meiclenini* T; *La Cíanan Doim líacc ... Macc Lénéni*, 'With Cianán of Duleek, Mac Léinín', MO.

1. MU 1.
2. Molanus, which cites Surius as source, is the only other *auctarium* to notice here the feast of Protasius of Milan; the feast usually falls on 19 June, as above, together with that of Gervasius.

3. Cianán was patron of Duleek in the Meath barony of Lower Duleek, whereas Mac Léinín, better known as Colmán, was founder-patron of Cloyne, later a diocesan see, in the Cork barony of Imokilly.

Sources: **1**. Dubois, *Martyrologe*, 347. **2**. Dubois, *Martyrologe*, 344. **3**. Stokes, *Martyrology*, 236; Stokes, *Martyrology of Gorman*, 224; *DIS*, 166–7, 185–6.

[25 November] G Septimo Calendas Decembris 25

1. In Monte Sinai, sanctissimae Catharinae uirginis et martyris.
2. In Hybernia, sancti Finchue abbatis et confessoris.
3. Apud Aemiliam, sanctae Jucundae virginis.

² *Fincuanini* T; *Findchú ó Bríg gobann*, 'Fionnchú from Brigown', MO.

1. The cult of Catherine became popular after the arrival of her relics in the Benedictine monastery of Trinité-du-Mont, near Rouen, towards the middle of the eleventh century. Most *auctaria* locate her in Alexandria, but Molanus, which also places her first, likewise refers to Mount Sinai.
2. Fionnchú was patron of the church of Brigown in the Cork barony of Condons and Clangibbon.
3. Molanus, which uses the same words, is among the few *auctaria* to commemorate here the feast of Iucunda (Gioconda) of Reggio Emilia in Italy.

Sources: **1**. *AASS*, Iun. VII, 699–700; Overgaauw, *Martyrologes*, 1079; *BiblSS*, iii, 954–63. **2**. Stokes, *Martyrology*, 236; Stokes, *Martyrology of Gorman*, 226; *DIS*, 335–7. **3**. *AASS*, Iun. VII, 700; *BiblSS*, vi, 485.

[26 November] Sexto Calendas Decembris [26] A

1. Natalis beati Petri episcopi Alexandriae et martyris.
2. Eodem die, depositio sancti Conradi episcopi Constantiensis et confessoris.

1. MU 1 (25 November). As Overgaauw suggests, the switch of the feast to this day may have been due to Franciscan influence. Molanus has it in first place.

2. Molanus, which has much the same text, is among the few *auctaria* to notice the feast of Conrad, patron of Konstanz and Freiburg im Breisgau; the saint occupied the see from 934 until his death in 976. He was canonized in 1123.

Sources: **1**. Dubois, *Martyrologe*, 348; Overgaauw, *Martyrologes*, 1083. **2**. *AASS*, Iun. VII, 702–3; *BiblSS*, iv, 201.

[27 November] B Quinto Calendas Decembris 27

1. In Antiochia, sancti Basilei episcopi et sancti Saturnini martyris.
2. Eodem die, sanctae Ode uirginis, filiae regis Scotorum, quae apud Rhodium in Taxandria Brabantiae patrona quiescit.

1. Molanus, which uses the same words, is among the few *auctaria* to commemorate the feast of these two saints; they are otherwise found in MH on 21 November, in the company of Auxilius.
2. This feast is otherwise on this day in Molanus, which has much the same text, and Bruxellensis. According to her Life, which was written by an Augustinian canon, Oda of Sint-Oedenrode was the daughter of an Irish king.

Sources: **1**. *AASS*, Iun. VII, 704–5; *BiblSS*, ii, 948–9. **2**. *AASS*, Iun. VII, 704–5; *BiblSS*, ix, 1093–6; *DIS*, 518.

[28 November] Quarto Calendas Decembris 28 C

1. Apud Corinthum, natalis beati Sosthenes, discipuli sancti Pauli apostoli.
2. Romae, beati Gregorii papae, qui rexit Ecclesiam annis decem.

1. MU 1.
2. Molanus and almost all other *auctaria* commemorate here the feast of Pope Gregory III (†741) who showed great interest in the progress of the Church in northern Europe.

Sources: **1**. Dubois, *Martyrologe*, 349. **2**. *AASS*, Iun. VII, 707; Overgaauw, *Martyrologes*, 1085; Kelly, *Dictionary*, 88–9.

[29 November] D Tertio Calendas Decembris 29

1. Vigilia sancti Andreae apostoli.
2. Romae, natalis sancti Saturnini martyris et sancti Sysinnii diaconi.
3. Eodem die, obitus venerabilis Idae.

1, 2. MU 1, 2, with the omission here in 2 of the precise location (*via Salaria*).
3. This feast is also in Molanus, which identifies the saint as *de Niuella*, 'of Nivelles'. However, the feast of this saint normally fell on 10/11 December.

Sources: **1**. Dubois, *Martyrologe*, 350. **2**. *AASS*, Iun. VII, 710; *BiblSS*, vii, 640–1.

[30 November] E Pridie Calendas Decembris 30

1. In ciuitate Patras, natalis sancti Andreae apostoli.
2. Eodem die, passio sanctae Justinae uirginis et martyris.
3. Apud Santonas, sancti Troiani episcopi et confessoris.

1. MU 1, with omission here of the location of the *civitas* in the province of Achaia.
2. Molanus and most other *auctaria* notice here the feast of (the otherwise unknown) St Iustina.
3. MU 2.

Sources: **1, 3**. Dubois, *Martyrologe*, 351. **2**. *AASS*, Iun. VII, 710; Overgaauw, *Martyrologes*, 1089.

[1 December] F Calendis Decembris 1

1. Ciuitate Narnia, sancti Proculi presbiteri.
2. Ipso die, sancti Euasii episcopi et confessoris.
3. Item, translatio sancti Mauri martyris.

1. MU 6.

2. The feast of this saint, who was venerated in Casale Monferrato of Piedmont, found its way into a few *auctaria*, including Molanus, which has the same wording as MReg.

3. Several *auctaria*, including Molanus, commemorate the translation of the relics of Maurus, whose name, according to Overgaauw, may have been borrowed from an entry in MA.

Sources: **1**. Dubois, *Martyrologe*, 351. **2**. *AASS*, Iun. VII, 715–16; *BiblSS*, v, 375–6. **3**. *AASS*, Iun. VII, 715–16; Overgaauw, *Martyrologes*, 1091.

[2 December] Quarto Nonis Decembris 2 G

1. Romae, passio sanctae Bibianae martyris.
2. Item, sancti Pontiani martyris.
3. In India, ciuitate Cantana, obitus beati Francisci Zaiuerii.

1. MU 2.

2. Several *auctaria*, including Molanus, notice the feast of Pontianus of Rome, who may be the same as the third-century pope of that name.

3. Molanus likewise commemorates Francis Xavier, who died in the Far East in 1552.

Sources: **1**. Dubois, *Martyrologe*, 352. **2**. *AASS*, Iun. VII, 717. **3**. *AASS*, Iun. VII, 717.

[3 December] A Tertio Nonis Decembris 3

1. In Anglia, depositio sancti Birini episcopi Dorcestriensis.
2. Mediolani, sancti Mirocletis archiepiscopi et confessoris.
3. Eodem die, sancti Sophoniae prophetae.

1. Molanus, which has the same text, is among several *auctaria* that commemorate Birinus, founder and first bishop of the West Saxon see at Dorchester-on-Thames.

2. Molanus, which uses the same words, is the only other version of MU to notice the feast of Mirocles, an early fourth-century bishop of Milan.

3. Molanus is again the only other version of MU to notice the feast of the prophet Sophonias.

Sources: **1**. *AASS*, Iun. VII, 719; Overgaauw, *Martyrologes*, 1094–5; *EncASE*, 67. **2**. *AASS*, Iun. VII, 719; *BiblSS*, ix, 501–2. **3**. *AASS*, Iun. VII, 719; *BiblSS*, xi, 1280–2.

[4 December] Pridie Nonas Decembris 4 B

1. In Tuscia, sanctae Barbare uirginis et martyris.
2. In Anglia, sancti Osmundi episcopi et confessoris.
3. In Hybernia, sancti Berchani confessoris.
4. Apud Floriacum monasterium, translatio sancti Benedicti abbatis.

³   *Fer dá lethe* MO.

1. Although at 16 December in MU, Barbara is placed here in most *auctaria*, including Molanus.
2. Molanus, which has the same text, is the only other *auctarium* to notice the feast of Osmund, bishop of Salisbury; the saint died in 1099.
3. Bearchán, alias Fear Dá Leithe, was attached to the church of Clonsast in the Offaly barony of Coolestown.
4. Molanus, which uses the same words, is among a large number of *auctaria* that commemorate the feast of Benedict's translation to Fleury in France on 4 December.

Sources: **1**. Dubois, *Martyrologe*, 360; *AASS*, Iun. VII, 720–1; Overgaauw, *Martyrologes*, 1095–6. **2**. *AASS*, Iun. VII, 722; Farmer, *Dictionary*, 303–4. **3**. Stokes, *Martyrology*, 236; Stokes, *Martyrology of Gorman*, 224; *DIS*, 97–8. **4**. *AASS*, Iun. VII, 720–2.

[5 December] C Nonis Decembris 5

1. In Africa, apud Coloniam Thebestinam, natalis sanctae Crispinae martyris.
2. In Italia, sancti Dalmatii martyris.
3. Cappadociae, sancti Sabbae abbatis et confessoris.

¹   *In apud* (crossed out) *Africa* MS.

1, 2. MU 1, 2.
3. Molanus and several other *auctaria* likewise contain the feast of
Sabas who died in Jerusalem in 532.

Sources: **1, 2.** Dubois, *Martyrologe*, 354. **3.** *AASS*, Iun. VII, 723;
Overgaauw, *Martyrologes*, 1098; *BiblSS*, xi, 533–5.

[6 December] Octauo Idus Decembris 6 D

1. Natalis beati Nicolai episcopi Myreorum Lyciae.
2. In Hybernia, sancti Gabbani confessoris.
3. In Affrica, sanctarum Dionisiae, Datiuae et sociorum.

² *In Hibernia, sancti Gobbani confessoris* COW; *Gotpani* T; *Féil Gobbáin
... maccu ... Láme*, 'Feast of Gobán of Maca Láimhe', MO.

1, 3. MU 1, 2, with *Myreorum Lyciae* here, as in Molanus.
2. Gobán was patron of Killamery in the Kilkenny barony of Kells.

Sources: **1, 3.** Dubois, *Martyrologe*, 354; *AASS*, Iun. VII, 724. **2.**
Stokes, *Martyrology*, 250; Stokes, *Martyrology of Gorman*, 232; *DIS*,
367–8.

[7 December] E Septimo Idus Decembris 7

1. Mediolani, ordinatio beati Ambrosii episcopi.
2. Apud Alexandriam, natalis beati Agathonis martyris.
3. In pago Meldicensi, sanctae Pharae uirginis.
4. In Hybernia, sancti Butii confessoris.

⁴ *Butcii* MS; *Buti* T; *ó Mainistir ... Buiti*, 'Buithe from Monasterboice', MO.

1. Most *auctaria*, including Molanus, which has the same wording as
MReg, notice the feast of the ordination of Ambrosius of Milan on this
day. Molanus also places the feast first.
2, 3. MU 1, 3.
4. Buithe was founder-patron of Monasterboice in the Louth barony
of Ferrard. Grevenus (*In Hibernia, Boetii confessoris*) also notes the
feast.

Sources: **1**. *AASS*, Iun. VII, 727–8; Overgaauw, *Martyrologes*, 1100. **2, 3**. Dubois, *Martyrologe*, 355. **4**. Stokes, *Martyrology*, 250; Stokes, *Martyrology of Gorman*, 234; *AASS*, Iun. VII, 728; *DIS*, 131–3.

[8 December] Sexto Idus Decembris 8 F

1. Conceptio sacratissimae Virginis Mariae genetricis Dei et Domini nostri Jesu Christi.
2. Treuiris, sancti Eucharii episcopi et confessoris.
3. Eodem die, sancti Macarii martyris.
4. In Hybernia, sancti Nofraigii abbatis.

4 *Buaid nIchtbrichtáin,* 'The triumph of Ecgberht', MO.

1. This feast, which was proclaimed for the Church as a whole in 1439, is in almost all *auctaria*, but not in Molanus.
2. Several *auctaria*, including Molanus, likewise commemorate Eucharius, the first bishop of Trier, who is supposed to have lived towards the end of the third century.
3. MU 2, with the omission here of the location (*apud Alexandriam*).
4. The form of the name, which is Anglo-Saxon in origin (Ecgberht), is very corrupt in MReg.

Sources: **1**. *AASS*, Iun. VII, 729–30; Overgaauw, *Martyrologes*, 1102–3. **2**. *AASS*, Iun. VII, 729–30; Overgaauw, *Martyrologes*, 1103; *BiblSS*, v, 137–9. **3**. Dubois, *Martyrologe*, 355. **4**. Stokes, *Martyrology*, 250; Stokes, *Martyrology of Gorman*, 234.

[9 December] G Quinto Idus Decembris 9

1. Natalis sanctae Leocadiae uirginis.
2. In Affrica, sanctorum Petri, Successi et Bassiani martyrum.
3. In Hybernia, sancti Modimmoci abbatis et confessoris.

3 *Modimoci* T; *féil* mo *Dímóc* MO.

1. MU 1.

2. Molanus has the same spelling of *Bassiani* as here, unlike other *auctaria* which prefer the form *Bassini*.
3. Modhíomóg, alias Díomán, was attached to the church of Clonkeen in the Limerick barony of Clanwilliam.

Sources: **1**. Dubois, *Martyrologe*, 356. **2**. *AASS*, Iun. VII, 731–2; Overgaauw, *Martyrologes*, 1105. **3**. Stokes, *Martyrology*, 250; Stokes, *Martyrology of Gorman*, 236; *DIS*, 266–7.

[10 December] Quarto Idus Decembris 10 A

1. Romae, sancti Melchiadis papae et martyris.
2. Viennae, sancti Syndulphi episcopi et confessoris.
3. In Hispania, ciuitate Emerita, passio sanctae Eulaliae uirginis et martyris.

1   *Melchiades* MS.

1. Most *auctaria*, including Molanus, notice the feast of Melchiadis (†314), the first pope to occupy the Lateran palace.
2. Molanus is among the few *auctaria* to notice the feast of Sindulfus of Vienne, whose name also figures in the third recension of MA.
3. MU 2.

Sources: **1**. *AASS*, Iun. VII, 734–5; Overgaauw, *Martyrologes*, 1107; Kelly, *Dictionary*, 26–7. **2**. *AASS*, Iun. VII, 731–2; Dubois and Renaud, *Martyrologes*, 412; *BiblSS*, xi, 1212. **3**. Dubois, *Martyrologe*, 356.

[11 December] B Tertio Idus Decembris 11

1. Romae, natalis sancti Damasi papae.
2. Item, passio sancti Thrasonis martyris.
3. Item, Danielis prophetae.
4. In Hybernia, sancti Mosenochi confessoris.

4   *In Hibernia, sancti Mofenochi confessoris* COW; *Mosenoci* T; *lam Shenóc Mugnai*, 'with Mosheanóg of Ballaghmoon', MO.

1, 2. MU 1, 2.

175

3. Most *auctaria*, including Molanus, follow MA in locating the feast here; MU has it on 21 July.
4. Seanán, alias Mosheanóg, was venerated at Ballaghmoon, adjoining Dunmanoge (fort of Mosheanóg) in the Kildare barony of Kilkea and Moone.

Sources: **1, 2**. Dubois, *Martyrologe*, 357. **2**. *AASS*, Iun. VII, 736–7; Overgaauw, *Martyrologes*, 1109; Dubois and Renaud, *Martyrologes*, 413. **3**. Stokes, *Martyrology*, 251; Stokes, *Martyrology of Gorman*, 236; *DIS*, 499.

[12 December] Pridie Idus Decembris 12 C

1. Apud Narbonam, sancti Pauli episcopi et confessoris.
2. In pago Uimacensi, S. Uualerici episcopi et confessoris.
3. In Hybernia, sancti Finniani abbatis.

³ *In Hibernia, sancti Finniani doctoris* COW; *Finniani* T; *Findén ... Clúana Iraird*, 'Finnian of Clonard', MO.

1, 2. MU 1, 5. Valéry (Walericus) of Le Vimeu in Picardy is described here as a bishop, as against Usuard's *presbiter* and *abbas* of some *auctaria*.
3. Finnian was patron of Clonard in the Meath barony of Moyfenrath Upper. Both Bruxellensis (13 December) and Grevenus (*In Hybernia, Finniani abbatis et confessoris*) also note the feast in the same words.

Sources: **1, 2**. Dubois, *Martyrologe*, 357–8; *AASS*, Iun. VII, 738; Overgaauw, *Martyrologes*, 1110. **3**. Stokes, *Martyrology*, 251; Stokes, *Martyrology of Gorman*, 236; *AASS*, Iun. VII, 739, 741; *DIS*, 319–21.

[13 December] D Idibus Decembris 13

1. Apud Syracusas Ciciliae, natalis sanctae Luciae uirginis et martyris.
2. In pago Pontino, sancti Judoci confessoris, filii regis Scotiae peregrini.

1. MU 1.

2. Most *auctaria* note this feast, but the wording here is very close to Molanus which reads *Britonum* for MReg's *Scotiae*.

Sources: **1.** Dubois, *Martyrologe*, 358; *AASS*, Iun. VII, 740. **2.** *AASS*, Iun. VII, 742; Overgaauw, *Martyrologes*, 1112.

[14 December] Decimo Nono Calendas Januarii 14 E

1. Apud Antiochiam, natalis sanctorum martyrum Drusi, Zosimi et Theodori.
2. In Hybernia, sanctorum abbatum et confessorum Betani et Columbani.

[2] *In Hibernia, sancti Columbi* (*Columbani* O; corrected from *Columbani* C) *abbatis* COW; *Betani, Columbani* T; *Báethán Clúana ... Colomb ... Tíre*, 'Baodán of Cloney, Colum of Terryglass', MO.

1. MU 3 reads *In Antiochia.*
2. These saints belong more properly on the previous day. They were patrons respectively of Cloney in the Kildare parish of Kilberry, barony of Narragh and Reban West, and Terryglass in the Tipperary barony of Ormond Lower.

Sources: **1.** Dubois, *Martyrologe*, 359. **2.** Stokes, *Martyrology*, 251; Stokes, *Martyrology of Gorman*, 238; *DIS*, 85–6, 209–11.

[15 December] Decimo Octauo Calendas Januarii 15 F

1. Apud Affricam, beati Valeriani episcopi et confessoris.
2. In territorio Aurelianensi, sancti Maximi confessoris.
3. Eodem die, sancti Flannani episcopi et confessoris.

[3] *Flannani* T; *la féil Flaind ... Bennchuir*, 'with the feast of Flann of Bangor', MO.

1, 2. MU 1, 2. *Aurelianensi* agrees with Grevenus and Molanus, against Usuard's *Aurelianensium*. In 2, MReg, in common with some *auctaria*, reads *confessoris* for *abbatis* of MU.
3. MReg's particular interest in Flannán of Killaloe is evident from the inclusion at 26 August above of the (otherwise unattested) feast of

his translation, and from the apparent substitution here of his name for that of Flann, abbot of Bangor in Co. Down. In MO and MG, but not in MReg, Flannán's main feast falls on 18 December.
Sources: **1**, **2**. Dubois, *Martyrologe*, 359–60; *AASS*, Iun. VII, 744; Overgaauw, *Martyrologes*, 1114–15. **3**. Stokes, *Martyrology*, 252; Stokes, *Martyrology of Gorman*, 240; *DIS*, 346–9.

[16 December] Decimo Septimo Calendas Januarii 16 G

1. Trium puerorum Ananiae, Asariae et Misaelis.
2. Viennae, beati Adonis episcopi.
3. In Scotia, natalis beati Beani, primi episcopi Aberdonensis et confessoris.

1. MU 1.
2. Molanus and Grevenus likewise commemorate Ado of Vienne, whose martyrology was the principal source of MU.
3. Both Grevenus and Molanus likewise have the feast of Beanus, with each reading *Hibernia* for MReg's *Scotia*.

Sources: **1**. Dubois, *Martyrologe*, 360. **2**. *AASS*, Iun. VII, 748. **3**. *AASS*, Iun. VII, 748; *BiblSS*, ii, 986–7.

[17 December] A Decimo Sexto Calendas Januarii 17

1. Translatio sancti Ignatii episcopi et martyris.
2. Eodem die, beati Lazari, quem Dominus resuscitauit a mortuis.
3. Andaniae, transitus beatae Beggae uiduae.

3 *Beggsa* MS.

1, 2. MU 1, 2.
3. Most *auctaria*, including Molanus, notice the feast of Begga, sister of Gertrude of Nivelles, and first abbess of Andenne in the diocese of Liège.

Sources: **1, 2**. Dubois, *Martyrologe*, 360–1. **3**. *AASS*, Iun. VII, 749–50; Overgaauw, *Martyrologes*, 1118; *BiblSS*, ii, 1077–8.

[18 December] Decimo Quinto Calendas Januarii 18 B

1. Apud Macedoniam, ciuitate Philippis, sanctorum martyrum Rufi et Sozimi.
2. In Africa, passio sancti Moysetis martyris.
3. Turonis, sancti Gatiani episcopi et confessoris.

1, 2, 3. MU 1, 2, 3. In common with MReg, Molanus and a few other *auctaria* read *Gatiani* for the more usual *Catiani*.

Sources: **1, 2, 3**. Dubois, *Martyrologe*, 361; *AASS*, Iun. VII, 750; Overgaauw, *Martyrologes*, 1119.

[19 December] C Decimo Quarto Calendas Januarii [19]

1. Apud Aegyptum, beati Nemasii martyris.
2. Ciuitate Nicea, sancti Darii martyris.
3. In Hibernia, sanctae Samtannae uirginis.

[3] *In Hibernia, sancte Samtannae* [*Samtamne* O] *virginis* COW; *Samthannae* T; *Samthann Clúana Brónaig*, 'Samhthann of Clonbroney', MO.

1, 2. MU 1, 2.
3. Samhthann was attached to the church of Clonbroney in the Longford barony of Granard.

Sources: **1**. Dubois, *Martyrologe*, 361. **2**. Stokes, *Martyrology*, 252; Stokes, *Martyrology of Gorman*, 242; *DIS*, 545–6.

[20–31 December are missing from the manuscript, but see Appendix 2]

APPENDIX 1:
Necrology and Diary of the Regensburg *Schottenkloster*

(The necrological notices are usually added below the martyrological entries, whereas the diary notices are normally inserted at the bottom of the page. Punctuation and capitals of the manuscript are preserved here.)

FEBRUARY

1. Cras hodie (*crossed out*) in monasterio inferiori: statur pro choro et in Sarching – id est in die purificationis Beatae Virginis.
3. In die sancti Blasii in monasterio inferiori statur pro choro.
4. Hodie obiit Reverendus Pater f. Vitus Linex ex monasterio inferioris Altahae.
5. In die cinerum habetur anniuersarium Domini Ambrosii Strauß, canonici apud S. Joannem, qui contulit 50 fl. Monasterio, unde annuatim accipimus a quodam rustico 2 fl. cum dimidio ut in Registro habetur.
9. Anniversarium Domini Ambrosii in die cinerum.
11. Hodie obiit Reverendus Pater Godehardus Gober ex Nideraltaha.
23. In die sancti Mathiae celebrare debemus in parochiali ecclesia in Sarching.
24. Celebratur in Sarching.

MARCH

21. Hodie statur pro choro in Monasterio inferiori.
25. Hodie statur pro choro in Monasterio inferiori et in Sarching.
27. Nota quod sis festis et dominicis mobilibus viz dominica Reminiscere. oculi. Indica In quadragesima celebramus in ecclesia Sarching.

APRIL

2. Hodie obiit Reverendus pater Benedictus Kotpatius prior monasterii Inferioris Altahae.
3. Hodie obiit Reverendus pater f. Benedictus Katpatius prior monasterii Inferioris Altahae.
9. Hodie obiit F. Leopoldus Pollinger ex Nideraltah.
10. Hodie, obiit F. Leopoldus conuersus cognomine Pollinger ex Monasterio inferioris Altahae.
19. Hodie, obiit R. P. fr. Mathaeus Wagner ex monasterio Rottenburg.

MAY

1. Hodie (crossed out).
2. Hodie habentur uigilia Philippi Nynehalleri, qui aedificari fecit tabernaculum nostrum sacrum, et contulit monasterio pro semetipso 60 fl.
3. Hodie celebramus in ecclesia Sarching.
5. Hodie obiit R. P. Stephanus Haldmyger? ex monasterio Rottenburg?
14. Hodie obiit Hieronimus Abbas Sancti Emerani 1609.

JUNE

1. Hodie obiit Reverendus pater f. Cristophorus ex Monasterio S. Emmerani.
21. Hodie habentur uespere in Monasterio Superiori (Inferiori *crossed out*) ad S. Achatium.
22. Hodie celebratur in monasterio superiori sacrum ad S. Achatium.
27. Hodie habentur uespere in Monasterio inferiori pro fundatrice hora i (?).
28. Hodie habentur anniuersarium fundatricis in Monasterio inferiori.

JULY

1. Hodie obiit R. P. Marcus Carhe ex monasterio Rottenburg?.
4. Hodie celebratur offerendum? ad S. Udalricum in capella Sarching.
11. Hodie legitur sacrum de quodam defuncto.
18. Hodie obiit f. Georgius Purhober? laicus ex monasterio Rottenburg.
21. Hodie habentur vigiliae fundatricis in monasterio inferiori.

23 Hodie obiit R. P. Utilo Ryß ex monasterio inferiori Altae.
26. Hodie obiit R. P. Godeardus Fistfer? ex Nideraltiha et f. Adamus Hüfer ibidem.
Hodie habentur uigiliae nobilis D. Joannis a Stingelhame?

AUGUST

11. Hodie obiit R. P. Thomas Neagricolae ex Monasterio inferioris Altahae.
12. Hodie, debemus interesse primis uesperis in monasterio inferiori.
13. Hodie, debemus legere sacrum in monasterio inferiori de Sancta Katharina.
15. Hodie, stamus pro choro in monasterio inferiori et in Sarching.
16. Hodie, habentur uigiliae Domini Petri ad Sanctum Joannem quondam canonici.
21. Hodie, obiit f. Martinus Awer presbiter ex monasterio Rottenburg?.
22. Hodie obiit R. P. f. Henricus Mauritius Schopperus ex monasterio inferioris Altahae.

SEPTEMBER

4. Hodie obiit R. P. Abraham Horterich ex monasterio inferioris Altaha.
8. Hodie stamus pro choro in monasterio inferiori et in Sarching.

OCTOBER

1. Hodie obiit R. P. Casparus Primsperg? ex monasterio Rottenburg?.
4. Hodie obiit R. P. Joannes Casparus ex monasterio S. Emmerami.
5. Hodie obiit R. P. Andreas Zimmerman ex Nideraltaha, et R. P. Exuperantius Wagner ibidem.
8. Hodie debemus interesse primis uesperis et in die celebrare in monasterio inferiori.
13. Hodie obiit R. P. Thomas Renner ex monasterio Rottenburg. Item R. P. Joannes Hand Pherr? et Martinus Hag famulus ibidem.
15. Hodie in monasterio inferiori stamus pro choro.
28. Hodie tenemus celebrare sac[r]um in ecclesia parochiali in Sarching.
30. Hodie obiit f. Nicolaus Smeling ex monasterio inferioris Altae.

NOVEMBER

1. Hodie statur pro choro in monasterio inferiori et in Sarching.
2. Hodie statur pro choro in Sarching
7. Hodie obiit R. P. Joannes Walkherus abbas ad S. Jacobum in Erfurt.
25. Hodie statur pro choro in monasterio inferiori.
29. Hodie obiit R. P. Jacobus Gruener ex Monasterio inferioris Altaae.
30. Hodie tenemus celebrare in ecclesia parochiali in Sarching.

DECEMBER

2. Hodie obiit R. P. Georgius Miltaler prior inferioris Altahae.
6. Hodie in monasterio inferiori statur pro choro.

APPENDIX 2:
Irish Saints in CSOW and T
on Days now lacking in MReg

January

2. Muchullini [corrected from Muchilini], Manchini T/Manchine MO.[1]
10 Diarmetii T/Diarmait MO.
12. Langeni T/Laidcenn MO.
15. In Hybernia, sanctae Ydae virginis gloriosae in miraculis CS/Itae T/Íte MO.

December

23. In Hibernia, sancti Mothtionochi confessoris O/M'themnióc [MO].
29. In Hibernia, sancti Airarani [Atrerani corrected from Atrarani O] confessoris CSO/Airerán MO.[2]
30. In Hibernia, sancti Ailbae [Ailde O] confessoris CSO/Ailbe MO.

---

[1] T's 'Muchullini' derives erroneously from the placename 'Dísert Meic Ciluirn/Cuilinn' in the notes to MO.
[2] The W manuscript of Hermann's martyrology is defective here and on the following day.

APPENDIX 3:

Daily Excerpts from the Rule of St Benedict (20.1–4.12) and from the Pseudo-Bernard *Documenta pie seu religiose vivendi* (5–19.12)

(Dates are in *italic*; chapter numbers in roman)

January *20–31*:   Chapter 2.
February *1–6*:   Chapter 3; *7–23*: Chapter 4; *24–28*: Chapter 5.
March *1*:   Chapter 5; *2–4*: Chapter 6; *5–31*: Chapter 7.
April *1–2*:   Chapter 7; *3*: Chapter 8; *4*: Chapter 9; *5*: Chapter 10; *6*: Chapter 11; *7*: Chapter 12; *8*: Chapter 13; *9*: Chapter 14; *10*: Chapter 15; *11*: Chapter 16; *12*: Chapter 17; *13*: Chapter 18; *14*: Chapter 19; *15–16:* Chapter 20; *17–18*: Chapter 21; *19–21*: Chapter 22; *22–3*: Chapter 23; *24–6*: Chapter 24; *27*: Chapter 25; *28*: Chapter 27; *29*: Chapter 26; *30*: Chapter 27.
May *1–2*:   Chapter 27; *3–5*: Chapter 28; *6*: Chapter 29; *7*: Chapter 30; *8–14*: Chapter 31; *15–17*: Chapter 32; *18–21*: Chapter 33; *22–24*: Chapter 34; *25–31*: Chapter 35.
June *1–5*:   Chapter 36; *6*: Chapter 37; *7–11*: Chapter 38; *12–15*: Chapter 39; *16–19*: Chapter 40; *20–23*: Chapter 41; *24–7*: Chapter 42; *28–30*: Chapter 43.
July *1–3*:   Chapter 43; *4–7*: Chapter 44; *8–9*: Chapter 45; *10*: Chapter 46; *11–12*: Chapter 47; *13–24*: Chapter 48; *25–29*: Chapter 49; *30–31*: Chapter 50.
August *1*:   Chapter 51; *2–4*: Chapter 52; *5–16*: Chapter 53; *17–19*: Chapter 54; *20–31*: Chapter 55.
September *1–3*:   Chapter 55; *4–5*: Chapter 56; *6–10*: Chapter 57; *11–28*: Chapter 58; *29–30*: Chapter 59.

October *1–2*: Chapter 59; *3–6*: Chapter 60; *7–13*: Chapter 61; *14–17*: Chapter 62; *18–24*: Chapter 63; *25–31*: Chapter 64.

November *1–2*: Chapter 64; *3–10*: Chapter 65; *11–13*: Chapter 66; *14–16*: Chapter 67; *17–18*: Chapter 68; *19–20*: Chapter 69; *21–23*: Chapter 70; *24–26*: Chapter 71; *27–29*: Chapter 72; *30*: Chapter 73.

December *1–4*: Chapter 73; *5–19*: Extracts from a text on the spiritual life attributed to Bernard of Clairvaux, beginning *Si plene uis assequi quod intendis*, and ending *et pro quam modica delectatione tanta mala patuntur*.

BIBLIOGRAPHY

Anderson, A. O. and M. O. Anderson, ed. and trans., *Adomnan's Life of Columba* (Edinburgh, 1961; rev. edn Oxford, 1991).

Baumann, F. L., ed., *Necrologium Tegernsee / Necrologium monasterii s. Emmerami Ratisbonensis*, Monumenta Germaniae Historica; Necrologia Germanica 3 (Berlin, 1905), pp. 136–57, 301–34.

Best, R. I. and H. J. Lawlor, ed., *The Martyrology of Tallaght*, Henry Bradshaw Society 68 (London, 1931).

Bieler, L., ed., *The Patrician Texts in the Book of Armagh*, Scriptores Latini Hiberniae 10 (Dublin, 1979).

Borst, Arno, 'Die Sebaldslegenden in der mittelalterlichen Geschichte Nürnbergs', *Jahrbuch für fränkische Landesforschung* 26 (1966–7), 19–178.

Breatnach, P. A., ed., *Die Regensburger Schottenlegende – Libellus de fundacione ecclesie Consecrati Petri. Untersuchung und Textausgabe*, Münchener Beiträge zur Mediävistik und Renaissance-Forschung 27 (München, 1977).

Colgan, J., *Triadis, Thaumaturgae seu Divorum Patricii, Columbae et Brigidae, Trium Veteris et Maioris Scotiae seu Hiberniae, Sanctorum Insulae, Communium Patronorum Acta* (Louvain 1647; repr. Dublin, 1997).

De Gaiffier, B., 'Le Martyrologe de le Légendier d'Hermann Greven', *Analecta Bollandiana* 54 (1936), 316–58.

Delehaye, H. et al., eds, *Propylaeum ad Acta Sanctorum Decembris. Martyrologium Romanum*, Société des Bollandistes (Brussels, 1940).

Delehaye, H. and H. Quentin, *Acta Sanctorum Novembris, tom. II, Pars posterior. Commentarius perpetuus in Martyrologium Hieronymianum*, Société des Bollandistes (Brussels, 1931).

De Rossi J.-B. and L. Duchesne, eds, *Acta Sanctorum Novembris, tom. II, Pars prior. Praemissum est Martyrologium Hieronymianum*, Société des Bollandistes (Brussels, 1897, repr. 1971).

Dold, A., 'Wessobrunner Kalendarblätter irischen Ursprungs', *Archivalische Zeitschrift* 58 (1962), 11–33.

Dubois, J., ed., *Le martyrologe d'Usuard: texte et commentaire*, Subsidia Hagiographica 40 (Brussels, 1965).

Dubois, J. and G. Renaud, *Edition pratique des martyrologes de Béde de l'anonyme Lyonnais et de Florus* (Paris, 1976).

Du Sollier, J. B. See Sollerius.

Farmer, D. H., *The Oxford Dictionary of Saints* (Oxford, 1978).

Flachenecker, H., *Schottenklöster: Irische Benediktinerkonvente im hochmittelalterlichen Deutschland* (Paderborn, 1995).

Flachenecker, H., 'Monastischer Austausch und Inkulturation in süddeutschen Territorien. Die Schottenklöster im Hoch- und Spätmittelalter', *Blätter für deutsche Landesgeschichte* 137 (2001), 101–16.

Flachenecker, H., 'Benedictine Monks from Rosscarbery in Würzburg – a Remarkable Cultural Exchange in the Middle Ages', *Journal of the Cork Historical and Archaeological Society* 123 (2018), 5–18.

Forbes, A. P., *Kalendars of the Scottish Saints* (Edinburgh, 1872).

Freise, E., D. Geuenich and J. Wollasch, eds, *Das Martyrolog – Nekrolog von St Emmeram zu Regensburg*, Monumenta Germaniae Historica; Libri Memoriales et Necrologia; Nova Series III (Hannover, 1986).

Grosjean, P., 'Catalogus codicum hagiographicorum latinorum Dubliniensium', *Analecta Bollandiana* 46 (1928), 81–148.

Grosjean, P., 'Notes d'hagiographie celtique', *Analecta Bollandiana* 61 (1943), 91–107.

Grosjean, P., 'S. Patrice d'Irlande et quelques homonymes dans les anciens martyrologes', *The Journal of Ecclesiastical History* 1 (1950), 151–71.

Grosjean, P., 'Sur les éditions de l'Usuard de Jean Molanus', *Analecta Bollandiana* 70 (1952), 327–33.

Grosjean, P., 'La prétendue origine irlandaise du culte de S. Joseph en Occident', *Analecta Bollandiana* 72 (1954), 357–62.

Heist, W. W., ed., *Vitae sanctorum Hiberniae e codice olim Salmanticensi*, Subsidia Hagiographica 28 (Brussels,1965).

Hennig, J., 'St. Albert of Cashel: A Study in the History of Diocesan Episcopacy in Ireland', *Medieval Studies* 7 (1945), 21–39.

Hochholzer, E., 'Ein Martyrologfragment aus Regensburg mit irischen Heiligen aus dem 11. Jahrhundert', *Studien und Mitteilungen zur Geschichte des Benediktinerordens und seiner Zweige* 116 (2005), 33–64.

Kelly, J. N. D., *The Oxford Dictionary of Popes* (Oxford, 1986).

Levison, W., 'Das Werden der Ursula-Legende', *Bonner Jahrbücher* 132 (1927), 1–164.

Mac Airt, S. and G. Mac Niocaill, ed., *The Annals of Ulster (to A.D. 1131)* (Dublin, 1983).

Macquarrie, A., ed., *Legends of Scottish Saints; Readings, Hymns and Prayers for the Commemorations of Scottish Saints in the Aberdeen Breviary* (Dublin, 2012).

McCulloh, J. M., 'Herman the Lame's Martyrology through Four Centuries of Scholarship', *Analecta Bollandiana*, 104 (1986), 329–70.

McCulloh, J. M., 'Jewish Ritual Murder:William of Norwich, Thomas of Monmouth, and the Early Dissemination of the Myth', *Speculum* 72 (1997), 698–740.

Miesges, P., *Der Trierer Festkalender. Seine Entwicklung und seine Verwendung zu Urkundendatierungen. Ein Beitrag zur Heortologie und Chronologie des Mittelalters* (Trier, 1915).

Migne, J.-P., ed., *S. Bernardus, Clarae-vallensis abbas*, Patrologia Latina 184 (Paris, 1879).

Molanus, Ioannes, *Usuardi Martyrologium quo Romana Ecclesia ac Permultae Aliae Utuntur ... ac Aliunde* (Louvain, 1568; 1573, 1583).

Morsbach, P., *Ratisbona Sacra: Das Bistum Regensburg im Mittelalter.* Ausstellung im Diözeanmuseum Obermünster anlässlich des 1250 jährigen Jubiläums der kanonischen Errichtung des Bistums Regensburg durch Bonifatius 739–1989 (Munich, 1989).

Ó Riain, D., 'The Early History and Architecture of the Irish Benedictine Monasteries in Medieval Germany' (PhD thesis, University College Dublin, 2008).

Ó Riain, D., 'New Light on the History of St Mary's Priory, Rosscarbery', *Journal of the Cork Historical and Archaeological Society* 113 (2008), 56–68.

Ó Riain, D., 'The *Magnum Legendarium Austriacum*: A New Investigation of One of Medieval Europe's Richest Hagiographical Collections', *Analecta Bollandiana* 133 (2015), 87–165.

Ó Riain, D., 'The *Schottenklöster* and the Legacy of the Irish *sancti peregrini*', in W. Keller and D. Schlüter, eds, *'A Fantastic and Abstruse Latinity': Hiberno-Continental Cultural and Literary Interactions in the Middle Ages* (Münster, 2017), pp. 141–64.

191

Ó Riain, P., ed., *Corpus Genealogiarum Sanctorum Hiberniae* (Dublin, 1985).

Ó Riain, P., 'St. Abbán. The Genesis of an Irish Saint's Life', in D. E. Evans et al., ed., *Proceedings of the Seventh International Congress of Celtic Studies, Oxford, 1983* (Oxford, 1986), 159–70.

Ó Riain, P., *Anglo-Saxon Ireland: The Evidence of the Martyrology of Tallaght*, H. M. Chadwick Memorial Lectures, 3 (Cambridge, 1993).

Ó Riain, P., '*Codex Salmanticensis*: A Provenance *inter Anglos* or *inter Hibernos*?', in T. Barnard, D. Ó Cróinín and K. Simms, eds, *A Miracle of Learning. Essays in Honour of William O'Sullivan* (Aldershot, 1997), pp. 91–100.

Ó Riain, P., *Feastdays of the Saints: a History of Irish Martyrologies*, Subsidia Hagiographica 86 (Brussels, 2006).

Ó Riain, P., ed., *Beatha Ailbhe: The Life of Saint Ailbhe of Cashel and Emly*, Irish Texts Society 67 (London and Dublin, 2017).

Ó Riain, P., 'The Feast of the Dedication of St Peter's' (forthcoming).

Ó Riain, P., D. Ó Murchadha and K. Murray, eds, *Historical Dictionary of Gaelic Placenames: Foclóir Stairiúil Áitainmneacha na Gaeilge*, i, ii, iii, iv, v, Irish Texts Society (London, 2003, 2005, 2008, 2011, 2013).

Ó Riain-Raedel, D., 'Aspects of the Promotion of Irish Saints Cults in Medieval Germany', *Zeitschrift für celtische Philologie* 39 (1982), 220–34.

Ó Riain-Raedel, D., 'Twelfth- and Thirteenth-Century Irish Annals in Vienna', *Peritia* 2 (1983), 27–36.

Ó Riain-Raedel, D., 'Das Nekrolog der irischen Schottenklöster', *Beiträge zur Geschichte des Bistums Regensburg* 26 (1992), 7–119.

Ó Riain-Raedel, D., 'Irish Benedictine Monasteries on the Continent', in M. Browne and C. Ó Clabaigh, eds, *The Irish Benedictines: A History* (Dublin, 2005), pp. 25–63.

Ó Riain-Raedel, D., 'Cashel and Germany: the Documentary Evidence', in D. Bracken and D. Ó Riain-Raedel, eds, *Ireland and Europe in the Twelfth Century: Reform and Renewal* (Dublin, 2006), pp. 176–217.

Ó Riain-Raedel, D. and P. Ó Riain, 'Irish Saints in a Regensburg Litany', in E. Purcell, P. MacCotter, J. Nyhan and J. Sheehan, eds, *Clerics, Kings and Vikings: Essays on Medieval Ireland in Honour of Donnchadh Ó Corráin* (Dublin, 2015), pp. 55–66.

Overgaauw, E. A., *Martyrologes manuscrits des anciens diocèses d'Utrecht et de Liège*, 2 vols. (Hilversum, 1993).

Pfeil, B., *Die 'Vision des Tnugdalus Albers von Windberg'. Literatur- und Frömmigkeitsgeschichte im ausgehenden 12. Jahrhundert* (Frankfurt am Main, 1999).

Picard, J.-M. and Y. de Pontfarcy, *The Vision of Tnugdal* (Dublin, 1989).

Plummer, C., ed.,*Venerabilis Baedae Historiam Ecclesiasticum Gentis Anglorum Historiam Abbatum Epistolam ad Ecgbertum una cum Historia Abbatum Auctore Anonymo* (Oxford, 1896).

Price, L., *The Place-names of County Wicklow*, 7 vols (Dublin, 1945–67).

Quentin, H., *Les martyrologes historiques du Moyen Âge. Étude sur la formation du martyrologe romain* (Paris, 1908; repr. Spoleto, 2002).

Sollerius/Du Sollier, J. B., ed., *Martyrologium Usuardi Monachi ...*, in *Acta Sanctorum* Iunii VI/VII (Antwerp, 1714–17).

Stokes, W., ed., *Félire húi Gormáin: The Martyrology of Gorman*, Henry Bradshaw Society 9 (London, 1895).

Stokes, W., ed., *Féilire Oengusso Céli Dé: The Martyrology of Oengus the Culdee*, Henry Bradshaw Society 29 (London, 1905; repr. Dublin, 1984).

Watson, W. J., *The History of the Celtic Placenames of Scotland* (Edinburgh and London, 1926; repr. Dublin, 1986).

Weber, S., *Iren auf dem Kontinent. Das Leben des Marianus Scottus und die Anfänge der irischen «Schottenklöster»* (Heidelberg, 2010).

Wilson, H. A., *The Calendar of St. Willibrord*, Henry Bradshaw Society 55 (London, 1918; repr. Woodbridge, 1998).

INDEX SANCTORUM

Aaron, cum aliis in Britannia, Iun. 22[1]

Abbanus, ab. in Hibernia, Mar. 16[2], Oct. 27[2]

Abdon, Romae, Iul. 30[1]

Abilius, ep. Alexandriae, Feb. 22[2]

Abraham, patriarcha, Oct. 9[1]

Achatius, et socii, m., Iun. 22[3]

Achilleus, m. Romae, Mai. 12[1]

Acobranus, ab. in Hibernia, Ian. 28[3]

Adalbertus, ep. et m. Prussiae, Apr. 24[2]

Adbeus, ab. in Hibernia, Mai. 24[3]

Ado, ep. Viennae, Dec. 16[2]

Adrianus, m. apud Nicomediam, Sep. 8[2]

Aegidius, ab., Sep. 1[3]

Aenanus *see* Enanus

Aereranus, ab. in Hibernia, Aug. 11[3]

Aethelbertus, rex et m., Herefordiae, Mai. 20[4]

Agabus, propheta apud Antiochiam, Feb. 13[1]

Agapitus, in Phrigia, Mar. 24[1]

Agapitus, m. apud Praenestinam civitatem, Aug. 18[1]

Agatha, v. et m. Catanae, Feb. 5[1]

Agatho, m. apud Alexandriam, Dec. 7[2]

Aggaeus, propheta, Iul. 4[1]

Agnes, v. et m. Romae, Ian. 21[1], Ian. 23[1], Ian. 28[1]; translatio, Sep. 2[3]

Agricola, Bononiae, Nov. 4[1]

Ailbae, Dec. 30 (p. 185)

Ailbeus, in Hibernia, Sep. 12[2]

Ailitherus, ab. in Hibernia, Mai. 12[4]

Airaranus, Dec. 29 (p. 185)

Albanus, m., Iun. 21[3]

Albertus, pater ordinis Carmeli, Apr. 8[2]

Albinus, m. in Britannia, Iun. 22[1]

Albinus, m., translatio in Colonia, Apr. 16[1]

Aldelmus, ep. in Britannia, Mai. 26[1]

Aldetrudis, v., Feb. 25[2]

Alexander, ep., Mar. 18[1]

Alexander, m., Mai. 13[3]

Alexander, ep. apud Alexandriam, Feb. 26[1]

Alexander, m. Bergami/Pergami, Aug. 26[2]

Alexander, m. Lugduni Galliae, Apr. 24[1]

Alexander, m. Romae, Mai. 3[2]

Alexander, m. Niveduni, Iun. 6[3]

Alexius, Iul. 17[1]

Amantius, m. Niveduni, Iun. 6[3]

Ambrosius, ep. Caturcensis, in territorio Bituricensi, Oct. 16[1]

Ambrosius, ep. Mediolanensis, pro victoria, ipso invocato Feb. 21[2]; festum eius, Apr. 4[1]; conversio Augustini per eum, Mai. 5[2]; ordinatio eius, Dec. 7[1]

Amos, propheta, Mar. 31[1]

Anacletus (Cletus), papa et m. Romae, Apr. 26[2], Iul. 13[2]

Ananias, Ian. 25[2]

Ananias, Azarias et Misael, Dec. 16[1]

Anastasius, monachus et m. Romae, ad aquas Salvias/Salinias, Ian. 22[2]

Anastasius, papa, Romae, Apr. 27[1]

Anastasius, m. Salonae, Aug. 21[2]

Anatholius, ep. Constantinopolis, Iul. 3[3]

Andreas, apostolus, in civitate Patras, Nov. 30[1]; vigilia, Nov. 29[1]

Anicetus/Nicetus, papa et m. Romae, Apr. 17[1]

Anna, mater Mariae, Iul. 26[1]

Anna, prophetissa, Sep. 1[2]

Anselmus, ep. Cantuariae, Apr. 21[2]

Anselmus, ab. in Lirino, Nov. 18[3]

Anthymus, pr. Romae, Mai. 11[1]

Antoninus, m. Romae, Aug. 22[4]

Antonius, m. apud Alexandriam, Feb. 14[2]

Antonius, in Padua, Iun. 13[1]

Apollinaris, Aug. 23[2]

Apollinaris, ep. in Galliis, Oct. 5[2]

Apollinaris, ep. apud Ravennam, Iul. 23[1]

Apollonia, v. et m. apud Alexandriam, Feb. 9[1]

Apollonius, m. apud Aegyptum, Apr. 5[1]

Apollonius, m. apud Aegyptum, Iun. 5[1]

Apollonius, senator, Romae, Apr. 18[1]

Apostoli, discipulus eorum, Nov. 3[1]; divisio, Iul. 15[2]

Apuleus, m., Oct. 7[2]

Aquilinus, ep. Ebroicensis, Oct. 19[1]

Aquilinus, m. Romae, Feb. 4[2]

Arbogastus, apud Argentinam, Nov. 7[2]

Arca, egressio de, Apr. 28[2]

Aretas, m. Romae, Oct. 1[1]

Aretius, m. Romae, Iun. 4[2]

Artemius, ep. Arvernensis, Ian. 24[2]

Asaphus, ep. in Scotia, Mai. 1[3]

Ascensio *see* Iesus Christus

Athanasius, ep. Alexandriae, Mai. 2[1]

Atticus, in Phrigia, Nov. 6[1]

Auctor, ep. Metensis, Aug. 10[3]

Augulus, ep. et m. Augustae, in Britanniis, Feb. 7[1]

Augustinus, ep. in Africa, Aug. 28[1]; conversio eius, Mai. 5[2]; mater eius, Apr. 9[2]; translatio, Feb. 28[2]

Augustinus, primus ep. Anglorum, Mai. 26[2]

Aurea, v. Parisius, Oct. 4[2]

Auspicius, ep. Treverensis, Iul. 8[1]

Avitus, ep. Viennensis, Feb. 5[2]

Azarias/Asarias, cum Anania, Dec. 16[1]

Baithenus, ab., Iun. 9[3]

Baithenus, ab. in Hibernia, Feb. 19[3]

Baithenus, ab. in Hibernia, Iun. 18[3]

Baithenus, ab. in Hibernia, Oct. 6[3]
Baithenus, in Hibernia, Mai. 22[3]
Balbina, v. Romae, Oct. 6[2]
Barbara, v. et m. in Tuscia, Dec. 4[1]
Barnabas, apostolus, Iun. 11[1]
Barrinnus, ab. in Hibernia, Nov. 8[2]
Barrinnus, in Hibernia, Mai. 21[3]
Barrus, ep. in Hibernia, Sep. 25[3]
Bartholomeus, apostolus, Aug. 24[1]; vigilia, Aug. 23[1]
Basileus, ep. in Antiochia, Nov. 27[1]
Basileus, m. Romae, Mar. 2[2]
Basilides, m. Romae, Iun. 12[1]
Basilius, ep., Apr. 12[2]
Basilius Caesariensis, Mar. 9[2], Iun. 14[3]
Basilla, v. et m. Romae, Mai. 20[1]
Bassianus, m. in Africa, Dec. 9[2]
Bassus, m. apud Alexandriam, Feb. 14[2]
Bavo, in portu Ganda, Oct. 1[3]
Beanus, ab., in Hibernia, Aug. 8[3]
Beanus, ep. Aberdonensis, Dec. 16[3]
Becanus, ab., in Hibernia, Mai. 26[4]
Becanus, heremita, in Hibernia, Apr. 5[2]
Beda, venerabilis, pr., Mai. 10[3], 27[2]
Begga, vidua, transitus, Andaniae, Dec. 17[3]
Benedicta, v., Iun. 29[3]
Benedictus, ab., apud Cassinum, Feb. 10[1], Mar. 21[1], Mai. 22[2], Oct. 5[1]; translatio apud Floriacum, Iul. 11[1], Dec. 4[4]; octava, Iul. 18[3]
Benedictus, in pago Pictavensi, Oct. 23[2]
Benignus, in Thomis Scythiae, Apr. 3[1]
Beoanus, ep. in Hibernia, Mar. 8[3]

Berchanus, in Hibernia, Dec. 4[3]
Bernardinus Senensis, Mai. 20[3]
Bernardus, primus Clarauallis ab., Aug. 20[2]
Bertholdus, ordinis Carmeli, Mar. 29[2]
Bertinus, elevatio corporis, in monasterio Scithiu, Iun. 15[2]
Betanus, ab., in Hibernia, Dec. 14[2]
Betharius, ep., Carnoti, Aug. 2[3]
Bibiana, m. Romae, Dec. 2[1]
Bibianus see Vivianus
Birinus, ep. Dorcestriensis in Anglia, Dec. 3[1]
Blasius/Blastus, m. Romae, Iun. 17[1]
Blasius, ep. et m. apud Sebasten, Feb. 3[1]
Blathmethus, ep., Iul. 9[3]
Bonaventura, cardinalis et ep. Albanensis, Lugduni, Iul. 14[1]
Bonifacius, de Britanniis, Iun. 5[2], Sep. 28[2]
Bonifacius, diac. et m. apud Africam, Aug. 17[1]
Bonifacius, m., Mai. 14[1]
Bonifacius, papa, Romae, Oct. 25[2]
Bonifacius nonus, papa, Oct. 7[4]
Brainus, in Hibernia, Mai. 18[3]
Brechanus, ab. in Hibernia, Sep. 5[2]
Brendanus, ab. in Scotia, Mai. 16[1]
Brictius, ep. Turonensis, Nov. 13[1]
Brigida, v. in Scotia, Feb. 1[2]
Brigitta, vidua, Romae, Iul. 23[2]; canonizatio, Oct. 7[4]; mater Catharinae, Mar. 24[2]
Briocus, ep., Mai. 1[5]
Brocanus, ab., in Hibernia, Sep. 17[3]
Brocanus, in Hibernia, Iul. 8[4]

Bruno, ep. Coloniae, ad sanctum Pantaleonem, Oct. 11[3]

Bruno, institutor Carthusiensis, in Calabria, Oct. 6[1]

Burchardus, ep. apud civitatem Würzburg, Oct. 10[3]

Butius, in Hibernia, Dec. 7[4]

Cairech Dergan, Feb. 9[3]

Caius, apud Corinthum, Oct. 3[2]

Caius, papa, Romae, Apr. 22[1]

Calixtus, papa et m. Romae, Oct.14[1]

Caminus, ab. in Hibernia, Mar. 24[4]

Candida, v., Aug. 29[3]

Canicus (Kainnicus), ab. in Scotia/Hibernia, Oct. 11[1,4]

Cantianus, m., Aquileiae, Mai. 31[2]

Cantius, m., Aquileiae, Mai. 31[2]

Caprasius, m., Agenni, in Gallia, Oct. 20[1]

Carnachus, Mai. 16[2]

Carpophorus, Romae, via Lavicana, Nov. 8[1]

Cassianus, ep. Augustoduni, Aug. 5[3]

Castor, m. Tarsi Ciliciae, Apr. 27[2]

Castulus, m., Romae, Mar. 26[1]

Catharina, filia Brigittae, abbatissa, Mar. 24[2]

Catharina (Katarina) Senensis, Romae, Apr. 29[2]

Catharina, v. et m. in Monte Sinai, Nov. 25[1]

Cecilia, v. et m. Romae, Nov. 22[1]

Ceddeus, ep., Mar. 3[3]

Cele, ab. in Hibernia, Mar. 3[2]

Celerinus, diac. in Africa, Feb. 3[3]

Ceolfridus, ep. in Glasconia, Sep. 25[2]

Chlotildis (Crotildis), regina, Iun. 3[3]

Chorentinus, ep. in Britannia, Mai. 1[2]

Chrisantus, m. Romae, Oct. 25[1]

Chrisogonus, m. Romae, Nov. 24[1]

Christiana, filia regis Angliae, in civitate Tenremundae, Iul. 26[2]

Christina, v., Tyri, Iul. 24[2]

Christophorus, m., Iul. 25[2]

Ciprianus see Cyprianus

Ciriacus see Cyriacus

Cirillus see Cyrillus

Cirinus, m. Romae, Iun. 12[1]

Clara, v., in Assisio, Aug. 12[1]; translatio, Oct. 2[3]

Clarus, monachus et m. in Nortmannia, Iul. 18[2]

Clemens, ep., papa et m., Nov. 23[1]

Clemens, pr. apud Lugdunum Galliae, Ian. 20[3]

Cleophas, m., Sep. 25[1]

Cletus see Anacletus

Coemanus, ab., Iun. 12[2]

Coemgenus, ab.in Hibernia, Iun. 3[4]

Colmanus, ab. in Hibernia, Mar. 30[2], Mai. 24[3], Mai. 26[3], Sep. 26[3], Nov. 1[2]

Colmanus, ep. in Hibernia, Iul. 31[4]

Colmanus, in Hibernia, Mai. 21[3]

Colmannus, in Hibernia, Oct. 27[3]

Colomannus, m. apud Medelicam, Oct.13[3]

Columba, ab. in Hibernia, Sep. 7[3]

Columbanus, ab. in Hibernia, Dec. 14[2]

Columbanus, ab. in Hibernia, Feb. 18[3]

Columbanus, ep. in Hibernia, Aug. 8[2]

Columbanus, in Scotia, Ian. 22[3]

Columbanus Scotus, ab. Bobiensis, Nov. 21[2]

Columbus, ab. in Hibernia, Iun. 7[3]

Columkille, ab. in Scotia, Iun. 9[2]

Comgallus, ab., Mai. 9[3]

Comganus, ab. in Hibernia, Feb. 27[2]

Concordia, nutrix Hyppoliti et m. Romae, Aug. 13[1]

Conlaidus, ep. et m. in Hibernia, Mai. 2[2]

Conradus, ep. Constantiensis, Nov. 26[2]

Constantia, m. apud Nuceriam, Sep. 19[1]

Corbinianus, ep. Frisingae, Sep. 8[3]

Cordula, v. et m. Coloniae, Oct. 22[2]

Cormacus, ab. in Hibernia, Iun. 21[2]

Cormacus (Cormakus), in Hibernia, Feb. 17[3], Mai. 11[2]

Cornelius, papa, Romae, Sep. 14[2], Sep. 16[1]

Coronati, quatuor, Romae, Nov. 8[1]

Cosmas, eremita, Sep. 2[2]

Cosmas, m. apud civitatem Aegeam, Sep. 27[1]

Crato, m. Romae, Feb. 15[2]

Crescens (Cressens), discipulus Pauli in Galatia, Iun. 27[1]

Crescentia, m. in Sicilia (Cicilia), Iun. 15[1]

Crispus, apud Corinthum, Oct. 3[2]

Crispus, pr. Romae, Aug. 18[2]

Cronanus, ab. in Hibernia, Feb. 10[3]

Cronanus, ab. in Hibernia, Iun. 22[2], Nov. 1[2]

Cronanus (Cronanus), in Hibernia, Apr. 28[3]

Crotildis *see* Chlotildis

Crumenus, ab. in Hibernia, Iun. 28[3]

Crux, sancta, inventio, Mai. 3[1]; exaltatio, Sep. 14[1]

Cuacha, v. in Hibernia, Apr. 29[4]

Cuaeranus, ab. in Scotia, Sep. 9[2]

Cuangusus, ab. in Hibernia, Mar. 13[2]

Cuannus, ab. in Hibernia, Feb. 4[3]

Cuannus, ab. in Hibernia, Apr. 10[3]

Cuannanus, in Hibernia, Iul. 10[3]

Cuminus, ab. in Hibernia, Feb. 24[3]

Cummenus, ab. in Hibernia, Nov. 12[4]

Cummenus, in Hibernia, Mai. 29[3]

Curphinus, ab. in Hibernia, Iul. 20[3]

Cuthbertus, ep. Lindisfarnensis et anchorita, Mar. 20[1]

Cuthburga, v. et regina in Anglia, Aug. 31[2]

Cyprianus (Ciprianus), in Africa, Sep. 14[3]

Cyprianus, m., Sep. 26[1]

Cyriaca, m. Romae et translatio Vesaliae, Aug. 21[1]

Cyriacus (Ciriacus), diac. Romae, Mar. 16[1], Aug. 8[1]

Cyrillus (Cirillus), ep., Iul. 9[1]

Cyrillus, ep. Alexandriae, Ian. 28[2]

Daganus, ab. in Scotia, Sep. 13[3]

Daigeus mac Karill, ab. in Hibernia, Aug. 18[3]

Dalmatius, m. in Italia, Dec. 5[2]

Damasus, papa, Romae, Dec. 11[1]

Damianus, m. apud civitatem Aegeam, Sep. 27[1]

Damianus, miles et m., Feb. 12[3]

Daniel, propheta, Iul. 21[1], Dec. 11[3]

Daria, v. Romae, Oct. 25[1]

Darius, m. Niceae, Dec. 19[2]

Datianus, m. Romae, Iun. 4[2]

Dativa, in Africa, Dec. 6[3]

Dativus, m. in Africa, Feb. 12[2]

Dauid, ep. in Britannia, Mar. 1[2]

Demetria, v., Iun. 21[1]

Demetrus, in Africa, Aug. 14[3]

Desiderius, ep. apud Lugudunum, Feb. 11[1]

Desiderius, m. et ep. apud Lingones, Mai. 23[1]

Deusdedit, archiep. Cantuariae, Iul. 15[3]

Diarmetius, in Hibernia, Iul. 8[4]

Diarmetius, Ian. 10 (p. 185)

Diogenes, in Macedonia, Apr. 6[2]

Dionisia, in Africa, Dec. 6[3]

Dionisius, apud Armeniam minorem, Feb. 8[1]

Dionisius, ep., apud Alexandriam, Nov. 17[2]

Dionisius, ep., apud Corinthum, Apr. 8[2]

Dionisius, ep. et m. apud Parisium, Oct. 9[2]; inventio, Apr. 22[3]

Dionisius, m. in Phrigia, Sep. 20[1]

Dionisius Areopagita, Oct. 3[3]

Dioscorus, lector et m. in Aegypto, Mai. 18[1]

Dogranus, ab., in Hibernia, Nov. 4[3]

Domangartus, ab. in Hibernia, Mar. 24[4]

Dominica, v. et m. in Calabria, Iul. 5[3]

Dominicus, Bononiae, Aug. 3[1]; translatio, Mai. 25[4]

Dominus see Iesus Christus

Domitilla, v., Mai. 12[3]

Domitius (Domitianus), m. apud Syriam, Iul. 5[1]

Domnolus, ep. Viennensis, Iun. 16[1]

Donatianus, ep. in Africa, Sep. 6[1]

Donatilla, apud Africam, Iul. 30[3]

Donatus, ep. et m. apud Tusciam, Aug. 7[1]

Donatus, m., Mar. 1[1]

Donatus, m. apud Africam, Apr. 7[1]

Donatus, m. Romae, Feb. 4[2]

Donatus, m. in Sicilia, Oct. 5[1]

Donnanus, cum sociis in Hibernia, Apr. 16[2]

Dormientes, septem, apud Ephesum, Iul. 27[2]

Dorothea, m. apud Aquileiam, Sep. 3[2]

Dorothea, v. et m. apud Caesaream Cappadociae, Feb. 6[1]

Dorotheus, m. apud Nicomediam, Sep. 9[1], Oct. 24[2]

Droctoueus, ab., Parisius, Mar. 10[2]

Drusus, m. apud Antiochiam, Dec. 14[1]

Dubliteranus, in Hibernia, Mai. 15[2]

Dunchadus, ab. in Hibernia, Mai. 25[2]

Eadmundus, rex et m. in Anglia, Nov. 20[3]

Edbertus, ep. Lindisfarnensis in Anglia, Mai. 6[2]

Ediltrudis, regina et v. in Britannia, Iun. 23[2]

Eduardus, rex in Britannia, Mar. 18[2]

Edus, ep. in Hibernia, Nov. 10[2]

Egbertus, monachus et pr. in Hibernia, Apr. 24[2]

Eleazarus, apud Parisium, Sep. 27[2]

Eleutherius, papa et m., Mai. 26[4]

Eleutherius, m. cum aliis apud Nicomediam, Oct. 2[1]

Eleutherius, m. apud Parisium, Oct. 9[2]; inventio, Apr. 22[3]

Eliseus, propheta, Iun. 14[1]

Elphegus, ep. Cantuariensis et m. in Anglia, Apr. 19[2]

Emeramus, ep. et m., apud Ratisbonam, Sep. 22[1]

Emerentiana, v. et m. Romae, Ian. 23[1]

Emilianus, apud Armeniam minorem, Feb. 8[1]

Emilius, m. in Sardinia, Mai. 28[2]

Enanus (Aenanus), ab. in Hibernia, Aug. 19[4], Sep. 18[3]

Enanus (Aenanus), ab. in Hibernia, Ian. 30[4]

Enna, ab. in Hibernia, Mar. 21[2]

Enodius, ep. Ticini, Iul. 17[2]

Eoganus, ep. in Hibernia, Aug. 23[4]

Eolangus, ab., in Hibernia, Sep. 5[2]

Epimachus, m. Romae, Mai. 10[2]

Epiphanius, m. et ep. apud Africam, Apr. 7[1]

Erasma, m. apud Aquileiam, Sep. 3[2]

Erasmus, ep. et m. in Campania, Iun. 2[1]

Erconualdus, ep. Londoniae in Britannia, Apr. 30[2]

Ercus (Hercus), ab. in Hibernia, Mai. 12[4]

Erhardus, ep., translatio eius, Oct. 8[2], octava translationis eius, Oct. 15[4]

Ericus, rex et m. in Suecia, Mai. 18[2]

Ermenilda, v. in Britannia, Feb. 13[3]

Esdras, propheta, Iul. 13[1]

Etbinus, ab. Nectensis in Britannia, Oct. 19[3]

Etchenus, ep. in Hibernia, Feb. 11[2]

Ethelburga, v. et abbatissa in Anglia, Oct. 11[2]

Eucharius, ep. Treverensis, Dec. 8[2]

Eugenius, ep. Toletanus, Nov. 13[3]

Eulalia, v. in Hispania, Feb. 12[1]

Eulalia, v. et m. Emeritae in Hispania, Dec. 10[3]

Eulogius, pr. et m. Cordubae, Sep. 20[3]

Euphemia, m., apud Aquileiam, Sep. 3[2]

Euphronius, ep. Turonensis, Aug. 4[2]

Eusebius, ep. Romae, Sep. 26[2]

Eusebius, monachus et m. in Campania, Nov. 5[2]

Eusebius, pr. Romae, Aug. 14[2]

Eustachius, ep. apud Antiochiam, Iul. 16[1]

Eustachius, ep. Turonensis, Sep. 19[3]

Eustachius, pr., in Syria, Oct. 12[2]

Eutichius, m., Apr. 9[1]

Eutichius, m. in Sicilia, Oct. 5[1]

Evagrius, Thomis Scythiae, Apr. 3[1]

Evaristus, papa et m. Romae, Oct. 26[2]

Evasius, ep., Dec. 1[2]

Eventius, apud Ticinum, Sep. 12[1]

Eventius, ep. Viennensis, Feb. 3[2]

Eventius, m. Romae, Mai. 3[2]

Exuperantia, v., Trecas, Apr. 26[3]

Exuperius, ep. Tolosanus, Sep. 28[1]

Ezechiel, propheta, Apr. 10[1]

Fabianus, papa et m., Romae, Ian. 20[1]

Fabius, m. apud Caesaream, Iul. 31[1]

Fachneanus, ab. in Hibernia, Aug. 14[4]

Faelanus, ab. in Hibernia, Iun. 20[2]

Falbus, ab. in Hibernia, Mar. 22[2]

Fancha, v. in Hibernia, Ian. 21[3]

Fara *see* Phara

Faustinus, m. Brixiae, Feb. 15[1]

Faustus, m. in Hispaniis, Oct.13[1]

Fechenus, ab. in Hibernia, Ian. 20[4]

Felicianus, ep. et m. apud Mindam, Oct. 20[2]

Felicianus, m. Romae, Iun. 9[1]

Felicissimus, m. apud Africam, Oct. 26[1]

Felicitas, Iul. 10[1]

Felicitas, apud Carthaginem, Mar. 7[2]

Felicitas, mater septem martyrum, Nov. 23[2]

Felicula, v. Romae, Iun. 13[2]

Felix, Feb. 26[2]

Felix, in Africa, Mar. 23[1]

Felix, ep. in Anglia, Mar. 8[1]

Felix, ep. et m. apud Nolam, Nov. 15[1]

Felix, m. apud Nuceriam, Sep. 19[1]

Felix, m. Mediolani, Iul. 12[1]

Felix, m. in Sardinia, Mai. 28[2]

Felix, papa et m., Mar. 31[2]

Felix, papa et m. Romae, Mai. 30[1]

Felix, papa et m. Romae, Iul. 29[1]

Felix, pr. Romae, Aug. 30[1]

Felix, pr. et m., in Campania, Nov. 5[2]

Felix IV, papa Romae, Oct. 12[1]

Ferdachrichus, ep. in Hibernia, Oct. 6[3]

Fergnanus, ab. in Hibernia, Mar. 2[2]

Fergnanus, in Hibernia, Oct. 11[5]

Ferndrudis (Frindrudis?), v., Iun. 30[3]

Fiachra, in Hibernia, Apr. 29[4]

Fiachraig, ab. in Hibernia, Feb. 8[4]

Fiachraigus, ab. in Hibernia, Oct.12[4]

Fiacrius, filius regis Scotorum, in territorio Meldensi, Aug. 30[3]

Fiacus, ab., in Hibernia, Oct. 12[4]

Filia Feradaigae, v. in Hibernia, Mar. 23[2]

Filiae Baitae, in Hibernia, Mar. 29[4]

Filiae Comgalli, in Scotia, Ian. 22[3]

Filii Felicitatis, septem, Iul. 10[1]

Filii Israel, transitus per Mare Rubrum, Mar. 25[4]

Filii Nesani, in Hibernia, Mar. 15[2]

Finanus, ab.in Hibernia, Apr. 7[2]

Finbarrus, ab. in Hibernia, Iul. 4[2]

Finbarrus, ep. in Scotia, Sep. 10[3]

Finchua, ab.in Hibernia, Nov. 25[2]

Fingenus, ab. in Hibernia, Nov. 12[4]

Finnanus, ep. in Scotia, Feb. 16[3]

Finnanus, in Hibernia, Mar. 16[2]

Finnianus, ab., in Hibernia, Dec. 12[3]

Finnicha, v. in Hibernia, Feb. 2[3]

Finsiga, v. in Hibernia, Oct.13[2]

Fintanus, ab. in Hibernia, Feb. 21[3]

Fintanus, ab. in Hibernia, Oct. 10[4]

Fintanus, pr. in Scotia, Feb. 17[1]

Fintanus Meeldubius, in Hibernia, Oct. 20[3]

Flannanus, ep. in Hibernia, Dec. 15[3]; translatio, Aug. 26[3]

Florentinus, ep. Treverensis et m., Oct. 17[3]

Florentius, ep. in pago Pictavensi, Sep. 22[2]

Florentius, Hoya Insula, translatio vel natalis, Iun. 27[2]

Florentius Scotus, ep. apud Argentinam, Nov. 7[2]

Foillanus, ep., Fossis, Oct. 31[2]

Fortchernus, in Hibernia, Oct. 11[5]

Fortunatus, Feb. 26[2]

Fortunatus, m. Romae, via Aurelia, Oct. 15[1]

Franciscus, in Assisio, Oct. 3[1]

Franciscus de Paula, Apr. 2[1]

Franciscus Zaiverius, in India, Dec. 2[3]

Fredesuuida, v. Oxoniae, Oct. 19[2]

Frindrudis *see* Femdrudis

Fronto, ab. apud Alexandriam, Apr. 14[2]

Furudranus, ab. in Hibernia, Iun. 18[3]

Gabbanus, in Hibernia, Dec. 6[2]

Gabinus, m. Romae, Feb. 19[1]

Gallicanus, m. in Alexandria, Iun. 25[1]

Gallus, pr. in Alemannia, Oct. 16[2]; translatio, Oct. 23[3]; discipulus eius, Sep. 6[2]

Garbanus, ab. in Hibernia, Iul. 9[2]

Gatianus, ep. Turonensis, Dec. 18[3]

Gaudentia, v. Romae, Aug. 30[2]

Gaudentius, ep. apud Novariam, Aug. 3[2]

Gedeon, propheta, Sep. 1[1]

Genesius, m. Romae, Aug. 25[1]

Genovefa, Parisiis, translatio, Oct. 28[2]

Georgius, m., Apr. 24[1]

Gerardus, ep. et m. in Hungaria, Sep. 24[3]

Gerlandus, ep. Agrigentini in Sicilia, Feb. 25[3]

Germanus, ep. in Africa, Sep. 6[1]

Germanus, ep. Romae et Coloniae, Apr. 16[1]

Germanus, Parisiis, transitus, Mai. 28[1]

Gervasius, m. Mediolani, Iun. 19[1]

Gildas, ab. in Britannia, Ian. 29[2]

Glyceria, m., Mai. 13[2]

Godricus, eremita in Anglia, Mai. 21[2]

Gordianus, m. Romae, Mai. 10[2]

Gregorius, ep. apud Neocaesaream Ponti, Nov. 17[1]

Gorgonius, m. apud Nicomediam, Sep. 9[1]

Gregorius, frater Basilii, ep. apud Nissenam, Mar. 9[2]

Gregorius, pontifex, doctor et apostolus Anglorum, Romae, Mar. 12[1]; ordinatio, Sep. 4[3]

Gregorius secundus, papa, Romae, Feb. 13[2]

Gregorius tertius, papa, Romae, Nov. 28[2]

Gregorius Nazianzenus, Mar. 29[3], Mai. 9[1]

Gregorius Traiectaensis, ep., Aug. 25[3]

Grimbaldus, ab. in Britannia, Iul. 8[2]

Gullielmus, m. in Anglia, civitate Rossensi, Mai. 23[2]

Gunthildis, v., ex Scotia, Sep. 28[3]

Guthlacus, anchorita in Britannia, Apr. 11[2]

Hadrianus, Nicomediae, cum aliis viginti tribus, Mar. 4[2]

Helena, v., Autisiodori, Mai. 22[1]

Helena, v., in Suetia, Iul. 30[2]

Hemerius, ep. Cremonae, Iun. 16[2]

Heraclius, m. in Carthagine, Mar. 11[1]

Hercanus, ep. in Hibernia, Nov. 2[3]

Herculanus, m. Romae, in Portu, Sep. 5[1]

Hercus see Ercus

Hermenigildus, m. in Hispania, Apr. 13[1]

Hermes, Romae, Apr. 1[1], Aug. 28[2]

Heron, discipulus Ignatii, ep. Antiochensis, Oct. 17[1]

Hiacinthus, m., Iul. 3[2]

Hiacinthus, m., Romae, Sep. 11[1]

Hidulphus, apud Argentinam, Nov. 7[2]

Hidulphus, ep. Treverensis, Iul. 11[3]

Hieronimus, ep. Papiae, Iul. 22[2]

Hieronimus, pr. apud Bethleem, Sep. 30[2]

Hilarion, Oct. 21[1]

Hilarion Iunior, Mar. 28[3]

Hilarius, papa, Romae, Sep. 10[1]

Hiltrudis, v., Laetiis, Sep. 27[3]

Hippolytus see Hyppolytus

Hirlaheus?, Mai. 19[3]

Honoratus, ep. Ambianensis, Mai. 16[3]

Honorina, v. et m. in Nortmannia, Feb. 27[3]

Honorius, Cantuariae in Anglia, Sep. 30[3]

Huasunachus, ep., Mai. 16[2]

Hubertus, ep. Tungrensis, Mai. 30[3]

Hugo, discipulus, Iun. 3[2]

Hugo, ep. Lincolniensis, Nov. 17[3]

Hyppolitus (Hippolytus), al. Nonus, et socii, Aug. 22[3]

Hyppolitus, m. apud Antiochiam, Ian. 30[1]

Hyppolitus, m. Romae, Aug. 13[1]

Iacobus, apostolus, Iul. 25[1]; octava, Aug. 1[3]; vigilia, Iul. 24[1]

Iacobus, apostolus, Mai. 1[1]; vigilia, Apr. 30[4]

Iacobus, Hierosolimis, Ian. 30[2]

Iacobus, ep., Nisibi, Iul. 15[1]

Ianuarius, m. in Hispaniis, Oct. 13[1]

Ida, venerabilis, Nov. 29[3]

Iesus Christus (Dominus), ascensio, Mai. 5[1], Feb. 24[1]; conceptio Matris, Dec. 8[1]; crucifixio imaginis, Nov. 9[2]; evangelium, Mar. 17[1]; in ulnis Symeonis, Oct. 8[1]; latus perforatus, Mar. 15[1]; passio, Mar. 25[1]; praecursor, Iun. 24[1], Sep. 24[1]; resurrectio, Mar. 27[1]; resuscitatio Lazari, Dec. 17[2]; sepultura, Oct. 22[1]; transfiguratio, Aug. 6[1]

Iesus Naue, propheta, Sep. 1[1]

Ignatius, ep. Antiochenus et m., Feb. 1[1]; discipulus eius, Oct. 17[1]; translatio, Dec. 17[1]

Ignatius Loiola, Romae, Iul. 31[3]

Ioachim, pater Mariae, Mar. 20[2]

Ioannes, apostolus et evangelista, dormitio, Iun. 24[2]; dedicatio, Romae, Mai. 6[1]; discipulus eius, Ian. 26[1]; frater eius, Iul. 24[1]

Ioannes, ep. Eboracensis, Beverlaci, Mai. 7[2]

Ioannes, m. apud Nicomediam, Sep. 7[1]

Ioannes, m. Romae, Iun. 26[1]

Ioannes, papa et m., Mai. 27[3]

Ioannes, patriarcha Alexandriae, Ian. 23[3]

Ioannes, pr. Romae, Aug. 18[2]

Ioannes Baptista, Praecursor Domini, nativitas, Iun. 24[1]; vigilia, Iun. 23[1]; octava, Iul. 1[1]; conceptio, Sep. 24[1]; decollatio, Aug. 29[1]; inventio capitis, Feb. 24[2]; pater eius, Nov. 5[1]

Ioannes Chrisostomus, ep. Constantinopolitanus, Ian. 27[1]

Iob, propheta, Mai. 10[1]

Ioel, propheta, Iul. 13[1]

Ioseph, diac., Antiochiae, Feb. 15[3]

Ioseph, sponsus Mariae, Mar. 19[1]

Iosephus Iustus, Iul. 20[1]

Iouinus, ab., Iun. 1[2]

Iouinus, m. Romae, Mar. 2[1]

Iovita, v. et m. Brixiae, Feb. 15[1]

Isaac, immolatio, Mar. 25[3]

Isaac(us), Mai. 30[2]

Isaias, propheta, Iul. 6[2]

Ismael, m., Iun. 16[3]

Iucunda, v., apud Aemiliam, Nov. 25[3]

Iudas (Thadeus), apostolus, Oct. 28[1]; vigilia, Oct. 27[3]

Iudocus, filius regis Scotiae, Dec. 13[2]

Iulia, v., Trecas, Iul. 21[3]

Iulianus, cum aliis in Britannia, Iun. 22[1]

Iulianus, in Africa, Feb. 19[2]

Iulianus, m. apud Aegyptum, Feb. 16[2]

Iulianus, m. Alexandriae, Feb. 27[1]

Iulianus, m. in Syria, Aug. 12[2]

Iulius, Ian. 31[1]

Iulius, papa, Romae, Apr. 12[1]

Iulius, senator et m. Romae, Aug. 19[1]

Iuonis, ep., translatio, Iun. 10[3]

Iuonis, pr., in Britannia Minori, Mai. 19[2]; translatio, Oct. 27[1]

Iusta, v. et m. in Hispania, Iul. 19[1]

Iustina, v., Sep. 26[1]

Iustina, v. apud Paduam, Oct. 7[3]

Iustina, v. et m., Nov. 30[2]

Iustinus, philosophus et m., Apr. 13[2]

Iustus, apud Treverim, Iul. 14[2]

Iustus, ep. in Britannia, Nov. 10[2]

Iustus, ep. Lugdunensis, Sep. 2[1]

Iustus, m., Nov. 2[2]

Iuvenalis, ep., Mai. 3[4]

Iuventius (Viventius), m. Romae, Iun. 1[3]

Kainnicus see Canicus

Karthagius, in Hibernia, Mar. 5[2]

Karthagus, ep. in Hibernia, Mai. 14[3]

Katarina see Catharina

Kenelmus, rex Merciorum et m., Iul. 17[3]

Kenfelaidus, ab. in Hibernia, Apr. 8[3]

Keranus, ab. in Hibernia, Nov. 10[3]

Kiaranus, in Hibernia, Mar. 5[2]

Kilianus Scotus, ep., Albiniaci, Nov. 13[2]

Kilianus, Scotus et m., in civitate Herbipoli, Iul. 8[3]

Kunigundis, v. Bambergae, Mar. 3[1]

Kyannanus, in Hibernia, Nov. 24[3]

Kyara, v. in Hibernia, Oct. 16[3]

Lachteanus, ab. in Hibernia, Mar. 19[3]

Maelaithgen, in Hibernia, Iun. 6[2]

Maenachus, ep. in Hibernia, Oct. 17[2]

Maglastianus, ep. in Hibernia, Ian. 30[3]

Maglorius, ep. in Britannia, Oct. 24[1]

Magnus, ab., Scotus et discipulus Galli, Sep. 6[2]

Magnus, m. Romae, Feb. 4[2]

Maicnisi, ep. in Hibernia, Sep. 4[2]

Maicnisus, ab. in Hibernia, Iun. 13[3]

Maida, v. in Hibernia, Ian. 27[4]. *See note at day*

Maimbodus, m. in Burgundia, Ian. 23[4]

Maknolochus, ep. in Hibernia, Ian. 29[3]

Manchinus, Ian. 2 (p. 185)

Mangoldus filius Gugonis, dux et m. in Hoyo, Feb. 9[4]

Mannea, uxor Marcellini, Tomis, Aug. 27[2]

Mansuetus, ep. in Africa, Sep. 6[1]

Manuel, m., Iun. 16[3]

Marcellinus, ep. Ebredunensis, Apr. 20[2]

Marcellinus, m., Romae, Iun. 2[3]

Marcellinus, pontifex, Romae, Apr. 26[2]

Marcellinus, tribunus et m., Tomis, Aug. 27[2]

Marcellus, m., Iun. 29[2]

Marcellus, m., Sep. 4[4]

Marcellus, m., Oct. 7[2]

Marcellus, in Africa, Feb. 19[2]

Marcianus, in Aegypto, Oct. 4[1]

Marcus, in Aegypto, Oct. 4[1]

Marcus, evangelista, apud Alexandriam, Apr. 25[2]; translatio, Ian. 31[1]

Marcus, m., Romae, Iun. 18[1]

Marcus, papa, Romae. via Appia, Oct. 7[1]

Margareta, regina in Scotia, Iun. 10[2], Nov. 16[3]

Margareta, v. et m. apud Antiochiam, Iul. 12[3]

Maria Aegyptiaca, in Palestina, Apr. 2[2]

Maria Magdalena, Iul. 22[1]; translatio, Mar. 19[2]

Maria Virgo, mater Christi, nativitas, Sep. 8[1]; octava nativitatis, Sep. 15[3]; annunciatio, Mar. 25[2]; assumptio, Aug. 15[1]; vigilia assumptionis, Aug. 14[1]; octava assumptionis, Aug. 22[1]; conceptio, Dec. 8[1]; presentatio in templo, Nov. 21[1]; purificatio, Feb. 2[1]; visitatio, Iul. 2[1]; sponsa Iosephi, Mar. 19[1]; filia Ioachim, Mar. 20[2]; filia Annae, Iul. 26[1]; Maria ad martyres, Mai. 13[1]; Maria ad nives, Aug. 5[1]

Marianus, in territorio Bituricensi, Aug. 19[2]

Marnanus, archidiac., Mar. 2[3]

Martellianus, m. Romae, Iun. 18[1]

Martha, soror Lazari, Iul. 29[2]

Martialis, m. in Hispaniis, Oct. 13[1]

Martianus, ep., Syracusis, Iun. 14[2]

Martianus, m. apud Aegyptum, Apr. 5[1]; Iun. 5[1]

Martinus, ep. Treverensis et m., Iul. 19[2]

Martinus, ep. Turonensis, Nov. 11[1]

Martinus, papa et m., Nov. 12[1]

Martyres, anonimi

    Mm. innumeres, apud Nicomediam, Oct. 2[1]

Mm., apud Tyrum, Feb. 20[1]

vii, Nov. 23[2]; diacones, Iun. 6[1]

ix, Mai. 17[1]

ix, in Africa, Mar. 22[1]

xii, fratres, Beneventi, Sep. 1[4]

xiii, apud Africam, Apr. 7[1]

xx, in Carthagine, Mar. 11[1]

xxiii, Sep. 8[2]

xxvii, Feb. 26[2]

xlii, in Perside, Mar. 10[1]

xl, milites, apud Sebasten, Mar. 9[1]

xlvii, Romae, Mar. 14[1]

lxxix, Feb. 21[1]

clxv, milites, Romae, Aug. 10[2]

ccc, apud Carthaginem, Aug. 24[2]

v m., Feb. 16[2]

xi m., vv. et mm., in Colonia, Oct. 21[2]

Marus, ep. Treverensis, Ian. 26[2]

Maternus, ep. Treverensis, Sep. 14[4]

Matheus, apostolus, Sep. 21[1]; vigilia, Sep. 20[2]

Mathias ep., Hierosolimitanus, Ian. 30[2]

Mathias, apostolus, Feb. 24[1]

Maurus, m. Romae, Nov. 22[2]

Maurus, m., translatio, Dec. 1[3]

Maxentia, filia regis Scotorum et m., in Scotia, Nov. 20[2]

Maxima, v. apud Africam, Iul. 30[3]

Maximinus, ep. Treverensis, Mai. 29[1], Sep. 12[3]

Maximus, in Africa, Feb. 18[2]

Maximus, in territorio Aurelianensi, Dec. 15[2]

Maximus, in Cordula (Corduba), Apr. 15[1]

Maximus, in Padua, Aug. 2[2]

Maximus, m. Romae, via Appia, Apr. 14[1]

Maximus, pr. et m. Romae, via Appia, Nov. 19[2]

Mecculinus, ep. in Hibernia, Sep. 7[2]

Medochus, ab. in Hibernia, Apr. 11[3]

Medranus, ab. in Hibernia, Iun. 8[2]

Meicleninus, in Hibernia, Nov. 24[3]

Melanphnus, Scotus, ab., Ian. 31[4]

Melchiades, papa et m. Romae, Dec. 10[1]

Melinus, ep. in Hibernia, Feb. 6[3]

Mellanus, ab. in Hibernia, Feb. 7[2]

Melruanus, ab. in Hibernia, Iul. 7[2]

Melrubus, ab. in Hibernia, Apr. 21[2]

Meltolinus, ab. in Hibernia, Nov. 8[2]

Mennas, m. in Scythia, Nov. 11[3]

Mernok, ab. in Hibernia, Aug. 18[3]

Methodius, ep., Sep. 18[1]

Michael, archangelus, in Monte Gargano, Mai. 8[2], Sep. 29[1]

Milburgis, filia regis Merciorum et v., Feb. 23[2]

Miletus, ep. Treverensis, Sep. 19[2]

Milites see Martyres

Mirocles/Mirocletes, archiep. Mediolani, Dec. 3[2]

Misael, cum Anania, Dec. 16[1]

Moacra, ab. in Hibernia, Mar. 3[2]

Mobi, ab. in Hibernia, Oct.12[4]

Mobiu, ab. in Hibernia, Iul. 22[3]

Mochaemochus, ab. in Hibernia, Mar. 13[2]

Mochellokus, in Hibernia, Mar. 26[3]

Mocholmok, ab. in Hibernia, Iul. 26[3]

Mochonnus, ep. in Hibernia, Mar. 8[3]

Mochritochus, in Hibernia, Mai. 11[2]

Mochtanus, ab., in Hibernia, Mar. 24[4], Aug. 19[4]

Mochtanus, in Hibernia, Mar. 18[3]. *See note at day*

Mochteus, ab., in Hibernia, Aug. 12[3]. *See note at day*

Mochua, Mai. 4[2]

Mochua, ab. in Hibernia, Mar. 30[2]

Mochua, ab. in Hibernia, Iun. 23[3]

Mochua, ab. in Hibernia, Aug. 6[3]

Mochuaroch, ab. in Hibernia, Feb. 9[2]

Modesta, m. in Nicomedia, Mar. 13[1]

Modestus, m. in Sicilia, Iun. 15[1]

Modimmocus, ab. in Hibernia, Dec. 9[3]

Modomnoc(h)us, ab. in Hibernia, Feb. 13[4], Mai. 18[3]

Mogoboc(h)us, ab., Feb. 11[3]

Moinennus, ab. in Hibernia, Mar. 1[3]

Molacus, in Hibernia, Ian. 20[4]

Moliva, v., Feb. 18[4]

Molivus, ab., in Hibernia, Iun. 25[2]

Mollingus, ep. in Hibernia, Iun. 17[3]

Molua, ab. in Hibernia, Aug. 4[3]

Momedochus, ab., in Hibernia, Mar. 23[2], Mai. 18[3], Aug. 13[2]

Monennus, ab. in Hibernia, Sep. 16[3]

Monica, mater sancti Augustini, Mai. 4[1]; translatio, Apr. 9[2]

Moninna, v., in Hibernia, Iul. 6[5]

Mono, m. in Nassonia, Oct. 18[2]

Montanus, monachus, translatio, Mai. 17[2]

Morandus, discipulus Hugonis, Iun. 3[2]

Mosenochus, in Hibernia, Dec. 11[4]

Mosilochus, in Hibernia, Iul. 13[3], 26[3]

Mothionochus, Dec. 23 (p. 185)

Moyses, m. in Africa, Dec. 18[2]

Muchullinus, Ian. 2 (p. 185)

Mundius, ab. in Hibernia, Oct. 21[3]

Murconus, ab. in Hibernia, Iun. 8[2]

Myron, m., Aug. 17[2]

Nabor, m. Mediolani, Iul. 12[1]

Nabor, m. Romae, Iun. 12[1]

Narcissus, ep. Hierosolimitanus, Oct. 29[1]

Nathi, ab. in Hibernia, Aug. 9[3]

Nazarius, m. Mediolani, Iul. 28[2]

Nazarius, m. Romae, Iun. 12[1]

Nechtanus, in Hibernia, Mai. 1[4]

Nemesius, m. apud Aegyptum, Dec. 19[1]

Nemesius, in Cypro, Feb. 20[2]

Neotus, sacerdos in Anglia, Iul. 31[2]

Nereus, m. Romae, Mai. 12[1]

Nesena, v. in Hibernia, Sep. 28[4]

Nessanus, ab. in Hibernia, Iul. 26[3]

Nessanus *see* Senanus

Nicander (Nicanor), m. apud Aegyptum, Apr. 5[1]; Iun. 5[1]

Nicander, m., Romae, Iun. 17[1]

Nicephorus, patriarcha Constantinopolis, Iun. 2[2]

Nicetius, ep. Treverensis, Oct. 1[5]

Nicetus *see* Anicetus

Nicolaus, ep. Myrorum Lyciae, Dec. 6[1]

Nicolaus, ep. Tolentini, Sep. 10[2]

Nicomedes, pr. et m. Romae, Sep. 15[1]

Nimpha, v. et m., Nov. 10[1]

Ninianus, ep. Candidae Casae, Sep. 16[2]

Noe, egressio de Arca, Apr. 28[2]

Nofraigius, ab. in Hibernia, Dec. 8[4]

Nonus *see* Hyppolytus

Novatus, Romae, Iun. 20[1]

Numerianus, archiep. Treverensis, Iul. 5[2]

Oda, filia regis Scotorum et v., apud Rhodium, Nov. 27[2]

Odger *see* Otgerus

Odo, ep. in Anglia, Feb. 7[4]

Odranus, in Hibernia, Oct. 27[3]

Oenimus, in Hibernia, Oct. 2[4]. *See note at day*

Oenus, in Hibernia, Ian. 20[4]

Olimpiades, in Cordula (Corduba), Apr. 15[1]

Omnes fideles defuncti, Nov. 2[1]

Omnes sancti, Nov. 1[1]; vigilia, Oct. 31[1]; Octava, Nov. 8[3]

Onesimus, Feb. 16[1]

Optatus, ep. Autisiodorensis, Aug. 31[3]

Oseas, propheta, Iul. 4[1]

Osmundus, ep. in Anglia, Dec. 4[2]

Osualdus, rex Anglorum, Aug. 5[2]

Osuinus, m. in Anglia, Aug. 20[3]

Oswaldus, ep. Vuigorniensis in Britannia, Oct. 15[2]

Otgerus (Odger), diac. in Britannia, Sep. 10[4]

Othmarus, ab. in Alemannia, Nov. 16[2]

Pachomius, Mai. 14[2]

Palladius, m., Iul. 6[4]

Pamphilus, m. Romae, Sep. 21[2]

Pancratius, m. Romae, Mai. 12[2]

Pantaleon, m. apud Nicomediam, Iul. 27[1]; Monasterium sancti Pantaleonis, in Colonia, Apr. 16[1]

Parmenas, diac., Philippis, Ian. 23[2]

Pascasius, Viennae, Feb. 22[3]

Pastor, m. Nicomediae, Mar. 29[1]

Paternus, ep. in civitate Constanciae, Sep. 23[3]

Patiens, ep. Lugdunensis, Sep. 11[2]

Patricia, m. in Nicomedia, Mar. 13[1]

Patricius, ab. in Hibernia, Aug. 24[3]

Patricius, ep. in Scotia, Mar. 17[1]

Paula, in Bethleem, Ian. 27[2]

Paulinus, ep. Eboracensis, Oct. 10[2]

Paulinus, ep. Treverensis, Aug. 31[1]

Paulus, apostolus, Romae, Iun. 29[1]; vigilia, Iun. 28[1]; octava, Iul. 6[1]; commemoratio, Iun. 30[1]; discipuli/socii eius, Ian. 24[1], Feb. 16[1], Iun. 27[1], Oct. 18[1], Nov. 28[1]

Paulus, diac. et m. Cordubae, Iul. 20[2]

Paulus, ep. Constantinopolitanus et m., Iun. 7[1]; translatio, Mai. 21[1]

Paulus, ep. Leonensis in Britannia minori, Mar. 12[3]

Paulus, ep. Narbonensis, Dec. 12[1]

Paulus, m. Romae, Iun. 26[1]

Pelagius, m., Legionensi civitate, Iun. 26[2]

Perfectus, pr. et m. Romae, Apr. 18[2]

Perpetua, Carthaginis, Mar. 7[2]

Perpetua, conjunx Petri apostoli, Nov. 4[2]

Perseveranda, v., Iun. 26[3]

Petronilla, Romae, Mai. 31[1]

Petrus, apostolus, Feb. 1[1], 2[2], Ian. 29[1], Mar. 14[1], Nov. 23[1]; natalis,

Ricardus, ep. Cicestriensis in Anglia, Apr. 3[2]

Robertus, ab. in Anglia, Iun. 7[2]

Robertus, in territorio Lingonensi, Apr. 29[3]

Rochus, in Galliis, Aug. 16[2]

Rogatianus, pr. et m. apud Africam, Oct. 26[1]

Rogatus, monachus et m. apud Africam, Aug. 17[1]

Romanus, ab. in Galliis, Mai. 22[2]

Romanus, ab. in territorio Lugdunensi, Feb. 28[1]

Romanus, m. apud Antiochiam, Nov. 18[1]

Romanus, miles Romae, Aug. 9[2]

Romanus Melodus, Oct. 1[4]

Ronanus, ep. in Hibernia, Feb. 7[3]

Ronanus, ep., in Hibernia, Nov. 19[3]

Ronanus, in Hibernia, Apr. 30[3]

Ronanus, in Hibernia, Mai. 22[3]

Ruadanus, ab. in Hibernia, Apr. 15[3]

Rufina, v., Iul. 10[2]

Rufina, v. et m. in Hispaniis, Iul. 19[1]

Rufus, m., apud Capuam, Aug. 27[1]

Rufus, m. Phillipis, Dec. 18[1]

Rumoldus, m. Mechliniae, Iul. 1[2]

Rumpharius, ep., apud Constantias inferioris Normanniae, Nov. 18[2]

Rupertus, ep. Vormatiae, Mar. 27[2]

Rusticus, ep. Arvernensis, Sep. 24[2]

Rusticus, ep. Treverensis, Oct. 14[3]

Rusticus, m., apud Parisium, Oct. 9[2]; inventio, Apr. 22[3]

Sabbas, ab. Cappadociae, Dec. 5[3]

Sabelis, m., Iun. 16[3]

Sabina, m. Romae, Aug. 29[2]

Saloma, Oct. 22[1]

Salomon, m. Cordubae, Feb. 8[2]

Sampson, ep. in Britannia minori, Iul. 28[1]

Samtanna, v. in Hibernia, Dec. 19[3]

Samuel, propheta, Aug. 20[1]

Sanctanus, ep. in Hibernia, Mai. 9[2]

Saranus, in Hibernia, Mai. 15[2]

Saturninus, Oct. 14[2]

Saturninus, in Africa, Mar. 22[1]

Saturninus, m. in Africa, Mai. 24[2]

Saturninus, m. in Antiochia, Nov. 27[1]

Saturninus, pr. et m. in Africa, Feb. 12[2]

Saturninus, m. Romae, Nov. 29[2]

Scetha, v. in Hibernia, Sep. 7[3]

Scholastica, apud Cassinum, Feb. 10[1]; translatio, Iul. 11[1]

Scira, v., in Hibernia, Mar. 24[3]

Sebaldus, Norinbergae, Aug. 19[3]

Sebastianus, apud Armeniam minorem, Feb. 8[1]

Sebastianus, m. Romae, apud Catacumbas, Ian. 20[2]

Secunda, v., Iul. 10[2]

Secunda, apud Africam, Iul. 30[3]

Segenus, ab. in Hibernia, Aug. 12[3]

Senachus, in Hibernia, Aug. 21[3]

Senanus, ep. in Hibernia, Mar. 1[3], Mar. 8[2]

Senanus (Nessanus?), ab. in Hibernia, Sep. 2[4]

Sennen, Romae, Iul. 30[1]

Septimus, monachus et m. apud Africam, Aug. 17[1]

Serapia, Romae, Sep. 3[1]

Serapion, ep. Antiochiae, Oct. 30[1]

Serapion, m. in Alexandria, Nov. 14[1]

Servatius, ep., Mai. 14[4]

Servilianus, m. Romae, Apr. 20[1]
Severianus, m., Sep. 9[3]
Severianus, Romae, via Lavicana, Nov. 8[1]
Severinus, ep. et m. Coloniae, Oct. 23[1]
Severus, ep. et m. Barcinonae, Nov. 6[3]
Severus, m. in Nicomedia, Oct. 24[2]
Severus, Romae, via Lavicana, Nov. 8[1]
Sexburga, vidua in Britannia, Iul. 6[3]
Sidonius, ep. Arvernensis, Aug. 23[3]
Sillenus, ab. in Scotia, Sep. 11[3]
Silvanus, in Africa, Feb. 18[2]
Silverius, papa, Romae, Iun. 19[2]
Silvester, ep. Cabilonensis, Nov. 20[1]
Silvester, in Reomago, Apr. 15[2]
Simeon *see* Symeon
Simon, monachus in Sicilia, Iul. 27[3]
Simon Cananeus, apostolus, Oct. 28[1]; vigilia, Oct. 27[4]
Simphorosa, cum septem filiis, via Tiburtina, Iul. 18[1]
Simplicius, ep. Augustodunensis, Iun. 24[3]
Sinchillus, ab. in Hibernia, Mar. 26[2]
Sinchillus, ab. in Hibernia, Iun. 25[2]
Sindulphus, ep. Viennensis, Dec. 10[2]
Sinecha, v. in Hibernia, Oct. 5[3]
Sisinnius, diac., Romae, Nov. 29[2]
Sixtus, papa, Romae, Mar. 28[1]
Sixtus, papa et m. Romae, Apr. 6[1]
Sixtus, papa et m. Romae, via Appia, Aug. 6[2]

Smaragdus, m. Romae, Aug. 8[1]
Socrates, in Britanniis, Sep. 17[2]
Sophonias, propheta, Dec. 3[3]
Sophronius, patriarcha Hierosolimorum, Mar. 11[2]
Sosimus, m. in Carthagine, Mar. 11[1]
Sosthenes, apud Corinthum, Nov. 28[1]
Sother, papa et m., Apr. 22[2]
Sother, v. et m. Romae, Feb. 6[2]
Sozimus *see* Zosimus
Spiritus sanctus, adventus, Hierosolymis, Mai. 15[1]
Stanislaus, ep. et m., Mai. 7[2]
Stephanus, in Aegypto, Apr. 1[2]
Stephanus, in Britanniis, Sep. 17[2]
Stephanus, papa Romae, in cimiterio Calixti, Aug. 2[1]
Stephanus, m. Tarsi Ciliciae, Apr. 27[2]
Stephanus, protom., Hierosolymis, Aug. 3[1]
Stephanus, thaumaturgus, Mar. 28[2]
Successus, m. in Africa, Dec. 9[2]
Sulpicius, m. Romae, Apr. 20[1]
Susanna, v. Romae, Aug. 11[2]
Swithunus, ep. Vintoniensis, Iul. 2[2]
Sy- *see also* Si-
Symeon, Oct. 8[1]
Symeon, ep. Hierosolymitanus et m., Feb. 18[1]
Symeon, ep. et m. in Perside, Apr. 21[1]
Symeon, monachus, Treveris, Iun. 1[1]
Syrus, apud Ticinum, Sep. 12[1]

Tassachus, ep. in Hibernia, Apr. 14[3]
Tecla, m. apud Aquileiam, Sep. 3[2]

Tecla, v., Sep. 23[2]

Tellius, ab. in Hibernia, Iun. 25[2]

Ternochus, in Hibernia, Feb. 8[3]

Thadeus *see* Iudas

Tharsitius, acolytus et m., Romae, Aug. 15[2]

Theobaldus, Iun. 30[2]

Theodarius, ep. Viennensis, Oct. 29[2]

Theodatus, apud Argentinam, Nov. 7[2]

Theodgarus, in Dania, Oct. 30[2]

Theodolus, m., Romae, Mai. 3[2]

Theodora, m., Romae, Apr. 1[1]

Theodorus, m., apud Amasiam, Nov. 9[1]

Theodorus, m. apud Antiochiam, Dec. 14[1]

Theodorus, ep. Papiae, Mai. 20[2]

Thomas, apostolus, translatio, Iul. 3[1]

Thomas, ep. Herefordensis, Oct. 2[2]

Thomas, ep. et m., translatio apud Cantuariam, Iul. 7[1]

Thomas Aquinas, doctor, Mar. 7[1]

Thrason, m., Dec. 11[2]

Tiburtius, m. Romae, Aug. 11[1]

Tiburtius, m. Romae, via Appia, Apr. 14[1]

Tigernachus, ep. in Hibernia, Apr. 4[2]

Timotheus, Aug. 23[2]

Timotheus, ep. Ephesinus et m., Ian. 24[1]

Timotheus, in Macedonia, Apr. 6[2]

Timotheus, m. Romae, Aug. 22[2]

Timotheus, pr., Iun. 20[1]

Tolanus, ab. in Hibernia, Mar. 30[2]

Toronanus, ab., Iun. 12[2]

Torpetus, m. in Tuscia, Mai. 17[1]

Transitus per Mare Rubrum *see* Filii Israel

Triphon, m., Nov. 10[1]

Troianus, ep. Santonensis, Nov. 30[3]

Turianus (Turiavus), ep. in Britannia minori, Iul. 13[4]

Tyrsus, et socii, mm., Treveris, Oct. 4[3]

Udalricus, ep., Iul. 4[3]

Ultanus, ep., in Hibernia, Sep. 4[5]

Urbanus, papa et m., Romae, Mai. 25[1]

Ursatius, in Nicea Bithyniae, Aug. 16[1]

Ursio, mon., Trecas, Sep. 29[3]

Ursus, m. in Galliis, Sep. 30[1]

Uu- *see* W-

Valentinus, ep. Treverensis et m., Iul. 16[2]

Valentinus, pr. et m. Romae, Feb. 14[1]

Valerianus, ep. apud Africam, Dec. 15[1]

Valerianus, m., Sep. 15[2]

Valerianus, m. Romae, via Appia, Apr. 14[1]

Valerius, ep. Treverensis, Ian. 29[1]

Valpurga, v., Feb. 25[1]

Veranus, ep., Lugdunensis, Nov. 11[2]

Verona, v. apud Lovanium, Aug. 29[4]

Victor, in Aegypto, Apr. 1[2]

Victor, m. in Galliis, Sep. 30[1]

Victor, m. Mediolani, Mai. 8[1]

Victor, Nicomediae, Mar. 6[1]

Victor, papa, Romae, Iul. 28[3]

Victor, Xanthis, Oct. 30[3]

INDEX LOCORUM

Aberdona, in Scotia, Dec. 16^3
Aegea, civitas, Sep. 27^1
Aegyptus, Feb. 4^1, 16^2, Apr. 1^2, 5^1, Mai. 18^1, Iun. 5^1, Sep. 13^1, Oct. 4^1, Dec. 19^1. *See also* Alexandria
Aemilia, Nov. 25^3
Africa, Feb. 3^3, 12^2, 18^2, 19^2, Mar. 22^1, 23^1, Apr. 7^1, Mai. 24^2, Iul. 30^3, Aug. 14^3, 17^1, 28^1, Sep. 6^1, 14^3, Oct. 26^1, Dec. 5^1, 6^3, 9^2, 15^1, 18^2
Agennum, in Gallia, Oct. 20^1
Agrigentum, in Sicilia, Feb. 25^3
Albanum, Iul. 14^1
Albiniacum, Nov. 13^2
Alemannia, Oct. 16^2, Nov. 16^2
Alexandria, in Aegypto, Ian. 23^3, 28^2, 31^2, Feb. 9^1, 14^2, 22^2, 26^1, 27^1, Apr. 14^2, 25^2, Mai. 2^1, Iun. 25^1, Sep. 13^1, Nov. 14^1, 17^2, 26^1, Dec. 7^2
Amasia, Nov. 9^1
Ambiani, in Galliis, Mai. 16^3
Andania, Dec. 17^3
Andela, in Germania, Sep. 18^2
Anglia (Angli), Feb. 2^4, 7^4, 9^4, 23^2, Mar. 8^1, 12^1, Apr. 3^2, 19^2, 21^3, 29^3, Mai. 6^2, 20^4, 21^2, 23^2, 26^2, Iun. 7^2, 8^1, Iul. 7^1, 14^3, 17^3, 31^2, Aug. 20^3, 31^2, Sep. 30^3, Oct. 2^2, 11^2, 12^3, Nov. 3^2, 20^3, Dec. 3^1, 4^2

Antiochia, Ian. 30^1, Feb. 1^1, 13^1, 15^3, 22^1, Mar. 5^1, Iul. 12^3, 16^1, Aug. 1^1, Oct. 17^1, 30^1, Nov. 18^1, 27^1, Dec. 14^1; cathedra sancti Petri, Feb. 22^1
Aquileia, Mai. 31^2, Sep. 3^2
Arduenna, Oct. 18^2
Argentina, Nov. 7^2
Armenia minor, Feb. 8^1, Mar. 9^1
Arverna, Ian. 24^2, 25^3, Aug. 23^3, Sep. 24^2
Assisium, Aug. 12^1, Oct. 2^3, 3^1
Augusta, civitas in Britanniis, Feb. 7^1
Augustodunum, Iun. 24^3, Aug. 5^3, Nov. 22^3
Aurelianis, Iun. 3^1, Iul. 29^3, Dec. 15^2
Austria, Nov. 15^3
Autisiodorum (Antisiodorum), Mai. 22^1, 27^1, Aug. 31^3

Bamberga, Mar. 3^1
Barcinona, Nov. 6^3
Bavaria, Sep. 22^1
Beneventum, Sep. 1^3
Bergamum (Pergamum), Aug. 26^2
Beritho, in Syria, Nov. 9^2
Bethleem Iudae, Ian. 27^2, Sep. 30^2
Beverlacum, Mai. 7^2

Fossae, Oct. 31[2]
Francia, Aug. 25[2]
Frigia *see* Phrigia
Frisia, Nov. 7[1]
Frisinga, Sep. 8[3]
Fulda, monasterium, Sep. 28[2]

Galatia, Iun. 27[1]
Galilea, Mar. 25[2]
Gallia, Apr. 20[2], 24[1], Mai. 16[3], 22[2], Iul. 11[1], Aug. 7[2], 16[2], Sep. 30[1], Oct. 5[2], 20[1], 29[2], Nov. 11[1]. *See also* Floriacum, Lugdunum
Ganda (Gandavum), Apr. 10[2], Oct. 1[3]
Gaza, Feb. 26[3]
Germania, Sep. 18[2], 28[2]
Glasconia, Sep. 25[2]

Herbipolis, Iul. 8[3]
Herefordia, Mai. 20[4], Oct. 2[2]
Hibernia, **Ian.** 20[4], 21[3], 27[4], 28[3], 29[3], 30[3,4], 31[3], **Feb.** 2[3], 4[3], 6[3], 7[2], 8[3], 9[2],10[3], 11[2], 13[4], 17[3], 18[3], 19[3], 21[3], 24[3], 27[2], **Mar.** 1[3], 2[2], 3[2], 5[2], 8[2], 13[2], 15[2], 16[2], 17[1], 18[3], 19[3], 21[2], 22[2], 23[2], 24[3,4], 26[2,3], 29[4], 30[2], **Apr.** 4[2], 5[2], 7[2], 8[3], 10[3], 11[3], 14[3], 15[3],16[2], 17[2], 21[2],24[2,3], 25[3], 28[3], 29[4], 30[3], **Mai.** 1[4], 2[2], 4[2], 9[2,3], 11[2], 12[4], 14[3], 15[2], 18[3], 21[3], 22[3], 24[3], 25[2], 26[3], 29[3], **Iun.** 3[4], 6[2], 7[3], 8[2], 11[3], 12[2], 13[3], 17[3], 18[3], 20[2], 21[2], 22[2], 23[3], 25[2], 28[3], **Iul.** 4[2], 6[5], 7[2], 8[4], 9[2], 10[3], 13[3], 20[3], 22[3], 26[3], 31[4], **Aug.** 4[3], 6[3], 8[2], 9[3], 11[3], 12[3], 13[2], 14[4], 15[3], 18[3], 19[4], 21[3], 23[4], 24[3], 26[3], **Sep.** 2[4], 4[2,5], 5[2], 7[2], 12[2], 16[3], 17[3], 18[3], 25[3], 26[3], 28[4], **Oct.** 2[4], 5[3],6[3], 10[4], 11[4,5], 12[4], 13[2], 16[3],
17[2], 20[3], 21[3], 25[3], 27[2], **Nov.** 1[2], 2[3], 4[3],8[2], 10[3], 12[4], 14[2], 19[3], 24[3], 25[2], **Dec.** 4[3], 6[2], 7[4], 8[4], 9[3], 11[4], 12[3], 14[2], 19[3]
Hierosolymae, Ian. 30[2], Feb. 18[1], Mar. 11[2], 27[1], Mai. 3[1], 15[1], Iul. 25[1], Aug. 3[1], Oct. 29[1], Nov. 21[1]
Hispalis, in Hispania, Iul. 18[1], Oct. 8[3]
Hispania, Feb. 12[1], Apr. 13[1], Iul. 19[1], 25[1], Oct. 13[1], Dec. 10[3]. *See also* Hispalis
Hoya, insula, Iun. 27[2]
Hoyum, Feb. 9[4]
Hungaria, Sep. 24[3]
Hus, terra, Mai. 10[1]

Illiricum, Iun. 3[1]
India, Dec. 2[3]
Israel, Mar. 31[1], Apr. 10[1]
Italia, Iul. 11[1], 18[1], 24[2], Nov. 21[2], Dec. 5[2]
Iudea, Iul. 6[2]

Laetiae, Sep. 27[3]
Legio, civitas, Iun. 26[2]
Leodium, Mai. 25[3], Sep. 17[1]
Lincolnium, in Britannia, Nov. 17[3]
Lindisfarnensis, Mar. 20[1], Mai. 6[2]
Lingones, Mai. 23[1], Aug. 20[2]; In Anglia {sic}, Apr. 29[3]
Lirinum, insula, Nov. 18[3]
Londonium, civitas in Britannia, Apr. 30[2]
Louanium, Aug. 29[4]
Lugdunum Galliae, Ian. 20[3], Feb. 11[1], 28[1], Apr. 24[1], Iul. 14[1], Sep. 2[1], 11[2], Nov. 11[2]

Macedonia, Apr. 6[2], Dec. 18[1]

220

INDEX NOMINUM

Caedocus, filius Alani regis, Nov. 3[2]
Carolus Crassus, in Germania, Sep. 18[2]
Celestinus, papa, Mar. 17[1]
Claudius Caesar, Feb. 14[1]
Constantinus, princeps, Mai. 3[2]
Diocletianus, Feb. 20[1], Iun. 22[1]
Gallienus, imperator, Aug. 24[2]
Gothi, Nov. 6[3]
Gugo, rex Anglorum, Feb. 9[4]
Helena, regina, inventio Crucis ab, Mai. 3[1]
Herodes, rex, Iul. 25[1]

Honorius, papa, Nov. 14[2]
Judei, Sep. 25[1]; in Syria, Nov. 9[2]
Licinus, rex, Mar. 9[1]
Malcolmus tertius, rex, Nov. 16[3]
Maximianus, imperator, May 13[3]
Nero, imperator, Sep. 3[2]
Ozias, rex Israel, Mar. 31[1]
Philemonus, Feb. 16[1]
Rogerius, comes, Feb. 25[3]
Scoti, rex eorum, Iul.1[2], Aug. 30[3]; Scotus, Iul. 8[3], Sep. 6[2]
Valentinianus, imperator, Oct. 15[3]
Valerianus, imperator, Aug. 24[2]

GENERAL INDEX

Blathmac, saint, July 9.3

Blois, France, Aug. 2.3

Bogha, daughter of Comhghall, Jan. 22.3

Bogland (WW), Apr. 29.4

Bohemia, 9, July 4.3

Bonaventure, of Bagnoregio, July 14.1

Boniface I, Oct. 25.2

Boniface V, Oct. 25.2

Boniface IX, July 2.1, Oct. 7.4

Boniface, saint, Feb. 13.2, Mar. 14.2, Aug. 25.3, Sep. 28.2

Book of Leinster, Apr. 16.2

Bourg, France, June 11.2

Boyle b. (RN), Mar. 8.3

Brabant, Apr. 4.2

Bratislava *see* Pressburg

Brendan, of Clonfert, Mar. 1.3, Apr. 7.2, May 16.1, Nov. 15.2

Breviary, of Aberdeen, Jan. 29.3, Feb. 7.3, 16.3, 18.3, Mar. 2.3, May 1.3, June 10.2, 25.2, July 6.4, Sep. 16.2, Nov. 16.3

Bricín, of Tomregan, Sep. 5.2

Brighid, of Kildare, Feb. 1.2, Mar. 5.2, May 2.2

Brigown (CK), Nov. 25.2

Briocus (Brieuc), of Saint-Brieuc, May 1.5

Britain (Britannia/Briton), Mar. 1.2,3, 2.2, Sep. 10.4, 28.2, Dec. 13.2

Brittany, Mar. 12.3, Mar. 26.3, May 1.5, July 1.3, Oct. 19.3, 24.1, 27.1

Brocán, of Mothel, July 8.4

Brocán, of Ros Tuirc, Sep. 17.3

Bruno of Calabria, Oct. 6.1

Bruno, of Cologne, Oct. 11.3

Budapest, Hungary, Sep. 24.3

Buithe, of Monasterboice, Dec. 7.4

Bunratty Upr b. (CE), Nov. 4.3

Burchard, feast of, Oct. 10.3

Burgundy, France, Jan. 23.4, Sep. 25.2

Burren b. (CE), July 9.3

Butter, R., ix, xi

Byzantine, June 2.2, Oct. 1.4

Caesarea, in Cappadocia, Oct. 24.3

Caimín, of Inis Cealtra (Holy Island), Mar. 24.4

Cainneach, of Kilkenny, Oct. 11.1

Cairneach, of Dulane, May 16.2

Calabria, Italy, July 5.3

Calixtus III, pope, Aug. 6.1

Candida Casa, Sep. 16.2

Canterbury, Feb. 7.4, Apr. 19.2, 21.3

cantus Romanus, Jan. 27.3

Caoimhghin (Kevin), of Glendalough, June 3.4

Caoireach Deargáin, of Cloonburren, Feb. 9.3

Caolán *see* Mochaoi

Caomhán Santleathan, of Ardcavan, June 12.2

Cappadocia, July 3.2, Oct. 24.3

Carmelite(s), Mar. 29.2, Apr. 8.2

Carbery East b. (CK), Aug. 14.4

Carbury b. (KE), June 6.2

Carlow co., Feb. 8.4, Apr. 11.3, 17.2, June 17.3

Carthach (Mochuda), of Lismore, Apr. 29.4, May 14.3

Carthach, of Seirkieran, Mar. 5.2

Carthage, Africa, Mar. 7.2

Carthusian(s), Oct. 6.1, Nov. 17.3

Dungannon Middle b. (TE), Sept 7.2,3

Dunganstown (WW), May 22.3

Dunleer (LH), June 18.3, Oct. 17.2

Dunmanoge (KE), Dec. 11.4

Dunwich, England, Mar. 8.1

Durham, England, May 21.2

Durrow (LS), Oct. 20.3

Durrow (OY), June 21.2, 25.2, Sep. 16.3

Dysert O Dea (CE), Mar. 30.2

Éanán, of Drumraney, Aug. 19.4, Sep. 18.3

Éanna, of Aran, Mar. 21.2

Earc, of Slane, Nov. 2.3

Earc, of Tullylish, May 12.4

Earconwald, of London, Apr. 30.2

East Anglia, England, Mar. 8.1, May 20.4

Ecgberht, Dec. 8.4

Echternach/Willibrord, calendar of, Feb. 1.2,2, Aug. 20.3

Edmund, king of England, Nov. 20.3

Edward the Martyr, Mar. 18.2

Egbert, of Iona (d. 729), Apr. 24.2

Eglish b. (OY), May 21.3

Eichstätt, Germany, 1, 7, Sep. 28.3. *See also* Manuscripts

Éidchéan, of Clonfad, Feb. 11.2

Eindhoven, in Brabant, Apr. 4.2

Eithne, and Soidhealbh, Mar. 29.4

Eleutherius, pope, May 26.4

Eliogarty b. (TY), Mar. 13.2, July 31.4

Ely, England, Feb. 13.3, July 6.3

Elzearius, of Ariano, Sep. 27.2

Emerentiana, of Rome, Jan. 23.1

Emlagh (LH), Sep. 11.3

Emlagh, (MH), Apr. 5.2

Emly (TY), Sep. 12.2

England, see Index Locorum, Anglia

English origin of saint, 9, Feb. 9.4, July 18.2, 26.2, Sep. 10.4, Nov. 20.3

Ennereilly (WW), Sep. 13.3

Ennisboyne (WW), May 22.3

Ennodius, of Pavia, July 17.2

Eoghan, of Ardstraw, Aug. 23.4

Eoghan see Mac Táil

Eoghanacht, of Cashel, Jan. 21.3

Eolang, of Aghabulloge, Sep. 5.2

Ephesus, July 27.2

Erentrudis, of Nonnberg, June 30.3

Erfurt, *Schottenkloster*, 1, 5, 184

Erhard, of Regensburg, 8, July 11.3, Oct. 8.2

Eric 'the Lawgiver', of Sweden, May 18.2

Ermengild/Ermenilda, of Ely, Feb. 13.3

Essex, England, Apr. 30.2

Etbin, saint, Oct. 19.3

Ethelburga, of Barking, Oct. 11.2

Eucharius, of Trier, Dec. 8.2

Euphemia, of Chalcedon, Sep. 3.2

Euphronius, of Tours, Aug. 4.2

Eupsychius, Apr. 9.1

Eusebius, Sep. 26.2

Eutichius, of Constantinople, Apr. 9.1

Evaristus, Oct. 26.2

Evenou, Jean, June 27.2

Évreux, France, Oct. 19.1

Exsuperantia, of Troyes, Apr. 26.3

Fachtna, of Ross, Aug. 14.4

Fáilbhe, of Iona, Mar. 22.2

Faolán, of Strathearn, June 20.2

Frankish, emperors, 4
Fredeswide, of Oxford, Oct. 19.2
Freiburg, Germany, Nov. 26.2
Freising, Germany, Sep. 8.3
Fuinche, of Cluain Caoi, Jan. 21.3
Fulda, Germany, Sep. 28.3
Furodhrán, of Dunleer, June 18.3
Fursa, of Péronne, Oct. 31.2
Füssen, Germany, Sep. 6.2

Gall(us), saint, 6, 8, Oct. 16.2, 23.3
Galway co., Feb. 9.3. Mar. 21.2,
    24.4, May 11.2, 16.1, Nov. 12.4
Garbhán, of Kinsaley, July 9.2
Garrycastle b. (OY), June 13.3
Gaudentius, of Novara, Aug. 3.2
Gaul/Gaulish, Mar. 8.1, Nov. 16.1
Gaultier b. (WD), July 4.2
Gaza, Palestine, Feb. 26.3
Geashill b. (OY), Mar. 26.2
Gebhard, of Sankt-Mang, 14
Gembloux, Belgium, Aug. 29.4
Gerardus, of Hungary, Sep. 24.3
Gerlandus, of Agrigento, Feb. 25.3
German/Germany, 2, 6, 9, 14, Jan.
    31.1, Mar. 14.2, Apr. 17.2, 24.2,
    Sep. 28.2,3, Oct. 1.2, 30.2
Gertrude, of Nivelles, 1, Mar. 17.1,
    Dec. 17.3
Gervasius, of Milan, Nov. 24.2
Ghent, Belgium, Apr. 10.2
Ghost saints, Jan. 27.4, Aug. 12.3
Giallán, of Killelan, Oct. 2.4
Giles, St, dedication, 1
Glasnevin (DB), Oct. 12.4
Glastonbury, England, Sep. 25.2
Glendalough (WW), June 3.4
Glyceria, of Heraclea, May 13.2
Gobán, of Killamery, Feb. 11.3,
    Dec. 6.2

Gobnaid, of Ballyvourney, Feb.
    11.3
Godric, of Finchale, May 21.2
Gorey b. (WX), Jan. 30.4, July 13.3
Gowran b. (KK), Nov. 8.2
Granard b. (LD), Dec. 19.3
Graystown (TY), Oct. 6.3
Great Island (CK), Mar. 15.2
Greek, church, Apr. 12.2
Gregorius Thaumaturgus, Nov.
    17.1
Gregory, abbot of St James, 2–3
Gregory II, Feb. 13.2
Gregory III, Nov. 28.2
Gregory VII, Sep. 24.3
Gregory, of Tours, Feb. 17.2
Gregory, of Utrecht, Aug. 25.3
Greven(us), Hermann, ix, xi, *et passim*
Grimbald, of Saint-Bertin, July 8.2
Grosjean, P., Aug. 24.3
Gunthildis, saint, 6, Sep. 28.3
Guthlac, of Crowland, Apr. 11.2

Heidenheim, Germany, Feb. 25.1
Helena, of Västergötland, July 30.2
Heraclea, Thrace, May 13.3
Hereford, England, Oct. 2.2
Hiacinthus, of Cappadocia, July
    3.2
Hidulphus, of Moyenmoutier, July
    11.3
Hieronymian, martyrology *see*
    Martyrology of Jerome
Hieronymus, of Pavia, July 22.2
Hilarion, of Pelecete, Mar. 28.3
Hiltrude, of Liessies, Sep. 27.3
Himerius, of Amelia, June 16.2
Hippolytus, of Rome, Aug. 22.3
Hochholzer, Elmar, 13.

Rome/Roman, 1, Apr. 9.2, 29.2, 30.1, May. 4.1, 13.2, 14.1, July 17.1, Aug. 21.1, 22.3; via Appia, Mar. 4.1; via Ardiatina, June 13.2, 18.1; via Latina, May 10.2; via Salaria, Nov. 29.1

Rónán, of Dromiskin, Nov. 19.3

Rónán, of Liathros, Apr. 30.3

Rónán, of Lismore, Feb. 7.3

Rónán, of Magheralin, May 22.3

Ros Deala, Aug. 24.3

Roscommon co., Mar. 8.3

Rosscarbery (CK), 2

Roscrea (TY), Apr. 28.3

Ross (CK), Aug. 14.4

Rosminogue (WX), Jan. 30.4

Rottenburg, an der Laaber, 5, 182–3

Rouen, France, Aug. 7.2, Nov. 25.1

Ruadhán, of Lorrha, Apr. 15.3

Rule, monastic, 4

Rumoldus, of Mechelen/Malines, July 1.2

Rupertus, of Salzburg, Mar. 27.2

Ruremonde see Roermond

Rusticus, of Clermont, Sep. 24.2

Rusticus, of Trier, Oct. 14.3

Sabas, of Cappadocia, Dec. 5.3

Saggart (DB), Mar. 3.2

Saint-Bertin, abbey of, Saint-Omer, France, July 8.2

Saint-Brieuc, France, May 1.5

Saint-Florent-le-Vieil, France, June 27.2

Saint-Lyé, France, Sep. 29.3

Saint-Malo, France, July 1.3

Saint-Pol-de-Léon, France, Mar. 12.3

Salzburg, Austria, Mar. 27.2, June 30.3

Samhthann, of Clonbroney, Dec. 19.3

Sankt-Mang, Regensburg, 14

Sárán, of Inis Mór, May 15.2

Sarching, Bavaria, 5, 181–4

Saturninus, of Africa, May 24.2

Sauget, J.-M., Mar. 28.2

Saxon, West, Dec. 3.1

Sázava, Czech Republic, July 4.3

Scarawalsh b. (WX), Oct. 27.3

Scattery Island (CE), Mar. 1.3, 8.2

Schottenkloster: Eichstätt, Sep. 28.3; Regensburg, passim, Aug. 23.3; Vienna, Nov. 15.3

Sciath, of Ardskeagh, Sep. 7.3

Scíre, of Kilskeer, Mar. 24.3

Scota, Nov. 20.2

Scotland/Scotic/Scotia, 4, Mar. 23.2, Apr. 21.2, June 20.2, 25.2, July 6.4, Sep. 28.2, Nov. 12.2, 15.2

Seanach, of Clonard, Aug. 21.3

Seanán see also Mosheanóg

Seanán, of Laraghbryan, Sep. 2.4

Seanán, of Scattery (Inis Cathaig), 3, Mar.1.3, 8.2

Sebald, of Nürnberg, Aug. 19.3

Séighín, of Iona, Aug. 12.3

Seirkieran (OY), Mar. 5.2

Sennen, of Rome, July 30.1

Seven Sleepers, of Ephesus, July 27.2

Severus, of Barcelona, Nov. 6.3

Sexburg, of Ely, July 6.3

Shannon, r., 3, May 12.4, Sep. 17.3

Shelmaliere East/West b. (WX), Apr. 23.3, June 12.2, Oct. 21.3

Sidonius, of Clermont, Aug. 23.3

Siena, Italy, Apr. 29.2, May 20.3

Silverius, pope, June 19.2